THE INSURGENTS

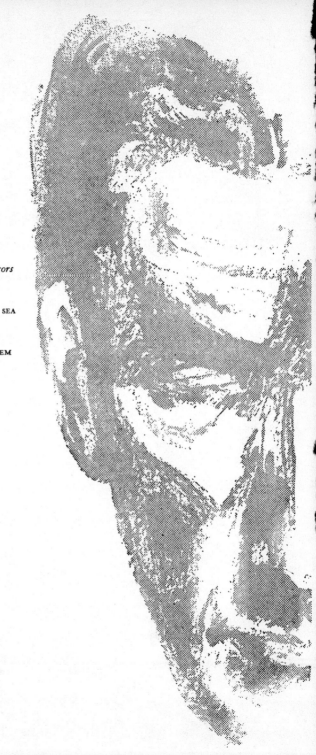

The Insurgents BY VERCORS

TRANSLATED FROM THE FRENCH BY RITA BARISSE

HARCOURT, BRACE AND COMPANY • NEW YORK

Foreword

In Venice there recently foregathered cultural personalities from East and West who, for thirty years, had been separated by the gaping rift of a world torn between capitalism and socialism—religion, atheism, humanism, racism—in order to search together, for the first time, the points on which they might agree. They promptly discovered one such point: they unanimously rejected my warning that, prior to all discussion, they would have to define what they called "culture," that is to say, what they called "man." Let's stick to concrete problems, they wisely declared.

They stuck to them so wisely indeed that for the rest of the week they agreed on no further point (except the date of the next meeting). This unheeded warning is the same that I have never stopped driving home in my writings for close to ten years.

My previous novel *You Shall Know Them* showed that to define Man by his physical traits—by zoology, physiology, and even psychology—is an impossible undertaking. Imagining the survival of an ape-men tribe halfway between the primates and Homo sapiens, a tribe which needs has to be determined from legal, social, religious standpoints, I pitted against one another zoologists, anthropologists, psychologists, priests, and philosophers, whose endless wrangling about the exact borderline between man and beast comically illustrated this impossibility.

This new novel again grapples with the problem of Man, but from quite a different angle. It tries to show that the answer cannot be found, either, in the knowledge, however complete, of our bodily person. Egmont, a physician turned poet, seeks this answer in a determined exploration of the mysteries of his own organism, of this carnal universe which constitutes his person but which, from birth to death, remains as alien to him as the bottom of the sea. Burrowing into uncharted regions, acquiring there unsuspected powers, he may perhaps discover the answer—but what is its use since he can bring back nothing usable? He rules over a new empire—but is he still a man? And while he is ever more deeply engulfed in unconsciousness, in a fantastic collusion with the mysteries of his body, mankind continues to grapple with its *human* problems on earth: a strike breaks out, a young girl struggles amid the cruel discoveries of love and death, an aged scientist deserts his peaceful laboratory to find the source of gladness in his solidarity with other men. . . .

"What distinguishes man from the beast is his unsubmissiveness to nature—even if he doesn't know it," says one of the characters. Without pretending that this may be a conclusive reply to this Great Question, I merely aim in this complex narrative to approach once again, though from an unusual angle, the fundamental notion of what we call *human,* a notion on which mankind *must* eventually agree if they want to understand each other at last, and live in peace.

THE INSURGENTS

. . . l'âme absente, occupee
aux enfers.

—PAUL VALERY

(La dormeuse)

Prologue

I wonder why Olga summoned me. She must have
known that where she herself had failed I could be of no help. She
had to open herself to someone, I suppose. Maybe she was hoping
unconsciously that by confiding in me she could avoid a more serious intervention. Anyway, it's from Olga I learned practically all I
knew, at least at that time. I had to piece together a thousand scattered fragments to try to form a coherent picture. It was not easy.
Happily, I have since had other sources.

Old Mirambeau also wrote me, at Olga's request no doubt. A
curious letter with its undertone of ill-concealed indifference, more
of a friendly suggestion than an urgent call: do come, this will interest you.

He related an odd mixture of events: a strike at Chaulieu that
was growing to the size of a major social movement, a hint at his
own biological work on the immortality of protoplasm, as if what
was happening to Egmont was mysteriously bound up with both
the strike and his experiments.

And, true enough, I found a group of people involved in all this,
and linked to one another, in spirit if not in substance, by Egmont's presence in the silent darkness where his body lay asleep.

Asleep . . . words play you false at once. In describing Eg-

3

mont's state, you can talk of anything but sleep. Besides, it is much too early. His story does not begin there. I am not the only one to think that its roots strike deep into remote frustrations. Hidden frustrations, for the success of his works has never diminished, and the renown of Egmont the poet, alias Dr. Daniel Roux, has grown ever more solid with the passage of time.

What did I know about him after all those years? I recall his last visit, when he was touching rock bottom perhaps, having just broken with "the party" and then learned from Olga that she would not resume their life together.

I heard, later, that he had regained his grip on himself. Was it Olga's doing? Certainly not—not then, at least. Only much later did the old affection that had for so long united them begin to re-assert itself. The means by which a man clings to life are much more devious. The fact was that the unexpected success on Broadway of some prewar play of his had enabled Egmont to acquire a modest place in the forest, an old farmstead, at some distance from Chaulieu. Half an acre of fields and woods surrounding an eighteenth-century-style brick-and-stucco building, rather dilapidated to look at, but still sound enough for Egmont to repair at little cost and make habitable.

Did he intend to feed his melancholy there in solitude? That's what his friends supposed, with some disquiet. The house once repaired, however, it appeared to their relieved surprise that it was not meant to be a retreat. They had always admired his taste as a collector. In the heyday of surrealism, his small flat in Chaulieu had first sheltered a collection of dry old vine stocks, picked up on the hills where ancient vineyards were dying a lingering death, and chosen for their strangeness, their animal or human likeness, their eerie or even diabolical evocative power. Later on, the shelves of his library sported showcases containing an armada of irides-

4

cent phials which, unearthed by him in some archaeological treasure hunts, gleamed in a mellow, submarine light with a smoldering fire that followed you about. He had abandoned all this to Olga at the time of their separation. And now they saw him slowly transform his house amid the elms and beeches into a natural history museum.

Where had he picked up this latest craze? I have often wondered if Mirambeau's biological studies had not at that time already exerted some influence on Egmont's mind. But Mirambeau won't have it: he purses his thick lips doubtfully whenever I suggest it. He says that it started quite simply with an old poacher-turned-gamekeeper, who looked after Egmont's lawn, bringing him some curious beasts one day. However this may be, Egmont eventually engaged the old man to live in, and between the two of them the house was invaded within a few years by an army of motionless animals: stuffed fish and fowl conquered the upper floor, mammals seemed to colonize the walls and floors downstairs. Crustaceans annexed the shelves of an entire room, insects all those of another. Snakes and batrachians slumbered in their bottles of spirit. Every week newcomers caused a moment's stir in this silent fixedness before turning to stone in the shadows.

Egmont rarely disturbed them: as his collection grew, his hobby of necessity yielded less enjoyment in use than in possession. He confessed with a smile that contemplating even the rarest pieces afforded him infinitely less pleasure than handling the innumerable index cards that he had compiled with young Pascale. Completely surrounded by his files, he felt at times as if he were ensconced in the very heart of Nature, whom he had effectively tamed and summarized. All the rest, those thousands of desiccated, stuffed, and sterilized animals down there below his feet, was a reserve comparable to the gold in the Bank of France: a mere presence required to guarantee his paper money, no more. But in the heart of his study, amid his countless files, there he could *hear* them live, in the swish of rustling wings, the throb of heartbeats, the rasp of scales, the visceral laments, and sometimes, for a few minutes, he would forget himself completely and no longer know where he was. This dizziness, this intoxication passed too quickly for his liking, and he hankered after it when he awoke to find himself back in his armchair, in front of his files, and inside the social entity christened Daniel Roux—Egmont in literature.

Were those moments of cosmic oblivion at the root of later events? It looks as if one could not deny the possibility of a link, of a deep-seated inclination. Olga later was to recall certain verses of his *Tenedos*:

> . . . *My night, sunlike into my flesh you burrow*
> *Bathing it in your almighty boredom*
> *More brilliant than an outburst of brasses*
> *You dazzle me and I walk like a blind man*
> *Within this fiery blaze of darkness* . . .

I was not thinking of those lines as I gazed at Egmont, motionless between his sheets. No, I did not think of them—and yet! Olga had taken me into the muffled room. It might have been a death chamber. The shutters closed, the curtains drawn. "For three months," she said. A pervasive scent, which was not unpleasant, was hovering in it. You sometimes smell it at a country grocer's: the log burning in the stove, the slow smoking of a leg of ham, a jar of olives, pepper, nut oil, jujubes. . . . Here there mingled with it the sweet fresh smell of a baby's skin. It was rather invigorating.

Egmont lay stretched out in marble stillness. You had to watch him for a long time to see that he was breathing. But the freshness

6

of his complexion, his lips, the firmness of the flesh, everything in this beautiful face glowed with the sap of life, with youthfulness. Was it the lighting? Did the soft, shaded lamp, standing on the antique chest in one corner, smooth out the wrinkles already hollowed by the fifties? I stepped closer, but no: Egmont really had shed fifteen years. I'd never known him to look so young. When he had last been to see me, he had, on the contrary, seemed far more than his age. I saw him again, slumped and hesitant, with that familiar gesture of his fingers over his face, as if they followed the trace of a tear along the heavy nose and the sagging cheeks.

Olga had left me alone. Alone with him, his immobility, alone in the silence and the semidarkness, and the tonic smell of hazelnuts, rustling leaves, and youthful flesh which familiarity was already dispelling. Mirambeau had told me too much for me to think I was simply facing a sick man ("His health? More flourishing than an athlete's. . . ."), not enough to prevent me from feeling surprise, anguish—or hope.

What strange words! What anguish, or what hope? For as I write them, I am not thinking of him, but of myself—of each and all of us. I watched the sheet over Egmont's chest rise slowly, imperceptibly, I waited to catch a tremor, a twitch of his face; but not a sign—it glowed, and that was all. The lamplight fastened on his Goethian forehead, a high, pure forehead that the closed lids prolonged like shells: an amber light that spread in a halo over his hair, the pillow, and part of the wall as if, like some faces by Rembrandt, the forehead did not receive the light but was the very source of it. I could not take my eyes away.

Olga returned. She remained standing at my side for a moment, gazing with me at this face. No doubt she was waiting for my questions. There were too many of them. The simplest would have been to say: "But what happened?" had it not meant asking everything at once. I suppose Olga understood my quandary. She broke the awkward silence.

"You are going to know everything, of course," she said. "Soon. I need time to collect myself. I am so grateful to you for not pressing me at once."

I was groping for words to discover, without worrying her, how much she worried.

"I am *not* worried," she declared slowly, in a low tone. "Not at all. It is much—" it was her turn to grope for words—"much deeper," she said, "much more overwhelming, it touches things that are so . . ."

But she did not find the word, and her hand moved as if to grip the empty air. She let it drop and murmured:

"Ah, and it's so deeply comforting too!"

She looked at me as if to explain herself. She half opened her lips, slowly drew in a breath of air—but shook her head mutely, and shut her eyes and mouth with such eloquent, such weary abandon that I put my arm around her shoulder and hugged her a little.

I was bewildered. I tried to understand this woman. We had been great friends once. I could have fallen in love with her, had I tried hard enough to break through her tough shell of skepticism and mental smugness: you easily get caught yourself in that game. She was a doctor—she knew Egmont from their hospital days when he was still practicing—and used to shock as well as amuse me by the way she spoke of her patients: "Cracked, all of them. It's true I'm treating them for bellyaches, and their brains are down there too. If I were to start sharing all their troubles . . ." She shared them sufficiently, though, for all her patients to be in-

8

fatuated with her. She was obliged to build up a defensive mechanism to save her mental balance. She found it in the form of a cool cynicism which she gradually extended to matters outside "shop." She treated poverty as she did disease, professing that nothing could be done about the world, or man, or the course of events. So she accepted as lesser evils the injustices, the infamies of the present, and refused to take up arms against them. We had quarreled over it hammer and tongs more than once.

This determined indifference lent her a stability that seemed proof against all things in life. For she stuck out the same stubborn chin against setbacks and adversity. One might have said that she countered them with an unalterable grin, a chuckle. If she ever cried, she hid it well.

And here I was holding pressed against me a woman who was shaken in her resolution and on the brink of tears. The same woman who, five or six years ago, had dropped Egmont with a brutal, almost cruel shrug of self-defense because, she said, she saw no point in crumbling with him. . . .

But she opened her eyes and smiled at me. Then gazing at him again:

"Now it is exactly, exactly as he wanted it," she whispered.

"As he wanted it . . ." I repeated to myself. I felt that this was the heart of the riddle.

"Look at this hand," said Olga, and she raised it between her two palms as if she were holding a priceless Soong bowl.

I did not remember Egmont having such beautiful hands. This one was firm, sinewy, with smooth, pearly skin.

Suddenly I saw this hand again, raking the sagging face with a limp finger as if tracing a tear. I recalled how prematurely old it had looked, already lined and freckled.

"It's unbelievable," I murmured.

"Isn't it?" said Olga with pride, but something broke in her voice.

"How you do love him, and with such courage," I said admiringly, yet compassion choked me.

Olga understood it so well that she stiffened a little, as if to defend her friend against me.

"I am so happy," she assured me, but it was pathetic. "I *am*."

Stroking her cheek with the fabulous hand she cast me a look of defiance.

PART ONE *Anabiosis*

Chapter One

In the winding lane, ribbed with shadow and pale sunlight, Egmont was walking down the steps. There were eight hundred and sixty of them. At Easter, the pilgrims would climb them on their knees. On each step they had to say an Ave Maria, a Pater Noster. At the top, brimming with darkness, gaped the porch of the red and black cathedral.

He came down the steps slowly. The friend he was on his way to see was dying of a tumor of the lung. Each step still to descend meant a sort of refuge. He was counting them mechanically. They were trodden down in the center. Faith wears out the stone, he thought; but the stone, he thought, outlives the pilgrims.

He suddenly saw again the chicken heart that Mirambeau had, for five years now, been keeping alive in a jar. There was said to be another in America that had gone on beating for over a quarter of a century. Generations of chickens had died in the meantime, heart and feathers, but that heart went on beating, would never stop. It outlived the chickens as the stone outlived the pilgrims.

He found it unbearable to picture his own heart beating in a jar till Kingdom come. Or, for that matter, the heart of that man waiting to die. In fact, everything was unbearable. So was the idea of those kneeling pilgrims muttering their eight hundred and sixty prayers for a thousand years on the steps hollowed by their resigned protest against the condition of man—without ever being vouchsafed an answer. . . . They had all died in pain and terror, but generations of pilgrims, with their millions of mocked hopes, had followed each other nonetheless with bullheaded obstinacy, indifferent to the rebuff of that black silence.

Halfway down, Egmont started looking out for the old, narrow oak door, wedged between two weather-beaten fluted piers. It stood ajar. The passage was dark and smelled of paraffin and cabbage. A twisting staircase disappeared amid the shadows between the walls.

He had expected to see a dying man in bed. He found him on his feet, dressed from top to toe, and wearing a stiff, detachable collar. Just as he was three months ago, when lecturing on physical chemistry at the university. He was not even sitting: standing up. Propped against the wall between the two windows, his legs planted apart. His neck was enormous, its skin gray and gritty, already moldering. However had he managed to fasten his collar?

Egmont wanted to smile. The sick man's glance would not permit it. It was suffused with pain.

A figure moved in the semidarkness. Egmont recognized a young teacher of the Jules-Ferry High School. What *was* his name? Closter Cloots. You can't forget a name like that. They shook hands. A dull, toneless, horribly rasping voice emerged from the tall body leaning against the wall:

"*Ave,* Egmont. *Moriturus te salutat.*"

"What are you talking about?" said Egmont. "You're getting better every day, that's plain. Splendid to find you up and about. But isn't it rather rash?"

"I'll be dead before tomorrow," said the sick man. "No," he said, "don't tire me. Don't oblige me. . . ." He said it so wearily that Egmont could do nothing but fall silent.

"I've been begging him to get back to bed," said Closter Cloots.

"No good," said the sick man in his muffled voice. "I shall fight to the finish. It's my Last Charge. Matter of self-respect."

Egmont cast a furtive questioning glance at Cloots.

"Don't understand?" said the sick man with a soundless, hoarse, horrible laugh. "My turn's come, but I won't play the game. You must never play the game. Y'understand? Never."

It makes no odds whether we do or not. As if we had the choice, thought Egmont, bewildered and oppressed.

"But you suffer needlessly," he stammered, and his voice was uncertain.

The sick man wanted to shake his head, but he grimaced, raising an emaciated hand to his monstrous neck. He said in that voice which despite his efforts was no more than a croak:

"A newborn baby also suffers needlessly, since life's a lost cause, anyway. You must keep fighting for lost causes until there's a change. Death is a dirty trick. Don't stand for it. Yours or anyone's. Don't compromise with it!" he shouted hoarsely. "Show it up, protest every time, say no!"

His fist made a downward gesture.

"I at least shall say no to the finish," he gasped.

"But why on your feet?" persisted Egmont in a hushed voice.

"So as to tear off its mask; so that it doesn't come disguised as deliverance. I force death to strike me down standing. Besides, I want it to be quite plain that there's no question of fear. On the contrary. Dying rather suits me." His voice changed. "So tired," he confessed. "Never got over Edmée, you know."

He took a breath with effort.

15

"I'm on my feet, and fully dressed, to show this: it's not I who am dying. No, I'm not dying, I am being killed. I myself, I am here, I am thinking, working—look," he said, motioning to the blackboard covered with chalk marks. "I'm studying new functions. On the variations of energy in polymeric systems. If someone steals up behind me and murders me while I'm at it, let him shoulder his crime. His responsibility must be clearly established."

"For whom?" muttered Egmont.

"For me, for everyone. So that others do as I do. So that they will understand—"

His voice became more and more stifled, his effort to speak ever more painful.

"—understand once for all that it isn't true that you have to resign yourself and bless providence. Not true," he repeated. "If you do, you're being a beast or a coward, sucking up to the brute to get into his good graces, to be let off more lightly. It's debasing."

He tried to clear his throat, closed his eyes in pain. His face was damp. Outside, the cathedral bells had started calling the faithful.

His fingers went up to his terrible neck as if groping to strangle it.

"See that?" he asked, but his voice was hardly audible. "It's been climbing stealthily from the armpits, day after day, for two months. And presently, tonight, or tomorrow—snap. Should I say 'amen' or shout 'murder'?"

A brief burst of laughter followed, sharp and cutting like broken glass.

"You wish I'd lie down? Like a cowed dog, offering his belly to his master's kicks, to soften him? Or say 'Praise be to God,' or else, with folded hands, *'Mehr Licht'*? Light, you mustn't ask for it . . ." He shouted: "You must snatch it!"

16

He seemed like Prometheus on his rock, while the bell's appeal filled the evening air, made the windows hum.

The room smelled of vinegar and, already, of faint decay. In the failing light the furniture seemed like crouching shadows, a pack of silent jackals, watching and waiting to tighten the circle around the man propped against the wall. And the man faced them, waiting for death. Egmont suddenly remembered a nameless photograph, the picture of a Resistance fighter who, with the Germans about to shoot, tauntingly bared his chest, laughing. Another fleeting memory crossed his mind: Valentin Feldman shouting to his killers: "Fools, it's for you I'm dying!" He looked at the moribund man and thought: But not he. Not even that consolation. We die for nobody. We are murdered at night, in silence. Our death is lost.

He saw the sick man totter. Closter Cloots quickly slipped forward. A glance stopped him. The man clutched the wall. He squared his legs, to hold himself up. He succeeded. His cracked, decaying lips wore a proud smile.

"Oh!" he said. "I'll stick it out."

He had no sooner spoken than a hiccup shook him. The spasm seemed to proceed from all parts of his body, and gather in his stomach for a moment before pressing violently against chest and throat. The jaw dropped open under the impact, and shut again. During that brief opening, a trickle of black, sticky blood spurted between the teeth, ran over his chin. It promptly spread a foul, stale odor. The sick man wiped it away with the back of his hand. He had closed his eyes. He seemed to be listening.

Egmont followed, spellbound, the progress of a new spasm. It was like an assault on a hill or a fortress. First the feet shook, then the knees. The hands, the elbows. The quiver traveled upward along the thighs, attacked the trunk at the waist, invaded the throat, jerking the head backward—the skull knocked slightly against the wall—and blood spurted between the lips. The man wiped it away.

He tried to speak: "As you came in, I was explaining to Cloots . . ." A new hiccup shook him, bringing more blood. "I was explaining that if one could put into an equation . . ." The hiccup bent him double. For a minute, a silent battle raged between the man who wanted to speak and the body which wouldn't let him, which pummeled him with its blows. Egmont, very pale and on the verge of nausea, kept thinking of the Gestapo. He thought: This is ghastly. Cloots, too, was of ashen pallor. The blows seemed to rain on the tensed carcass as on a boxer driven against the ropes. Arms and trunk writhed from side to side, and the foul blood gushed, spreading its stench, and the man wiped it off, and the skull drummed against the wall. Outside, the bells were still chiming, they chimed and their tragic peal seemed to accompany this dance of death. Egmont felt he heard in them now an undertone of frenzied rage and despair, like someone ringing the tocsin and charging heaven.

Chapter Two

Egmont and Cloots walked down the steps in heavy silence. The bells had stopped. Some women, late and trying to run up the steps in their haste, jostled them. The two men heard them pant in passing and were assailed by a hot, sour smell.

They reached the old Grand Square at the bottom without having uttered a word. They remained obsessed with that fallen body that had wished to raise itself alone, without their help. The dying man had succeeded. He had propped himself against the wall again, gasped for a while, and had then managed to resume: "I was explaining to Cloots . . ." and had started expounding to them, in hacked, choking scraps of phrases, his theory on the variations of energy. He had even dragged himself to the blackboard to scribble a formula. It had seemed to Egmont that the furniture had shrunk away in fear, with lowered head.

Afterward, burly old Mirambeau had arrived, panting from the three flights of stairs, and the sick man and he, both struggling for breath, had promptly resumed a discussion they had interrupted the day before. Faced with this preposterous effort, Egmont felt like screaming with anguish, but with disapproval too. An old nurse had finally put an end to the rebellion; she came to give the dying man an injection for his heart. The patient himself pulled up his sleeve over an arm that was so incredibly gaunt that it seemed impossible for the needle to squeeze between the bone and that dried parchment.

Egmont followed her into the kitchen. "But he's more than three-quarters dead!" he cried under his breath. The nurse nodded her long, horsy face: "He won't last the night." "Why don't you force him to lie down?" he said indignantly. But she looked at him in silence and slowly shook her head. Her eyes were full of a still incredulous certainty, a sort of fervor, an inarticulate admiration.

"What a man," murmured Cloots, as in a dream, as they turned into Grand Square. To anyone coming out of the lane, now almost dark, the square at first seemed dazzlingly bright. But once you were in it, the light was feeble.

"What's the good of making his horrible suffering worse when there's no hope?" grumbled Egmont, who could not rid himself of a dull rage.

Cloots suddenly stopped short on the curb and looked down at his feet.

"I'd like to show the same courage when my day comes," he said dreamily.

"That's an absurd wish," said Egmont. "It's no good to anyone."

"Who knows?" murmured Cloots. "To refuse and fight. Refuse uncompromisingly, to the very end. That's not a senseless example, if we only mind the lesson."

He lifted his head. He's aged a little, thought Egmont. They had not met for a long time. There is nothing like a medium-big town for losing sight of your friends: you keep waiting for an opportunity instead of provoking one. And so time passes.

Cloots was eying him quizzically. And always that faint ironic smile, reflected Egmont with slight irritation—a little lopsided smile under his ginger mustache.

"Damn odd though," muttered Cloots.

"What is?"

"Meeting you today like that, and in those circumstances. Imagine, I was just going to write to you."

Cloots had taken his arm, was pulling him along under the trees, as he used to do.

"And in those circumstances," he repeated with a sort of incredulous surprise. "Imagine . . ." he said again, but he seemed to hesitate. "I'm blurting it out point-blank, y'see, but I've been thinking of it for weeks. You've always had a critical acumen that impressed me. A knack of stripping down to the core, y'see, of telling the wheat from the chaff."

Yes, thought Egmont. Other people's wheat. As to my own poems, what are they worth?

"I need your advice," said Cloots. "As a critic and a writer," he explained.

Egmont remembered two or three quite neatly turned articles of Cloots's in the *Patriote Poitevin,* as well as a brief pamphlet published in Paris. And always that wise tenacity in remaining a schoolteacher. At the Liberation, the Ministry of Education had offered Cloots an undersecretaryship. "Why turn it down? You could make a success of it." Egmont remembered Cloots's smile. "I prefer my children, y'see?" With a hint in his voice that this wasn't all. But he had left it at that.

They had stopped under a lamppost. Cloots was smiling as usual. Egmont returned the smile and opened his hands expectantly. Cloot's grin broadened:

" 'I'm writing *Paludes. . . .*' "

"Like André Gide's hero?"

"Yes. Meaning that, like him, I'm not writing it. It's all still under my skullcap, y'see. I'd like to talk to you about it before taking the plunge into the inkpot."

"Whenever you like," said Egmont, "and with the greatest pleasure. But not here," he protested, "under this dusty lamppost!"

"I'm not yet clean out of my mind," said Cloots with a laugh. "And, anyway, you must be busy."

This time it was Egmont who took Cloots's arm. "Let's go and have a drink." They crossed the square. The lights of the *brasserie* blinked drearily. Egmont pushed the door.

The cashier at her desk bade them a smiling good evening. The light was brighter than Egmont had expected from outside, despite the tobacco smoke. There were pools of noise and pools of silence, a hubbub of voices, the hoarse, hilarious cries of card players, the click of billiard balls out of sight behind the plush seats and the dismal pillars.

Egmont ordered a chartreuse. Cloots was content with a beer. They glanced around them. No young people. Middle-aged men mostly. Opposite them, a straggly, tobacco-yellowed beard was quivering on the chin of an elderly man busily playing patience by himself; two others, whose eyes seemed to be vying for the ownership of the biggest pouches, were slobbering a little over their tales of hardship of life on a pension; yet another, with a vacant stare, kept stirring his spoon in his *pernod*.

"And there you are," said Cloots, with a discreet but expressive wave of his hand.

"Quite," said Egmont.

Cloots laughed briefly.

"We understand each other. How could you ever shake this fearful mass of indifference?"

"Must you? Besides, are you so sure it is indifference?"

"Resignation, then, at least. That's even worse."

They went on looking around. At one table, set back from the others, a hunched old man, with a bitter, drooping mouth and tired eyes behind his high-perched spectacles, was filling sheet after sheet of paper.

"Even that old newspaper hack," said Cloots, "what's to be done about him? Can there be anything he still believes in? Anything one can do to startle him?"

"What do you want to startle him for?" asked Egmont. What startled him was Cloots's youthfulness. How old could he be? Not much his junior. Close on forty, anyway.

"Because that's what I find so incredible, y'see. That people don't spend their time being startled. Here we are, living in utter darkness, with not one thing in life that isn't an insoluble mystery, and what happens? Nothing. See? Personally, I find that incredible. Don't you?"

"You can only marvel, you know, at things you're already familiar with. You've got to be Darwin to fret over not being able to explain the miracle that is an eye. How do you expect a poor bastard to worry about things of which he hasn't got the first notion?"

"It's not so much ignorance that surprises me," said Cloots, and he flung himself back to stretch out his legs under the table. "We can't all be encyclopedias. No: it's the way we put up with it, y'see? Everyone knows that he knows nothing, but he puts up with it. Oh, not just people like them," he said with a jerk of his chin, "but everybody, y'see, you and me. What I mean is that we're satisfied with what little we know. No, what I mean is . . . y'see, our mind ought constantly to hark back to this fundamental fact, this humiliating fact, that we don't know a thing, y'see, that nobody knows a thing, that one can't know a thing, that what minute shreds of knowledge we have were wrested by force after thousands of years of effort, hundreds of thousands. Wrested in an endless, exhausting struggle. We should be living in a state of constant indignation, simmering with revolt and rage. Instead, we mind our petty affairs, and that's all; we put up with it, y'see? We don't want to be uneasy, or amazed, or even merely disturbed. Things are as they are, therefore they're all right, so be a good fellow and scram."

The waiter brought them their drinks. He was marvelously bald. But across his bald dome he had pulled onto his forehead, with pathetic care, a wavy flourish of twenty or thirty hairs plastered down in the form of a harp, which underlined the gleaming nakedness of his scalp. He must have spent a considerable time each morning over this work of art.

Egmont gazed at it with admiration as he said:

"It's not as general, perhaps, as you like to make out."

"Our putting up with things?" asked Cloots. "No, of course not. We've just had a fine object lesson. Revolt isn't my invention. Almost everyone's gone through it some time. It has produced beautiful outcries. Some have even died of their suppressed rage. Others go on yelling all their lives. It's become quite the fashion, these days. But even they, y'see, even those who search . . . Take the scientists: they keep searching all the time. But try to trouble one of them with something outside his own cabbage patch, and he'll send you packing. And even in his own line if something new crops up and upsets his theories, he'll simply refuse to know it. If he doesn't go out of his way to suppress it. Isn't that so?"

"Yes, that happens. Still . . ."

"Mind you, I was talking of the ordinary run of people, including those with a certain amount of education," said Cloots, motioning with his head toward the old newspaperman.

He bent forward a little to say in a lowered voice:

"It's for all those people that I would like to write the tale I have in mind. But the trouble is," he added, pinching his nose, "I don't know whether it's any good. Nor what I can make of it."

"Your *Paludes?*"

"Yes. It's a tale of people who put up with things, who live and die without being surprised. Y'see? A bunch of addlepates."

He was watching Egmont as if to catch his reaction. When your head is full of an idea, you often expect your listener to be bowled over by the merest hint of it. Egmont knew this from his own experience. He tried his best:

"Where does it happen?" he inquired, to make a show of interest.

"On an island."

It would, thought Egmont, already bored.

"But not a desert island, by any means. On the contrary. It's rather an overcrowded island. In fact, it's a concentration camp. Y'see? A camp of slow death."

"Oh lord!" said Egmont. "What'll you use in lieu of a publisher?"

They both laughed wryly.

"*Ergo* I won't say it is one," Cloots explained. "People will guess it gradually."

"You've got a name for your island yet?"

"It's called Anabiosis."

"What does that mean?"

"Something like revival—when a wilted flower revives in fresh water."

"People revive in your concentration camp?"

Cloots again pinched his nose, in what seemed to be a habitual gesture.

"That is to say, people awaken there. They believe they are born, but in fact they wake up. Y'see? By dint of cross-checking and grubbing among old documents, I discovered that they were most probably imported by force from some vast, unknown, faraway continent. Some of those on the island have an inkling of it too. But it can't be proved."

"People don't remember?"

"No. First thing that happens when they arrive at the camp is a scalpel incision at the nth convolution of their brain, where the memory is situated. Y'see? Total amnesia. Everything has to be learned afresh: speaking, reading."

"Who wields the scalpel?"

"Nobody knows. Probably the *Jungfraus*—the young girls. The camp is guarded by young girls who, incidentally, are delightful, ravishing to look at. That's why people refuse to believe they're in a camp. To put it more correctly, it doesn't even occur to them. Y'see, they don't know that they're prisoners, either, nor that another kind of life is possible. That's what makes their condition so mysterious. Though at the same time it seems to them quite natural, y'see, since it's the only kind they've known for hundreds of generations. They don't imagine, they can't imagine any other. What made Buchenwald intolerable was that the prisoners weren't born there. If they'd lived there from father to son for twenty-five thousand years, they'd have got used to it, as we have to life on earth. 'That's life, old boy, nothing you can do about it. . . .'"

The revolving door opened to admit a youngster. He stopped for a moment, his eyes sweeping the café. His glance did not dwell on them nor on any of the others. It fastened on the eyes of a fellow of his age, half hidden by a pillar, and his lips curled up in a smile of youthful pleasure. Egmont's glance followed him.

"Young girls . . . why young girls?" he asked absently, but his heart twitched, as always, at the sight of such frail, transient youth.

"I told you: because they are pretty. Y'see, if our gardens, our landscapes resembled the frozen wastes of Labrador, if our trees, instead of flowering with cherry blossoms, were made of barbed wire, our fields and hills of tarred old felt, we'd look at Nature with different eyes, wouldn't we? And that would go, too, for our condition on this planet."

"Oh," said Egmont, "I see. Your *Jungfraus* are a symbol."

"You don't like that?" said Cloots.

"It depends. Kafka could afford them. Go on. So they are the *kapos,* the camp wardens, but nobody guesses it? No doubt they treat the convicts decently?"

"On the contrary, they're unimaginably cruel. Still, people adore them. They live in terror but they adore them. Perhaps because the girls' cruelty isn't obvious, y'see. And they are so pretty, so touching. Like roses, like chrysanthemums. Moreover, one can't do without them. They've got everything: food, material. Without them the camp would die in no time. It happens, mind you, that they whip a prisoner to death, without rhyme or reason, quite arbitrarily. But most of the time their cruelty remains rather passive. If you starve to death at their feet, or rot of typhus, they won't lift a finger. But break into their larder to pinch their preserves or some serum, and they won't do anything to stop you either. They're content to regarnish the shelves, untiringly."

"But why, for goodness' sake?" asked Egmont.

"Exactly, I'm asking you," said Cloots. "If I knew why, there'd be no need for me to write my book."

He took a few sips of his beer.

"Besides, y'see, they don't even see you: nobody's ever been able to catch their eye. What's more, they're completely deaf and dumb. No possible communication. Y'see?"

At the back, the two youngsters had spread some newspapers and magazines on their table. They were arguing with animation. One was pulling at his pipe with feigned casualness, but his eyes shone, narrowed, opened again. The other was waving his hands as if to reinforce his arguments. Opposite Egmont, a man and his wife, both fat and flabby, were looking at them too. They were gazing at them without tenderness, with a sort of dull, stern disapproval.

Closter Cloots motioned to Egmont to look out of the window at the night outside. The hill on which the town rose in tiers was lighting up with a thousand pinpoints. Egmont looked at its loveliness as it sparkled in the haze of the rising moon. Under its cool light the steeples and domes floated above a lake of blue shadows in which glistened the roofs.

"If you could see the cities of Anabiosis!" said Cloots playfully. Egmont turned toward him. "There, in their streets, between their walls, people forget for a time that they're scared," said Cloots. "They feel at home in them, among their own kind, y'see, like those in this café. The *Jungfraus* hardly ever intrude there—except in the shape of a steak or a cutlet. Here's to you," he said, raising his glass.

"What! People eat them?" cried Egmont.

"Oh, they don't eat them all. Merely the more stupid ones. Besides, even they are consumed only well disguised. The less they recognize the origin, the more refined people think they are. This isn't only cant: many an Anabiosian would rather starve to death than to have to slaughter them himself. They allot that task to some rough louts whom they despise for it into the bargain. Anyway, they rarely think of these things, y'see, even while they're munching the grilled flesh: it's been going on for so long. . . . Moreover, it's a sort of revenge they take on the others, perhaps."

"Which others?"

"Those who won't let themselves be gobbled up. Those who handle the scalpel and the syringe that dispenses slow death. Oh, but I haven't told you. As soon as they arrive, all the prisoners get a needle shot: into the kidneys, the prostate, the aorta, or elsewhere. Y'see? So they carry their death with them right from the start. But they don't know where. It remains a lottery for them, an accident. All they know is that they've got five or six years to live, at most, and then the pricked organ will give way under horrible pain, and they'll depart this life."

"But what a ghastly story!" exclaimed Egmont, half laughingly, half ashiver.

He had cried out rather loudly. People were looking at him. Fifteen or twenty pairs of sad eyes—except those of the two youngsters, whom nothing distracted from their ardent discussion of plans for the future. Egmont's heart tightened for them, their future was here, under his eyes: all this flesh marked by fatigue or sickness, by the approach of death, those glances veiled with bitterness and boredom, all those wrinkles of defeat at the corners of sagging mouths. . . . He shook himself.

"You think so?" Cloots was saying. "My Anabiosians think they're quite happy to have six years to live. Six years, y'see, is plenty of time to look ahead. Remember that in the old days, before they'd finally discovered the phials of antibiotics in the larder, the average expectation on Anabiosis was hardly three years. Besides, there are some tough ones who go on for eight, even ten years. They're the decennarians. They are feted, made a fuss of in the papers. And this gives the hope that with the advance of medicine people may normally live to be as old as they. Y'see? Some even claim that there's nothing to prevent people from living to the age of fifteen or twenty. But that's laughed at as a pipedream."

"People there feel like laughing?"

"Why ever not? They laugh and dance. We laugh at sixty, don't we? Yet what would people with six hundred years ahead of them think of us who laugh at death's door? No, as I said, six years to them seems fine. Y'see?"

"Still, why do they get killed off so early?"

"On account of the young'uns."

"Pardon?"

"That's their term for the fresh recruits. Have to choose, y'see. Question of organization. The camp can't expand. Therefore you either keep the same lot, but then you can't replace them, y'see, or where would you put the newcomers? Or else you import some every year, but in that case you've got to liquidate the others. For all sorts of reasons, a renewal was deemed preferable. But what is so comic, or rather tragicomic, is the fable those poor fellows have concocted to help them bear it."

The old man with the *pernod* was seized with a sudden fit of coughing. He was choking with asthma. He gripped the table to get back his breath. His neighbors averted their eyes—partly tact, partly disapproval at this exhibition of their common old age. The two young fellows looked at him with ill-concealed disgust.

"What fable?" asked Egmont.

"They've reversed the roles: they don't get liquidated to make room for the recruits, but they're given those recruits to console them for dying. . . . 'These children give us a new lease of life,' they say with emotion. Pathetic, isn't it?"

"And you think your readers will swallow this idea?"

"Oh," said Cloots, "you'll see they won't even tumble to the resemblance. . . . Have you ever seen people face up to an idea that shocks their feelings?"

It was true that Egmont felt shocked. Terribly shocked.

"Anyone on Anabiosis who talked as I do," Cloots went on, "would get himself torn to pieces, I know that. People cling to their fables more than to dear life."

Egmont wasn't listening. He felt terribly shocked.

"Special pleading, that's all," he rapped out in annoyance. "You kill them off at six, we are old at sixty. On the one hand your arbitrariness, on the other a biological fact. Your comparison won't hold water. Our children really do prolong our lives."

"That's exactly the answer he gets too," said Closter Cloots with a chuckle. He had settled back in his corner and, dangling a leg and sipping his beer in small gulps, was eying Egmont ironically.

"Who does?"

"One of our colleagues on Anabiosis. The chronicler of a dreadful camp where one's liquidated at the age of six months. . . . There's no shaking the idea: six years is the normal span of cellular aging. Death is inescapable, it's a biological fact. Children really do prolong our span of life. Everything goes to show it, and most of all the fact that it's been like that from time immemorial."

"What are you trying to argue? That we might live to be six hundred?"

"I don't want to argue anything. Just show things from an unexpected angle. Y'see? I've chosen six years because it's more striking. But six years or sixty, what's the difference? Merely that the former shocks your feelings. It disturbs you. And that's why the mind of man makes such slow progress. Nobody wants to be disturbed. Yet only those who call all things into question all the time ever advance."

"You want to call into question the duration of human life?"

"I? How'd I do it? I am a teacher of Latin. . . . I couldn't do it, not I. But a moment ago we saw a man who does: the man with the bottled chicken heart, your friend Mirambeau."

"I see!" cried Egmont. "So that's it. . . ."

"That *too*," said Cloots without wiping off his ironical grin. "Without Mirambeau's research, these ideas might possibly not have occurred to me. But with or without them, y'see, what does it matter? For if Mirambeau seeks to prove that living matter does not carry old age and death within itself, like a curse, it's because he first dared to ask himself what you refuse to face up to, y'see: Do we procreate because we die, or don't we rather die because we procreate?"

"You consider me very Anabiosian?"

"No more and no less than most. We all are. Take me, y'see: Why am I telling you my story instead of writing it? Because I'm afraid it might be idiotic."

"Certainly not idiotic—" started Egmont.

"But?"

". . . I see only too well what people will say."

"Oh," sighed Cloots, "they'll say *nothing*. That's the worst of it. Who'd dare to take such a story seriously?"

"That depends. . . . If you know how to tell it . . ."

The two young men were crossing the café on their way out, talking and laughing. Some old eyes followed them, and in them could be read no trace of benevolence, but a sort of unavowed disfavor. Egmont felt ill at ease.

"What do people do on your island?" he asked rather quickly.

"Same things as we do on earth. Or in a concentration camp. Everybody tries to muddle through. To suffer as little as possible. With the division that this implies: those who find it more expedient to muddle through *against* their fellows, and those who want to make a stand *all together*. There, as everywhere else, the choice determines their life."

Egmont said without quite knowing why:

"If life on Anabiosis is so much like ours, is it really worth while writing it?"

He blamed himself at once for this remark, but Closter Cloots seemed to take it quite differently.

"I hope, as you have seen," he said, "that people won't notice it right away. It'll strike them as revolting and absurd at first. Y'see? Later, I'd like them to—" he pinched his nose a little as if wondering whether to go on— "it won't be easy," he said, rubbing his small mustache with an air of amusement, "not easy at all, but I'd like my readers, in the long run, to feel as if they *were* on Anabiosis. Y'see? To get them to identify themselves eventually with the people on it. So that it'll all come to seem 'perfectly natural' to them too—as familiar, as normal, inescapable, and unalterable as what is happening here. So that when they put down the book in the end, they have to call both into question at once, y'see—that life and ours. All that they have in common that's so unaccountably odd, often infamous, unnecessary, arbitrary; in short, unbearable. Y'see?"

Definitely, thought Egmont: that story about the "children" still stuck in his gullet. He said—but perhaps merely to hurt Cloots:

"I'm afraid it all adds up to rather a lot of symbols."

"Well, how else do you want me to go about it," cried Cloots, "since people *will* bung up their eyes to shut out reality?"

Chapter Three

It was the habit of Paul Mirambeau, Fellow of the Institute of France and biologist of note, to leave his laboratory for ten minutes every morning to take a stroll in the Park des Recollets. Between him and the park lay only a tiny back garden planted with privet, spindle trees, and a wistaria which, facing north, flowered poorly. He had an intense dislike for this patch of green, finding it damp and depressing. He crossed it in four strides, opened the iron gate, and came out onto the circular avenue along which, in the old days, smart young dragoon officers used to canter on Sundays, before they and their garrison had disappeared and their barracks been turned into a workers' housing estate. Mirambeau crossed the deserted avenue and continued over the sparse grass of a lawn suffering from chronic scabies until he reached the edge of a pool where the lawn was better tended. He slowly walked two or three times around its mirror of still water, bordered with tall poplars and weeping willows. Sometimes, when he was busy with his thoughts, his stumpy legs, with their short steps, would carry him as far as the ruined pillars of an ancient monastery, now reduced to no more than a row of lopped columns stiffly rising from the lawn like a petrified battalion. Then he would leave the park and return along the quiet old canal, shaded by plane trees.

That morning, he was still strolling under the old trees, hardly yet in bud, when a figure hurried past him. That back . . . and that shaggy mane of changing hue . . .

"Pélion!"

The triangular back turned. The youthful face, with its firm, wide lips, showed less surprise than pleasure.

"Mr. Mirambeau! I was on my way to see you!"

A Burgundy accent was just noticeable in his liquid speech. The strong lips opened in a smile over very white teeth.

He fell in beside the burly man, but had to check the lively pace of his long legs to keep in step. This was always a slight torture.

"What's up?" asked Mirambeau.

"Oh, all sorts of things. Don't know where to begin, you know."

"Don't bother, then, as far as I'm concerned," said Mirambeau. "In the first place, I've a funeral on. Besides, I'm over my head in work. So whatever you ask, the answer is 'no' beforehand, I warn you."

"I know . . . I know . . ." said Pélion. "They're going to shoot four more in Madrid," he announced glumly.

"And of course you want me to sign a protest. One more. You people have plastered my signature on so many appeals that you've squeezed it dry of any efficacy it ever had. And that's all you have to show for it. You know jolly well that those four poor devils can't be saved."

"Perhaps not. But there are hundreds more left who'll go down the drain, one by one, if nobody protests."

Mirambeau walked on in silence.

"True enough," he conceded sulkily, "we haven't the right to despair. Our helplessness is discouraging, but to lose courage amounts to aiding and abetting, in the last analysis. What revolts me with those signatures," he said morosely, "is the way they provide you with a clear conscience at no expense. We should all sign 'Uriah Heep.'"

Pélion was used to these outbursts, which he considered as pure redundancy, and he never answered them.

"We'd also like you to . . ." he began, but broke off to start again cautiously. "We know how much time your work takes up, but if you could find an hour or two . . ."

"Come on, come on, cough it up," said Mirambeau. "I won't find an hour, nor even a minute."

"It's about an open letter."

"To be written to whom?"

"I dunno. To the President of the Republic. Never mind whom."

Mirambeau pulled his latchkey out of his pocket. Turning it in the keyhole, he said:

"I appreciate the honor. A thousand thanks. On what topic?"

"The H-bomb. The tests."

"What do you want me to tell the President about them?"

"That's *your* business," said Pélion bluntly as he followed him into the passage.

"Upon my word! Well, young fellow! . . ."

"You've nothing to say about the H-bomb?"

They went into the study. Its window overlooked the park. Mirambeau went to open it. He said quietly:

"I certainly have lots of things to say about it. But . . ."

"Well, then, say them, that's what we're asking," Pélion cut him short impatiently. Why does one always have to bully them, he thought. He'll write that letter in the end, anyway. What infernal bores they all are. . . . Mirambeau had sat down behind the long table covered with files and reports.

"It would take four hundred pages," he said, "to write about nothing but the biological effects. If you people are in a hurry, you'd better . . ."

"Who, we?" exploded Pélion. "You're not in a hurry yourself? Their stockpiles are big enough to destroy the whole human species and you're not in a hurry?"

"They've got the wherewithal to destroy it faster than they think, even without a war," admitted Mirambeau, huddled in his armchair, his big eyes resting thoughtfully on Pélion.

"Well, there you are, that's what you've got to tell 'em!" said the young man. "So why ask?"

"It won't stop anything," said Mirambeau wearily.

"Not writing it will even less," said Pélion, checking his temper—always trotting out the same things, he thought.

"All right, I'll draft it," sighed Mirambeau. "When d'you want it?"

"There'll be an international protest day in a month or six weeks. It would be fine if . . ."

"You shall have it. What else?"

"That's all," said Pélion, getting up. "At least, for you. As for me, I've got to dash off."

"You said there was so much you didn't know where to start."

Pélion seemed to waver, but decided:

"No, nothing you can do."

Mirambeau was enjoying himself. Very likely, he thought, this time it was for once a thing one really *could* do something about.

"Tell me anyway," he suggested with an engaging smile. He was fond of the boy. How old now? Twenty-five? Twenty-six?

Pélion was eying him as one examines a vase at an antique dealer's: a quick glance upward and down again to assess its value.

"Well then, in a couple of words," he conceded grumpily.

Those fits of his when impertinence got the better of deference always delighted Mirambeau: he knew that Pélion admired his knowledge and character, although pretending to scoff at his political inexperience.

"Why, are you so busy?" asked Mirambeau innocently.

"As busy as you," retorted Pélion.

What arrogance, thought Mirambeau, much amused. Why stand for the manners of an uncouth brat? No doubt because the brat was taking more on his shoulders than anybody else in sight.

"My time against yours, then," he proposed with a laugh. "Go ahead."

Pélion seemed a trifle shamefaced.

"Sorry. No, I'm not *so* busy, after all, but . . . I don't see how it can do any good."

"Telling me?"

"Yes."

"Supposing *I* said that?"

Pélion grinned.

"You're right, Mr. Mirambeau. It's about the Coubez factory," he said, sitting down again.

"Trouble brewing?"

"There will be. At least I hope so."

"With the Confédération Générale du Travail?"

"Sure."

"But I read somewhere that Coubez had announced a wage increase."

"Exactly," said Pélion, "but did you see for whom?"

"No. . . ."

"For all those who are members of the 'free' unions, as they call them—meaning the Catholic unions and Co. For the CGT members—nix. D'you realize what'll follow? Especially in this priest-ridden hole of a place, where the CGT is bottom dog."

"But that's illegal!" cried Mirambeau, flinging himself back and opening wide his goggle eyes.

"It's a question of a *raise*, Mr. Mirambeau. A bonus, a gift, anything you like."

"Still, it's discrimination," said Mirambeau. "The law's against—"

"Oh," said Pélion, "you can count on them taking the necessary precautions. They're granting the monthly bonus 'according to individual records,' as they say. But, by pure coincidence, 90 per cent of the 'free' brothers get it, and 90 per cent of the CGT ones have to lump it. It's as plain as a pikestaff, but what can you do? A lot of lawsuits? They're lost beforehand, as you can well imagine."

"Possibly, yes. Still, I'll think about it. Go on."

Pélion leaned forward, propping his elbow on the table.

"Do you see what they're up to? The management announces that all the records will be reviewed again next month, *after* the union elections. . . . You know how it worked in Italy?"

"Why Italy?"

"Because that's where the idea comes from. The Cambrini works near Rome. They dropped 60 per cent of their CGIL membership—that's their CGT."

"Just to get a bonus! Doesn't seem possible. . . ."

"Not only for that, actually: a big American offshore order was switched elsewhere on the pretext of security risks, and eight hundred workers were out in the street. They're poor over there, Mr. Mirambeau. Even poorer than here. And you know what unem-

ployment is like in Italy. Those who had a job were worried. At the
next elections they returned the right shop committee, right in
every sense of the word. . . . The offshore order was switched
back, the workers got signed on again, and except for a few hard-
bitten ones, the whole factory now pays its dues in the proper
quarters for the bonus."

"Still," said Mirambeau, "you're not going to tell me that here
in France . . ."

"People've got to eat, Mr. Mirambeau."

Some moments passed in silence.

"What do you plan to do?" asked Mirambeau at last.

"Strike, if we can. We've got to nip this in the bud. Coubez
aren't alone in this racket, you can be sure: they're merely testing
it out. The spot's well chosen—we're a century behind the times.
Class conscience is still pretty drowsy in this priest-ridden valley.
And if it comes off . . ."

"Pretty clever," murmured Mirambeau in a stricken tone.
"Would you get any support for a strike? Getting fat at the
CGT's expense must seem a godsend to the other unions."

"That's not so sure," said Pélion. "They know they're weak,
they're short of leaders and organizers. Everything's still to be
done in this dump. We've a hundred years to make up, I tell you.
They realize it's too risky to snipe at each other. No, what worries them rather is their rank and file, half of them unorganized.
And the temptation it means for all those poor blighters."

Mirambeau pondered, then said:

"You're going to talk to them?"

"Yes."

"Would you like me to, as well?"

Pélion promptly grasped Mirambeau's big hands in both of his,
and leaned forward over the table.

"You'd do that?"

"This isn't politics any more," said Mirambeau. And he added with a quizzical smile: "As you know I won't meddle in them. But this bird lime . . . They'll slide back twenty years if they're crazy enough to fall for it."

"Good for you, your understanding that."

"A scientist isn't necessarily a bigger fool than a weaver," said Mirambeau with a laugh. (Pélion had managed to set up a small weaving shed of his own.)

"Still, a weaver is closer to them, after all."

"You're your own boss. You earn your living. You could wash yours hands of it."

"A fellow must be off his rocker to think he stands alone," said Pélion. "I could never understand that sort of twirp."

"What sort?"

"Those who're happy if they have a car, a garden, a fishing rod, and let all the rest go hang. That kind of solitude is beyond me. Onanists, that's what they are. Like your friend Egmont."

"Leave Egmont out of this."

Mirambeau knew the dislike the two men harbored for each other. He regretted it without understanding its reasons. Pélion always harped on it, as if it were an obsession.

"That phony poet," he grumbled.

"What do you know about poetry?"

"Enough to be sure his isn't worth a damn. You know why he left us?"

"Roughly, yes."

"To get his play put on in America."

Mirambeau struck the table with his plump fist.

"He left you just because of that sort of slander. I can't blame him."

41

"Don't get sore," said Pélion.

"You can think what you like of Egmont, except that he's dishonest. You people are really discouraging."

"Don't get sore," said Pélion.

"You'll drive away your best friends."

"Don't get sore," said Pélion.

"Do you seriously believe what you said about Egmont?"

"We believe his play wouldn't have been put on if he'd stayed with us."

"That may be, but he didn't leave you to get it put on."

"*Fecit qui* . . . how does the Latin tag go? If he'd wanted to show he was on the level, he could have paid his dollars into the party coffer. Or to some charity, instead of buying himself a mansion."

"We aren't saints, any of us. There's no middle way for you: either saints or scoundrels. You people are tiring."

"That's what keeps us going," said Pélion mildly. "We'd have been gobbled up long ago if we'd stood for half-measures."

"Egmont isn't a man of half-measures."

"No. He's a recluse. That's no better."

"So am I," said Mirambeau.

"What?"

"I'm a recluse too. You know that."

"It's not the same . . ." said Pélion, scratching an ear lobe. "P'raps we need some, anyway."

"Recluses?"

"Those of your type, I mean. You like people."

"So does Egmont!" protested Mirambeau.

Pélion shook his thatch of hair.

"No," he said. "Liking people isn't like that. It doesn't mean only shedding tears over their misery. It also means fighting to make it stop."

"Crying over them is already better than blowing them to smithereens."

"You've got priests for that. Cry over them! What's the good of it if you let them be blown up? Sheer cant."

"What else do I do?" said Mirambeau. "Putting my signature at the bottom of a pamphlet won't put them on their feet."

"You're fighting against death and disease. You're fighting day and night. You're doing a job."

"So you think writing poems isn't doing a job?"

"Don't put words into my mouth, Mr. Mirambeau. You don't shut yourself up in your bottles to be left in peace."

"And Egmont does, in his poems?"

"He shuts himself up in anything within reach. He shuts himself up in his noble tears like a rat in a cheese. Anything serves him as a lock. His house in the woods. His stuffed animals."

"In fact, you mean I don't defend myself as well as he does?"

Pélion burst out laughing.

"You shout 'no' harder than most and then you go and do all you're asked—and even what you aren't asked. You'll come Sunday?"

"Sunday?"

"To the Coubez works. It was your own idea."

"So now you think I'm poking my nose into what isn't my business?"

"I think," said Pélion with sincerity, "you're terrific."

"Well, *you* are cyclothymic," said Mirambeau.

"I'm what?"

"One moment you think I'm a crashing bore, and the next you think I'm terrific."

43

"It isn't me, it's you," said Pélion. "Why do you always wait to be begged so? Instead of coming in with us once for all."

"If I started to explain, you wouldn't let me say three words before flying into a temper."

"All right then, don't. I say, Mr. Mirambeau," he started diffidently.

"What more?"

"You've never shown me your lab," said Pélion.

"You've never asked me to," replied Mirambeau.

He took Pélion's arm with a fatherly smile. And together they went out through the back garden.

Chapter Four

The sun already stood high: it had risen above the hill and was caressing the foot of the bed, but Egmont did not get up. Despite the late hour, he remained bogged in his inner night, amid the murky dregs of forgotten but oppressive dreams. He felt his whole body pervaded by a diffused unease that never left him, a vague nausea, a mushy anguish that weighed on his awakenings every morning.

Heavier today than ever, he thought, still in his half-sleep. That overarrogant, loathsome, monstrous death! In the early hours of the night, the nurse had found a chaotic scene reminiscent of some foul crime: the blackboard spattered with blood, and on the floor the convulsed body, as if gutted: its head in so vile a pool of stinking matter that the first thing to do was open all the windows. But the dead man's right hand still clutched a piece of chalk.

And that Clootsian universe! he thought with a shiver. That life is void of meaning, we know, but that it should also be that hideous Medusa . . . Can a simple change of perspective, a foreshortening, as it were, *create* horror, or mustn't the horror be already there in the germ? The word foreshortening called to his

45

mind the Christ of Milan: those huge, horrible feet . . . distortion or a revelation?

I'll go and see Mirambeau, he thought. If Cloots is right, if our organism does indeed age and die voluntarily, on account of that "make way for youth" with its smack of cannibalism . . . He raised his hand, which was already lined and flabby. Doubly vile old age, he thought, if it is also this treachery. Doubly cruel youth if it is also . . .

From the kitchen came the sound of coffee grinding. I oughtn't to, he thought. He told himself that he should get up, slip on his dressing gown. "I let her go on as if she were my daughter, or a serving-girl." Every morning, Pascale, the daughter of Dutouvet, the archaeologist, came and got his breakfast, brought it to him in bed. Every day he promised himself: "This is the last time." But the next morning he did not stir between his sheets: that weariness, that leaden anguish . . . "She is young," he'd pamper his tiredness, "so young. After all . . ." But this morning, the idea of that nimble youthfulness close by took on a tinge of ferocity.

There was a knock at the door. The young girl carried in a tray: black coffee, buttered toast, a boiled egg. . . . She knew she must also add, in a small saucer, half a tablet of orthedrine. It distressed her, but what good was it trying to stop him: he would merely help himself, and perhaps take a whole tablet, if not two. . . .

"Thank you, little one. Open the window, will you? It's so lovely out. . . ."

She opened it. The song of birds burst into the room as if she had turned the switch of some pastoral radio.

"You weren't too cold coming?"

She rode over from Chaulieu every morning on a motor scooter. There was ground frost sometimes as late as May.

She shook her head with a smile, without turning round. She

46

was sniffing the fragrance of the woods carried in by the breeze. Egmont stared at the graceful silhouette against the light, her head surrounded by its halo of soft flames in which the light glistened like dew. And he wondered, wondered, wondered, why she gave him so much of her time. "Gave" was the word; he only paid her a little pocket money, for form's sake. She came every day, tidied his papers, filed his mail, dealt with bores, and sometimes he even caught her mending his socks or his shirts. Once again he thought with a twitching heart that Pélion loved her, that young scoundrel. . . . Everybody knew it. Did she? Did she know it? And if she did . . .

"Pascale . . ." he started.

She turned round. She was smiling. But not at him: at the forest. She had not turned off her smile, that was all. He averted his head.

"Take the tray away," he said gruffly.

This time the smile was addressed to him, but it was not the same smile. A subtle change had come about in the lines at the corners of her eyes, in the height of her cheekbones drawn up as she smiled, in the contours of her mouth. It was as if they expressed a . . . yes, a feeling of slight, very slight pity. But also an unalterable wonder, an admiring awe that never left her in his presence. All this roused his anger.

She went out, came back, and stood leaning one shoulder against the doorpost. She was looking at him. She had not yet uttered a single word.

They were gazing at each other silently, he propped against his pillow, his hands flat on the counterpane, she slightly inclined toward one hip, so slim in her simple frock (gray or blue?) which fell in gentle folds. At last he said—he murmured, it was hardly meant for her:

"Who the devil do you take me for, anyway?"

47

The girl's eyes became round, not so much with surprise as with disquiet, with worry that crinkled the bridge of her nose.

"What glamour can you possibly see in middle age and, shall we say, talent? Why do you waste your time here? Hadn't you better send me some bespectacled old spinster instead, with nothing better to do?"

She said nothing. She just looked at him. Without a smile. She seemed perfectly calm. A frightening calmness. It was so eloquent that Egmont was almost relieved by it.

"Yet you don't *love* me," he said in a rather hoarse voice, stressing the word. He added slowly: "Do you?"

She remained motionless at first, continuing to gaze at him, as if she had not heard. And then she turned her head a little from right to left, but so slowly. . . . Egmont could have cried out. He controlled himself. And her eyes resting on him were so straightforward, so clear, so unsecret, eyes that were neither black nor brown but deep-hued, he thought, like plowed earth after rain.

I can't bear it any more, thought Egmont. Really I can't. I've got to bring it to a head today, now, at once. I'm becoming a laughingstock to my own self.

"Heaven's my witness," he said, "that I'm not keeping you here. I've not asked anything of you, you come every day of your own free will. The birds, the forest are my witness," he repeated.

She did not move. Only one hand was smoothing a fold of her dress as if to make sure it fell as it should. She had turned a little pale, that was all.

"Well, answer, for God's sake!" he shouted.

"I come of my own free will," she said, and her voice vibrated as softly as the muted reed of a harmonium.

"Why do you come?" he implored.

48

"You don't want me to come any more?"

"I don't know," said Egmont, and he forced himself at last to add: "You know that Pélion is in love with you."

"But Robert doesn't need me," she murmured after a moment.

"What does 'need' mean?" said Egmont slowly, staring at her fixedly, as if he wanted to nail her to the wall.

Once again she moved her head as if to say no; and suddenly she lowered her eyes, seemed to study the tips of her shoes, which she raised a little; then looked up again, and Egmont received their shaft of light full in the face once more.

"You do not love me," said Egmont, groping for words, "and yet if . . . if I were crazy enough to tell you . . . to ask you to marry me . . . You are eighteen, aren't you?"

Her head nodded yes as she murmured: "Not quite."

"You would do it . . ." he concluded, and one couldn't tell whether it was a question or an answer.

She did not turn away her clear, straight, unsecretive gaze.

"And yet," he went on—but once again was it a question or an answer—"and yet you love him."

She seemed, miraculously, even stiller than before. But at last she said in a toneless voice:

"I would marry you."

"What I'd like," said Egmont, almost through gritted teeth, "is to drill open that incredible brain of yours to see what's going on inside. Really . . ." he exploded.

"You do know," said Pascale simply.

"I don't!" shouted Egmont, furiously pounding his bed with his fist. "No, I don't. Nor do you, perhaps." He said with a painful sneer: "Need you, need you . . . What do you imagine?"

"You're too unhappy," she replied, and her voice suddenly cracked. And suddenly too, as if a button had been pressed to make it spurt, a tear—a single one—rolled down her nose.

Egmont gaped at it for a moment, but pulled himself together as if with a rein.

"And what could you do about it?" he cried roughly. He added at once more gently: "What do you know of it?"

Quite unexpectedly she left the doorpost at last, took three steps, and dropped to her heels at the foot of the bed. She buried her face in her arms, and her hair spread in disheveled curls.

"I heard you," she mumbled into the blanket.

"When? What?"

"With Daddy."

And she recited without raising her face:

> *"I'm a man who's been dead for years without number*
> *"Under wilted roses my heart lies in slumber."*

"That's from a poem by Cros," said Egmont softly.

"Yes. But you recited it for yourself."

She hasn't made this up, thought Egmont amazed. But when? He wondered again. What did she hear?

Like an echo, her father's voice came back to him, deep and calm, in his library so crammed with papers that one never found a place to sit.

"You no longer feel in tune with anyone, least of all with yourself," the voice said, and a forefinger went rooting in the middle of the little beard. The eyes could not be seen behind the steel-rimmed glasses that reflected the lamplight.

"That's true," confessed Egmont.

Since leaving the "party" a year previously, he had been groping in the darkness of a pathetic indecision.

"Why don't you go back?"

The question evidently concealed no ulterior motive: neither advice nor reproach.

"You know why," said Egmont. "For the same reasons that keep you from joining it. We are too strongly marked by our upbringing. We cannot manage to see things as they do. Nor keep an untroubled conscience when it comes to some of their fights. I'll tell you something: we are Forty-Eighters. We can't swallow their changing, contradictory truths. And even less that they, in turn, have adopted Maurras's advice: Don't argue with an opponent, dishonor him. As they've done with Tito, with so many others."

Dutouvet said simply:

"I've often wondered if that's really the way things are, seen from the inside."

"It's the way I saw them," sighed Egmont. "Maybe I saw them wrongly. But I can't see differently. And I can't pretend I have a clear conscience when in fact it's troubled. I'm not accusing them, mind you, I'm accusing myself, my own brain structure. What can I do about it?"

"Hillary said it would be too beautiful to die for an entirely just cause. Every cause remains human. And doesn't man's greatness lie in struggling amid his contradictions? What cause could be clear of this struggle? Doesn't real courage mean shouldering a cause despite its faults, its weaknesses?"

"But you yourself haven't taken the plunge either," said Egmont suavely.

"I didn't say I had that sort of courage. . . . But you had it once. It wasn't purblindness, surely? What has changed?"

Egmont sighed and said:

"I suppose what happens is that you think you have the necessary courage, and then experience shows you that you haven't."

But he leaned back, closed his eyes, and said with an even deeper sigh:

"Oh, and besides, there are other things too. . . ."

He felt the invisible gaze behind the glinting spectacles rest heavily on his face. Pascale's father slowly drew at his unlit pipe: he was no longer allowed to smoke and tried to deceive his craving with this ghost of a stale fragrance. . . . It made a sucking, monotonous noise.

"I wonder," muttered Egmont, "why we plod on so doggedly."

"At what?"

"Oh, at nothing, at life," said Egmont, and he quoted the verse:

"I'm a man who's been dead . . ."

"Do you really feel so hopeless?" asked his friend, stricken.

"Hopeless? No," said Egmont. "Hopelessness implies having hoped. Only one word fits me: bored. I'm so boundlessly bored that I no longer desire anything. Either to live or die."

"But that's abominable."

"It is rather," he admitted. "But you get used to it. Or more exactly, you fool yourself. You take an interest in this or that, an essay on Petrarch, a zoological collection like the one I've just started, and you get to believe in this self-deception. A way of killing time."

"That isn't true," protested Dutouvet. "Yesterday, on the platform, your indignation against those torturers in Morocco, that wasn't make-believe."

Egmont slowly raised his hand, let it drop again.

"There's no contradiction in that," he said. "When you get fed up with bloody bores, it can make you fighting mad."

"Yes, because, if it weren't for them, you'd have no cause to be fed up."

"I wouldn't be so bored if someone explained to me what it was all about, here on this planet. I'm fed up, like someone obliged to sit through the five acts of an interminable play in a foreign language, with no one to translate for him. It may amuse him for an act or two. But I find the third act already a bit on the long side. I'd like to be able to stroll around in the wings for a change."

He bent forward suddenly and said across the table:

"But the most staggering thing is that death frightens me. It scares me stiff. Isn't that amazing?"

Egmont was musing meanwhile: But how old could she have been at the time? Fourteen at most . . . and I'm getting on for fifty. He said:

"So you were eavesdropping?— Where did you hide?"

He did not notice that he had dropped into the "grown-up" tone that he had used when she was a little girl.

"I was doing my homework in the small study. I heard everything."

She had not lifted her head from her arms. The voice came to him muffled by her curls.

"For a long time I'd been copying out your poems in my copybook . . ." she said. "All of them. I still know them all by heart."

Heavens alive, thought Egmont, so that's what's behind it! And his heart was divided between a feeling of tenderness, of acute irony and a deep, aching pain. To be in love with an old, despairing poet, to fancy herself already his Antigone supporting him with her youth—and now she loved Pélion, but she wanted, wanted, wanted to remain faithful to her childhood.

He was going to call her name, when she suddenly cried out from the well of her folded arms:

"And I can't *bear* people to die!"

53

How does dying come into it? he wondered, but she went on: "Only yesterday, that friend of Daddy's. I liked him to come and see us. I was fond of him. He was handsome," she murmured, "his voice was musical. And his hand trembled like the wing of a bird whenever he raised it in talk. And he's dead," she cried. "They all die! And those who aren't dead will die too!"

He thought with anger that two years ago she had still been in Cloots's class. So this was the havoc wrought by that destroyer. . . .

But he saw she had lifted her head again. She remained squatting by the bedside, her chin on her forearms, and began:

> *". . . We've come out of the night, but you?*
> *To what night are you swept by this light*
> *in which gaily trail my first shouts*
> *and those mad bouts of laughter?"*

Egmont recognized a poem of his youth. Heavens! To hear it surging up from so long ago, and that this particular girl . . .

> *"Stop us! Do not believe our eyes,*
> *their looks are daggers in disguise. . . ."*

I wrote those words, thought Egmont. He was overcome with astonishment. So he too had shared one day that horrible intuition about murderous youth. . . .

> *"They are long, sharp weapons*
> *that slowly pierce your back. . . ."*

"Stop it," muttered Egmont, and Pascale obeyed. "So it was I who stuffed your head with this nonsense?" he said, aghast.

"When you die," said Pascale, "I think I'll kill myself."

Egmont smiled. She had found her fourteen years again.

"If I believed that for a second," he said without irony, "I'd wear a belt of thorns to the end of my days to punish myself. But *you* believe it no doubt, and that's already more than . . ."

"I'll kill myself because I love life and you don't, yet death frightens you. That's what's so utterly, utterly unbearable," she said without turning her eyes from him.

"You despise my fear?" said Egmont with an effort, after a long pause.

She protested without raising her voice:

"How can you think I'm so presumptuous? You are afraid because you know better than I what it means."

"Fear?"

"No, death. It's so very far from me. . . . But for you it's getting closer, and you're counting the days. Each season shortens your breath a little. It's horrible," she said, and buried her face again in her arms.

The silence lasted a very long time. At last Egmont said in a low voice:

"You'd guessed that I'd begun to love you?"

He saw the curls shake as her head nodded yes.

"And you so much wanted it to happen, once," he resumed. "You prayed heaven for it. And now it's happened. . . ."

He saw her press her head more tightly into her arms.

"It's so foolish to be stubborn," he murmured, but his heart ached.

"I'm not stubborn," he heard through the curls. "I love you."

A moment ago she had said she didn't.

"Come, come," he said moodily, "you love Pélion."

The curls did not stir. Egmont felt miserable. Almost as miserable as when Olga . . . Oh, why must Olga always loom in his thoughts? That affair was well and truly done with, settled and filed a good many years ago.

"I love you," said the childish voice from among the curls, "and you won't believe me."

Chapter Five

The road climbed up between the beeches. It was an old abandoned road along which the stagecoaches used to pass in days gone by. Grass had grown over it, but here and there a mossy paving stone jutted out, grazed a shoe.

The morning mist was of the kind that would lift later to reveal sparkling sunshine. For the time being it was like walking among memories: everything melted in a soft, suffused haze, under the pale blue sky. The trees materialized one by one, dim phantoms first, then strangely real. The leaves shed dewdrops that plashed on your back, your shoulder.

Ahead of Egmont walked the man carrying the urn, flanked by the potbellied notary, who was panting a little. In front of them, the undertaker was chatting with the police officer in an undertone: occasionally their subdued chuckles could be heard.

Egmont had fixed his gaze determinedly on the burly neck before him, with its ruddy flush between the peaked cap and the black cloth collar. He thought of nothing—he did not want to think. The urn was heavy, and the man changed it over from side to side at regular intervals. Egmont could guess which side it was on by the swelling of the man's neck. He felt Mirambeau's arm brush against his at times, and he heard his short breathing.

He wished that this breathlessness would continue to suspend all talk.

The group that followed them was whispering. Sometimes Cloots's voice could be recognized. Rather suddenly Egmont heard him protest loudly "Not at all!" and could not help listening. Mirambeau too had turned his head slightly.

"Who said anything of the sort?" Cloots was saying. "Certainly not he. 'To merge with nature'! You completely misunderstood. Don't you see he meant the very opposite?"

His will, they're still at it, thought Egmont. Can't they stop arguing about it. There were some half a dozen of them climbing up this ghost of a road, which led to the former quarry beyond the wood of Mauvoisin, in order to carry out the dead man's last wishes.

My ashes are to be thrown to the winds to be scattered.

The context was clear enough, though: *Nobody is to pay his respects to my carcass. It has killed me. You do not honor a killer: you annihilate him.*

And that ass, back there, who supposed . . .

"It would doubtless be more poetic," said a voice which Egmont recognized as belonging to Burgeaud the neurologist. "Universe, communion, immortality, the whole caboodle. But Mr. Cloots is right: it would be misconstruing him utterly."

"But why, then, have his ashes . . ."

"That is his last anger," said Burgeaud.

"Against whom?" asked the voice.

"Against whatever makes us confuse man with his mortal remains. His fratricidal remains. Even after they're reduced to ashes. I am charged to put in the urn, in their place, the manuscript of his work on *Periodic Ring Structures*. He's willing to have people come and pay their respects to that, recall his memory—even pray for it. But not over the remains of his murderer."

"It's just a paradox," said the voice.

"It wasn't for him," flung out Closter Cloots with sudden vehemence. "His terrible courage in death is proof of his sincerity—of the fierceness of his sincerity. Nobody has the right to call it in doubt."

"It's a paradox all the same," the voice persisted. "He was the first to know that the mind cannot exist without the body—that it exists *through* the body. This obsolete spiritualism . . ."

"What he deemed obsolete is precisely this *through*," said Burgeaud. "He said: *fettered to*. Just like the eye and the light. What blind man would raise a memorial to his cataract? Yet that is exactly, he used to say, what people do when they visit a grave."

They had left the wood behind at last. The plateau spread out before them in a straight sweep to the edge of the cliff. They had to leave the road and take a narrow footpath. Here and there, the broom was still in flower. The mist had dissolved. Under the cool sun they felt the breeze from the plain fanning their faces. The horizon rose in ripples to the foothills of the mountain range in its distant, almost invisible blueness. The clouds, in passing, dimmed and lit alternately the little white houses of a tiny village nestling in the crook of the river.

On the way back, Egmont kept silent. He was gloomy and sullen. The ceremony had exasperated him. By wanting to destroy the old rites, he thought, you create new ones that are just as silly. As for Cloots's intervention halfway through that mumbo jumbo! The urn bearer had started scattering the ashes in small handfuls with, admittedly, a somewhat solemn, pompous air. But was that a reason for wresting the urn from his hands, turning it upside down and emptying it into the ravine as if it were a garbage can? Whom did he want to impress with this melodramatic gesture? The ashes had swirled in the current of rising air, and some had come drifting back to the onlookers, who had felt them stinging their faces.

And what meaning was there in locking up in the urn that unprotesting manuscript which nobody would ever read? Who'd even care about its contents a quarter of a century hence? Assuming, that was, that the paper, too, hadn't crumbled to dust by then. Grotesque!

Egmont was walking alone, partly in protest, partly out of churlishness. The sun was now playing between the trees. The grass on the road, checkered with shadows, shone with a sparkling greenness. One's feet slid on the downward slope, over the dew and the slippery stones. He saw Cloots and Burgeaud grip old Mirambeau's arm now and then, as he slithered on his dumpy legs. All three were deep in conversation.

Egmont purposely did not listen. He did not think either. He refused to think, tired to death by the daily discovery that thought led nowhere. He looked at the trees, the trembling leaves with the glittering drops at the end of the branches, the soft-colored clouds gliding across the lavender sky. He tried to take pleasure in them, succeeded to some extent, but not very well. The bitter tang of vanity polluted everything, even beauty.

The road, emerging from the wood, dropped down to the ancient vineyards. It wound once or twice across the slope of the hill, and joined the highway at the war memorial, which stood outside the city walls, close to the cemetery.

The three men had stopped in surprise. Egmont, drawing level with them, stopped too. "What's going on?"

The highway, down below, was packed with a throng of people

carrying banners. They seemed excited. The noise of the crowd rose like the roar of breakers. Now and then, the roar was capped by shouts.

"It's those Reds brawling again," said the police officer jeeringly.

Mirambeau jerked his head around, but said nothing. Egmont remembered—having for many years taken part in it—that the workers of Chaulieu had their real May Day celebration on St. Gregory's Day. It was an old tradition which, handed down from the medieval guilds, had, oddly enough, survived here. Even the Communists had eventually adopted it, lest they should find themselves isolated. They weren't too numerous in Chaulieu, as it was.

The marchers would line up in procession in the Place Gambetta, follow the Avenue Louis-Blanc and the Cours Berthollet, place their wreaths on the memorial and—in principle—return to town, where they would disperse in Grand Square. In principle: because in fact they rarely got there.

Each year, the Communists suggested a truce for the May Day Demonstration to the trade unions: a procession without divisions and precedences, with one solid throng marching in brotherly unity behind the rows of red banners. Each year the proposal was turned down. And the selection of the group that was to head the march promptly became the subject of endless parleys and grim struggles that lasted for weeks without, usually, leading to results. So much so that two separate crowds would eventually be marching on either side of the boulevard, each behind its own flags, divided by a long and narrow moving crevice which the burghers of Chaulieu, sheltering behind their high windows, would laughingly call the *cordon sanitaire*.

They laughed even more when insults began to be exchanged across the narrow gap of the cordon. This rarely failed to happen. Shouts of "Social traitor!" or "Moscow lackey!" were sure to rise from the rival groups of workers—because of some private score to settle, trouble over a girl, a case of sneaking, a piece of double crossing. Their supporters would join in, gradually the ranks would catch fire, and rarely did the procession reach the war memorial before the bickering had turned into a brawl despite the leaders' ineffectual efforts.

This was the moment chosen by the forces of law and order— police or Compagnie Républicaine de Sécurité—to turn the occasion to their own account. Before the columns could realign to present a common front in defense, they would be broken up into fractions. The return to town resembled a rout, and the prefecture would, so to speak, hang out the flags.

Egmont's memories of these affrays were half unpleasant, half nostalgic, and there was no need to explain to him what was happening now before his eyes.

At the head, the two files were still marching in order, but they sprawled and writhed toward the back, like a crushed earthworm. As the procession neared the monument, however, the ranks attempted to close up again in a sort of respectful truce. It was this regrouping that the police were determined to prevent. Bursting out of barns and courtyards in which they had been biding their time, they had already sectioned off t⌐. head of the procession. A squad of them now streamed up the gap of the cordon and, laying about with their truncheons and rolled capes, started cracking up the two separate columns, splitting them into small, powerless, jumbled splinters. Another squad was adding to the commotion in the already fidgety tail end of the march, pulverizing it with gusto. A sort of froth had begun to form on its edges, lapping over the embankments of the road and flowing into the fields—they were those who wanted to get out of harm's way or who had already had their fill. The rest of the crowd reeled under the volley of truncheons and capes, tried to pull itself up here and there, collided with itself in violent jolts, as if shaken by hiccups—and for a moment Egmont saw again the dying man whose dust they had just scattered. He saw him in his agony, broken, battered to death by spasms and convulsions. He passed his hand over his face, as if he could still feel the sting of the ashes.

Meanwhile, without exchanging a word, Burgeaud and Mirambeau had flung themselves forward. They were hurtling down across the fields as fast as the old biologist's fat legs would permit them. Cloots did not follow. He came up to the motionless Egmont, stared with him at the two running figures. He muttered: "Why meddle? What's the good? . . ." Egmont felt angered—yet without cause, he had to admit, for he himself had been thinking along similar lines. The cause, no doubt, was that twisted smile under the small mustache.

The rest of their group moved on again, but at a dignified pace, watching Mirambeau and his companion drawing closer to the seething highway. But what can they hope for? thought Egmont, curious but worried. They're going to get themselves clouted like the rest. The punches he himself had received came back to his mind with amused complacency, but he feared them for the intrepid old scientist. Mirambeau was passing through the fringe of the lads already out of the fight, and was now elbowing his way through to the front. His elephantine figure enabled Egmont to follow him right into the heart of the fray, like a canoe riding on a whirlpool. He saw him work hard to get close to the police squad, which was merrily clubbing its way along, and grip one fellow by the shoulder. The policeman turned round enraged, his truncheon in the air. Egmont felt his own back jerk, as if under the impact of a sudden explosion, and his legs bounded forward to the rescue. But the truncheon there below did not come down, or rather it came down slowly, falteringly. . . .

Mirambeau, a Fellow of the Institute of France, was one of the prides of Chaulieu. The whole town knew his familiar figure, as also that of Burgeaud, the renowned neurologist. The constable, obviously perplexed, could not make up his mind. The other police, who had turned round in concert, also recognized the two men and hesitated in their turn. This indecision sealed their fate. Behind Mirambeau a wall had already formed, solid and intimidating. And behind the police, too, the people had rallied. Two seconds, and it was too late. The truncheons flew out of the policemen's hands as if by an electric shock. The squad was jostled, squeezed like a kernel, squirted and discarded on the roadside. Disarmed and deprived of their emblems of authority, they brushed their dusty caps with their sleeves amid the guffawing spectators, and promptly dwindled to their true size, that of ordinary men, and so they, too, started to laugh as if it had all been a huge joke.

A howl of victory and childlike joy went up around Mirambeau. The policemen who were still busy farther up instinctively felt a threat in their rear. They wanted to turn and face it. But for them, too, it was too late. You cannot switch from the offensive to defense without the punch passing over to the other side. The human wall that had lined up behind them carved through the moving mass with shouts of victory, made it clot, while the wall itself thickened and hardened as it moved on. The last policemen soon found themselves cast out on the roadside, as the others had been. And the whole delirious throng suddenly seemed to set as if frozen solid. Their shouts merged into a triumphant chant, while the banners, scattered a moment before, went up again at the head of the column, mingling at random, in a higgledy-piggledy, brotherly jumble.

And the procession started moving back to town—with no *cordon sanitaire*. They entered it singing with such fervor and stamping so forcefully that the windowpanes rattled as they passed. There was no flag-hanging at the prefecture that year.

Chapter Six

Egmont, too, followed the demonstration, but he was torn by conflicting emotions. At first he had felt elated, almost happy, as he had not done for a long time. But then Cloots had said: "Ugh, not for me" and had strode away with that irritating smile of his, leaving Egmont to feel rather a fool, with the edge taken off his pleasure. He would have liked to chant with the crowd but no sound would come. He squeezed through the ranks to try to reach Mirambeau. He caught up with him only when they were in sight of the Town Square. He found him together with Burgeaud, arms linked in Pélion's, and his brittle excitement ebbed and vanished.

But the old scientist had seen him and stopped to wait for him. He did not let go of Pélion's arm, and Pélion, frowning slightly, averted his head. For the space of a second Egmont, too, hesitated. Then he went toward the young man with outstretched hand and a smile. Mirambeau was delighted: patching it up? He was pained in his friendship for both of them by their antagonism. Pélion displayed some surprise and embarrassment, but he took Egmont's outstretched hand and shook it. Besides, he was bubbling over with enthusiasm at the victory of his side, and said excitedly:

"See that, Doctor?" (He pretended to see Dr. Roux exclusively in Egmont.) "I'm still all of a heap. What fame can do, by jiminy! Three cheers for science! Striking the cops dumb with awe! The Prof's worth his weight in gold."

"You people will have to rewrite your bible," said Egmont. "It's one up for individual enterprise over mass action."

"Sure: you've seen a swallow, so it's summer."

"I don't mind saying I'm pretty proud of my success," said Mirambeau. "But it's true that it doesn't prove anything. This is a small town, every policeman knows me. If this were Paris or if we'd been up against the cops of the C.R.S., I'd have waked up to find myself in the hospital. Besides, I doubt I'd have dreamed of meddling in that case."

Egmont felt a slight twinge of jealousy: Would the policemen have recognized him? You'd know whether they would or not if you'd acted like Mirambeau, instead of like Cloots. He wondered for a moment whether cowardice had held him back. Surely not, since not so long ago, before leaving the party . . . Why, then, had he not joined the fray? He shrugged his shoulders, he knew why well enough: the weariness of life.

"Well," said Burgeaud with a nonchalance that never failed him, "here we are safely home. Good-by, I'm off to the hospital."

"I say, he's waking up," said Pélion, looking after him. "This is the first time, as far as I know, that he's joined in a thing like that."

"What about me?" said Mirambeau.

"That's true," said Pélion with surprise, "but with you it seems so natural. Anyhow, Mr. Mirambeau, this has been a damn fine piece of work! You can't imagine what a blow it will be for those Coubez stinkers. You've achieved unity at the base! It's a miracle, if you think of it."

"Don't get excited," said Mirambeau. "It's merely unity against the cops. You'll have plenty of hard nuts to crack yet, don't worry."

During the last few days he had managed to collect a good deal of information on the wages question. The instigator of the whole scheme was the elder Coubez son, Antoine Coubez-Mallat, Christian Democrat deputy, forty years old, father of six, "tough but fair," aloof or hearty according to which way the wind blew, a worthy representative of that "intelligent right wing" which so well masters the art of withdrawing at low ebb in order to return on the flowing tide. He was well in with a lot of people in Paris, had means of exerting indirect pressure on the Chaulieu trade unions, invariably knew the exact state of the labor market, in fine, was perfectly equipped to launch an all-out paternalist offensive at the most opportune moment. The first chill of local unemployment had already made itself felt, it looked like wages would be frozen for a long time: the workers would be sorely tempted to yield to the lure of a bonus that had every appearance of a bounty.

"Sure, sure," said Pélion. "I know all that."

He always knows everything, thought Mirambeau with amusement, as the three of them were sauntering unhurriedly under the plane trees along the old canal.

"I even know something you don't," the young man went on, passing his fingers through his unruly shock of hair. He turned his head with a silent laugh: "There's a lockout at the Saint-Vaize distilleries."

Mirambeau slowed down to look at him. Egmont seemed miles away, in silent thought.

"The two hundred North Afs laid off at Saint-Vaize," said Pélion, "are going to be mighty tempted to seize their chance, if there's a strike here. It's easy to find people who'll make them believe their own bosses will climb down if they show Saint-Vaize that they can get a job in Chaulieu. Whereas we'll have to make them understand the opposite. Namely that Saint-Vaize and Chaulieu are hand in glove. Perhaps we'll have to drive it into their skulls by force. They'll take us for racialists. And who'll rub their hands in glee anyhow? Coubez and company."

They had arrived.

"May I come in with you?" said Egmont in an odd tone of voice. "I shan't disturb you?"

"Why, of course, do," said Mirambeau. "On the contrary, I'm delighted. So my old lab interests you?"

They went in, all three. Egmont started glancing around, obviously searching for something.

"Is that chicken heart of yours still beating?" he asked.

Mirambeau eyed him with a half-smile and he took him by the arm in silence and pushed him on.

Their heels rang out on the tiled floor, and a vibrant echo boomed back like the bass note of an organ. They walked past several tables piled with mixers, driers, balances, a paraphernalia of glass and metal instruments, attended to by white-coated young women.

Mirambeau stopped in front of the last bench. Its four sides were surmounted by tall glass panels, like an enormous aquarium turned upside down. Upon it were aligned a row of jars filled with cloudy liquids and connected with each other by a maze of glass and rubber tubes. In the center, a small copper and crystal pump set this circulatory system pulsating. It produced a constant, monotonous murmur of alternate sucking and gurgling.

Mirambeau pushed Egmont on again. He made him walk around the table. In one corner of the pseudo aquarium, another one, also upside down but much smaller, contained another cir-

68

culatory system around a single glass jar. Inside this jar was a heart.

A tiny, touching heart that throbbed away with a pathetic constancy and regularity. Egmont watched it silently, waiting for Mirambeau to speak.

"Is this what you wanted to see? It's been beating like this for over five years," he said. "I'm doing no more than repeat an old experiment. In another laboratory, in the States . . ."

"I know," said Egmont. "Another heart has been beating for thirty-four years."

"As long as that?" said Mirambeau.

"Eh?" said Egmont, disconcerted.

"Where d'you read that? In *Science in a Nutshell?* You may be right at that; thirty years or thirty thousand, what's the difference? That's not what matters. One fact has been proved, or as good as: it can be made to live as long as you like."

"Yes," said Egmont. "That's just it. If I remember rightly, though, there is one condition: it has to be fed on embryos."

"Well?" said Mirambeau.

"But the vitality of an embryo cell, its reproductive power, is twenty or thirty times that of an adult cell."

"Well?" said Mirambeau.

"So this eternal heart doesn't really prove anything, does it? Feed it on ordinary blood or plasma, and it'll age and die like the others, won't it?"

"Well?" said Mirambeau.

"It's my turn to say 'well?' What are you trying to prove?"

Mirambeau nodded and peered at him musingly.

"You're all the same," he muttered.

He glanced across at Pélion, but Pélion remained impassive. And suddenly the quiet paunch heaved with soundless laughter.

"My word," he cried, "if I am not mistaken, you have come to beard the lion in his den, to show him that he's wrong. Right?"

Egmont blushed. And then he too opted for laughter.

"I don't know," he said. "If I did . . ."

"All right, come and confess," said Mirambeau. "What's gnawing you? What have you been told?"

"Well, Cloots claims . . ."

"The Latin master!" said Mirambeau. "What does he understand about this stuff?"

"That's just it: how much *does* he understand?"

"Oh, I see. . . . Well, go ahead."

"Did he tell you about Anabiosis?"

"Whom didn't he tell?" said Mirambeau, grinning. He flung his short arms up into the air.

That'll teach me, thought Egmont, with annoyance.

"Well, then," he said out loud, "do you remember his story about the 'children'?"

"What children? No . . ."

"Well, the fresh recruits."

"Oh yes. Well, what of them? What's bothering you?" asked Mirambeau, and a twinkle of amusement gleamed in his bulgy eyes. "Study up on your Weisman. It's self-evident."

"That children—"

"—are the murderers of their fathers and mothers, why, of course. Involuntary homicide, I grant you. Most of the time, anyhow."

"Don't joke," said Egmont. "Do you mean to say this horrible assumption really squares with your research?"

"You'd have to know, first of all, what my research is," said Mirambeau with sudden seriousness.

"Exactly, if . . ."

"And to listen for a change, instead of running round in circles."

Egmont passed his hand over his forehead.

"Sorry," he said. "I . . . I find the condition of man hard enough to bear as it is, and if on top of that . . ."

"Donning a pair of blinkers certainly won't help you," said Mirambeau, looking at him quizzically.

Egmont stiffened slightly.

"A man like you, at any rate, should not treat it lightly, even in jest."

"I leave you to judge," said Mirambeau.

He took him by the arm again, and led him back to the first jars.

"In there are sample sections: liver, kidney, guts, skin. Fed on ordinary plasma. They age slowly, normally, like yours or mine. What's generally inferred from that? That the aging of cells is a biological necessity. Metchnikoff himself daren't doubt it."

He pointed beyond the jars to the one they had just left.

"Yet there we have a heart that doesn't age. Exceptional though it may be, it still proves that cellular aging is not a biological necessity after all. Not that we needed this heart to tell us that. The least neuron will do: a brain cell remains identical from birth to death, it is as permanent as a diamond splinter: it doesn't age, it doesn't reproduce itself, it doesn't die."

"What d'you mean, it doesn't die?" suddenly asked Pélion.

"It doesn't. It's we who die, the stopping of the heart kills it. That's not at all the same thing."

"What about senility?"

"One often tends to confuse the *accidental destruction* of small areas of the brain," said Mirambeau with emphasis, "with senescence of the brain cortex as a whole—which does not occur. An eighty-year-old neuron, unless destroyed by accident, is as fit and fresh as it was at thirty. Leonardo at eighty was in the full glory of his intelligence."

"I grant you that," said Egmont. "But—so what?"

"Nice of you, Doctor, to grant me a fact that's been established for half a century," said Mirambeau, whose mirth was now kindled by Egmont's resistance.

"Why don't you answer my question instead of teasing me?"

"I've already answered it, old chap: the abnormal behavior of my chicken heart and your neurons proclaims that there is nothing inevitable about the aging of a cell. If cells age, it's because they want to. They age *deliberately*."

"Just fancy that, deliberately," said Egmont sardonically—he couldn't help it. "And why do they do that, may I ask?"

"To make us die."

"Why, obviously! Suicidal maniacs, in short. It stands to reason."

"You're being damned sarcastic," said Mirambeau, but he seemed to be enjoying himself vastly.

"What's so funny?" grumbled Egmont.

"Not you, don't worry. Not even the face you pull—like a prim old maid with someone whispering a bawdy tale into her ear. No, what's funny is that you react so much like everyone else. It's becoming a joke. Come on," he said seriously, and he led him to another row of jars. "My personal part of the work is here: tissues put into a situation where—if I am right—they should lose just this will to age. If scientific discipline consists of checking a hypothesis by experiment, you'll admit that the success of the experiment lends weight to the hypothesis?"

Egmont grunted a vague, inarticulate assent.

"Thank you," said Mirambeau. "Your willingness to oblige is touching. Still you remember good old Lecomte du Noüy?"

"As much as most people," said Egmont.

"And his work on the rate of healing? That rate diminishes with age. It closely follows a graph which enables us to measure the age of a tissue by the time it takes to heal. Right. It's been presumed so far that the slowing down was due, briefly, to a sort of fatigue, wear and tear, or slow intoxication. I suppose—my school does—that it's due to nothing of the sort, but to a message, a signal, an order given to those tissues to slow down and eventually cease their activity."

"We're wading in metaphysics."

"Tut, tut, rude words right away. Try to be polite for a while. You admit that a living cell is a certain form of organization? You do? Good boy. Right. Imagine, now, a regiment doing a quick march. A command—or the absence of a command, and our unit changes to slow step, then to a stroll, and gradually it gets ever slacker until it breaks up in general disorder and stops being a unit altogether. Who has aged, who has died in all this? Nobody, except the regiment. A command has broken it up, another can put it together again, if necessary with a different batch of privates. Nothing metaphysical about that."

"Now we're wading in symbolism."

"*Nunc patienda censeo* . . . I shall now make you contradict yourself, your own assertions. What are you arguing? That keeping a chicken heart alive for thirty-four years does not prove anything because it's been fed on embryonic substances. That was indeed Carrel's experiment. A tissue fed, in vitro, on very young plasma accelerates its cellular increase, while the plasma of an old animal retards it. Nouy's and Carrel's graphs are complementary and coincide. That's it, isn't it?"

"Yes."

"I've got you there. Because what I'm doing, old man, is nothing more than to systematize those experiments. Here you have three samples of the same tissue, all three fed on the same organic fluid: neutral plasma. Incidentally, that plasma has been the very devil. Getting it neutral, I mean. Free of any kind of hormone. But that's by the way. Look at the tissue on the left: it's sprouting like a cluster of grapes. Here on your right: it's shriveling, a prey to macrophages. In the center: it's remained exactly like the sample controls. Yet they are all fed, I repeat, on one and the same fluid. What's happened?"

"I don't know."

"Only this: I have added to the substance on the left a trace, a few drops per gallon, of very young plasma; on the right, a drop of very old plasma. Well, those drops are all that's needed: my tissues obey them implicitly, as you can see. So much so that if I reverse the fluids, the aged tissue will promptly start to proliferate, and the young one will slacken its pace like an old mare. Does it seem clear to you this time? Are we still wading in metaphysics or symbolism? Do you still say: Fancy that?"

"You're sure of your results?" said Egmont after a pause, letting his finger glide limply alongside his nose.

"Now that's a strategic withdrawal if I ever saw one. . . . I admit my results still need more checking by numerous tests over many years. But five years already isn't too bad. Mind you, even without me, one might have guessed at the truth. It's been admitted for quite a while that humoral traces actually issue orders to the fetus cells to make them specialize as liver, kidney, or eye tissue, to make them grow or stop growing. There's nothing revolutionary about admitting that an 'order' of the same kind later commands them to slow down or disband."

"But, good lord, why give such an order? And why this obedience? It's contrary to all this . . . to the life force. . . ."

74

"You've heard of La Palice?"

"Was he a biologist?"

"No," said Mirambeau with a chuckle, "a rabid logician rather. 'A quarter of an hour before his death, he was still a living man. . . .' If past generations had gone on living after they had procreated, this little planet would by now look like the Marx Brothers' cabin: all treading on each other's toes. And since you people can't be much relied on to commit hara-kiri to make room, it must needs be left to your cells to take the initiative. That's the whole story."

Egmont shook his head, his eyes fixed on the jars, and said: "Too tall to swallow: it's absurd. Why the dickens produce offspring if there's really the choice of living eternally?"

"I didn't say that the choice was ours. Once again consult La Palice, that much-maligned author. An animal species made up of permanent and hence—as we have seen—descentless individuals would not stay the course for long: accidents, disease, the struggle for life would wipe out those individuals, one by one. Without mentioning the need for adaptation. For the survival of the species it is therefore necessary that those individuals give birth to others. But, in exchange, they must automatically age and die. We assert nothing more than that."

"I don't know," said Egmont slowly after a pause, "if that's a wholesome truth to assert, even less to broadcast. . . . Mother love is perhaps a fond illusion, but if you start shaking its foundation—"

"You have small faith in the virtues of truth," said Mirambeau unsmilingly. He gazed at Egmont with a gravity which, in his heavy, bulging eyes, verged on reproof. "I have no children," he went on, "but if I had, it seems to me that I would love them more dearly in the light, even the cruel light, of this truth than in the barren shelter of a soothing illusion. Wouldn't you?" he said to Egmont. "Why," he continued more firmly, "why should I love them less? They share our fate, they too, in their turn, will have children to whom they will give life. . . . 'Give life,' these words contain, perhaps, a terrible double meaning. But doesn't it amount to prizing mother love even more highly when it implies consenting to give everything—even one's existence?"

"Still . . . all the same . . . " started Egmont, and he felt as if a merry-go-round were whirling in his head. "Still, it raises questions without end. Were it only for . . . what does medicine become in all this?"

"Why, medicine?" said Mirambeau.

"Because I am still a doctor after all. And if you're right, if it's true that the species is *against* the individual, that nature and the species are *in favor* of age and death, in favor of cancer, angina pectoris, all the infirmities which, according to you, help to play off one generation against another, by what right does a doctor prolong a life which the species no longer wants?"

"Professor Leriche would have answered: the sacred character of human life. . . ."

"—clashes with the imperatives of the species, you said so yourself. 'Clear out and make room for your son.' How do you reconcile this contradiction? Your work, even more than ours—the work of surgeons and physicians—aims at prolonging life. And suppose you succeed one day, you or your fellow scientists? It's not altogether unthinkable, is it?"

"Not altogether, no. But it's still a far cry," he answered with a chuckle.

"No matter, the principle remains the same: what will be the price to pay for your success? As you go on lengthening the life of one generation, the next one will necessarily have to be reduced in number, if not suppressed entirely."

"No doubt."

"But you go on searching all the same."

"I do."

"How do you come to terms with the sacred character of human life?"

"Negation of a negation. Our friend Pélion should be able to answer that one," said Mirambeau with a wink.

"Come again," said Pélion blandly, in his slightly slurring voice. He walked toward the door. "I'm only a rank-and-filer. You'd have to put that one to our party pundits." His hand was on the doorknob. "I've got to make a lot of phone calls. And look in at the union branch. May I phone you toward two?"

Egmont raised his head. His glance searched Pélion, found him. His expression had oddly changed.

"You're going?" he said.

"As you see."

"Can you spare me ten minutes?" said Egmont with a pallid smile.

Pélion raised one eyebrow, in surprise and embarrassment.

"Hadn't you better see Fernand . . ." he suggested.

Fernand was the secretary of Egmont's former cell.

"Nothing to do with that," said Egmont without ceasing to smile, but his cheek twitched with the strain.

Pélion looked hard at him for some time.

"Now?" he said at last, but he, too, had gone pale.

"If you don't mind."

"All right, then," said the young man, and he opened the door to let him pass. Egmont walked out in front of him, forgetting to take his leave. Mirambeau followed them from his window with a worried look.

Chapter Seven

Shall we go into the park?" suggested Egmont.

Pélion opened his broad hands with an air of indifference. They passed through the damp back garden, one behind the other, and across the deserted riding track. Pélion gazed without affection at the stooping back before him, at the neck already lined and reddening below the graying hair. Then they slowly climbed the hill, side by side.

Egmont said to himself, as he had done at sixteen: Now. Then: No . . . at the tree up there, the one with tattered bark . . . But they passed the tree without Egmont's managing to speak. No farther than that bench, he decided, that's my last try. If I funk it this time, I'll quit. Even if Pélion thinks I'm crazy.

However, the bench approached inexorably, and all thought went blank; there was that bench, that BENCH, that BENCH. . . . When they reached it, Egmont heard himself say, to his vast surprise:

"You did not say anything at Mirambeau's. It all seemed just empty talk to you, I expect?"

"Not at all," said Pélion. "It was absorbing."

Egmont raged inwardly: Coward, he cursed himself, but he could not help going on:

"Nevertheless, you must be saying to yourself . . . well, that these are perfectly idle worries: to trouble about so remote a contingency is like being scared of the ghost of a man who isn't even dead. Everything in due time, to put it more plainly. Isn't that it?"

"N . . . no," said Pélion, trying to put his thoughts honestly. "That's not it exactly. I'd be more inclined to think that one man can't do everything, can't know everything. He can't even worry about everything. Struggling where he stands demands enough time and trouble to—"

"You cannot imagine," said Egmont, without letting him finish, "how . . . how unbearable this prospect seems to me."

"What prospect?"

"Precisely today," continued Egmont. "At this very moment."

What's he driving at? thought Pélion, and he was perturbed.

"That people of our age," answered Egmont belatedly, "of Mirambeau's and mine, must get used to the idea that you people . . . you the young, will one day . . ."

He made a gesture with his fingers and wrist as if flicking crumbs from a table.

"Just today," repeated Egmont in a low tone. And suddenly he rapped out aggressively, perhaps desperately: "What are you waiting for?"

Pélion stopped dead, staring at Egmont aghast. What does he want? Expect me to throw him into the canal to finish him off?

They came to the edge of the pool. But Egmont swung round to face him. He stamped the ground with his foot, like a nervous horse.

"What are you waiting for to take Pascale away from me?" he cried. "Don't you see that you two are torturing me?"

The last words Pélion would have expected. Pascale! He stammered:

"But she . . ." He was going to say: "She is in love with you," but was stopped by the look on the face before him. It was the very face of defeat: dun-colored and, at the temple, a small zigzag vein that throbbed. . . . But proud in defeat, Pélion said to himself. The eye had not lost its look of haughty domination, of aloof disdain, which Pélion found so insufferable. "Pascale and I . . ." Pélion repeated to himself. We're torturing him . . . he thought, and a surge of unexpected affection for this man transfixed before him lifted his two hands, as if to take him by the shoulders. He checked himself. First, he thought, it isn't true, more's the pity. "Pascale and I . . ." What's he imagining? The truth is that the one she loves is this old geezer.

Egmont did not know why Pélion had blushed. "Old geezer," Pélion was suddenly appalled at having thought it with such aversion. As if, in doing so, he had assumed a murderer's livery. . . . It was quite true that listening to Mirambeau a moment ago had rather altered the face of things. This revulsion of youth for senile weakness, for its decrepitude, was just as vile and ignoble as the torturer's for the victim he had himself degraded. Never again, he thought. His hands rose once more, hesitantly touched Egmont's forearms, which hung limp and heavy down his sides.

"Heaven knows," he started, but the rest choked in his throat. He shook his hand with pathetic vigor. "Pascale doesn't love me, she's fond of me, that's all," he managed to bring out, and he felt empty. His hands dropped inert.

What was going on in that man's mind? If he'd been talking to a marble statue, it couldn't have shown less response. Had he even heard him?

Something, however, moved in this face of stone. A flicker of the lips. The rest of the face did not even quiver, but the lips shook with tiny jerks, and Pélion thought he heard at last ". . . told you so?"—heard it less than he guessed it.

"That she doesn't love me, the way you mean? No need for her to tell me so," sighed Pélion grimly, "you can see it with your naked eye."

Egmont closed his eyes. The small vein at his temple throbbed, throbbed pitifully. . . . At last the lips in the blind face murmured:

"But you love her?"

Pélion felt anger rise in his breast and then recede and dissolve. Now that we've got this far . . . he thought with a shrug.

"Yes, of course, I love her."

"Take her away," said the lips, still almost without stirring.

"But since I'm telling you—"

"Take her away," said Egmont more loudly, and his eyes flashed. "Are you going to stand there like a stick?" he shouted. "Don't you understand that I'm tearing my heart out? What more do you want? Must I lead her myself, deposit her in your arms?"

"Doctor, I . . ."

"Shut up!" shouted Egmont, beside himself. "Come on," he ordered with such authority that Pélion surrendered without even realizing it.

Egmont started walking so quickly that Pélion at first was left behind. He had to run a few paces to catch up with Egmont, who was striding ahead.

They left the park without a word, walking down at a fast trot toward Grand Square. Pélion's heart was pounding so fast that it made him breathless. He's taking me to her, to her father's, he thought. He stopped still.

"What's the matter?" said Egmont irritably.

"Where are you taking me?"

Egmont's mouth opened as if to release a flood of curses. But it stayed open and silent. And then he went to lean against the plinth of a stone building, vermiculated from top to bottom.

"So you want to drain me of all my strength?"

Pélion shook his head. He took a step forward, and also leaned his back against the stone wall.

"No," he said faintly, "but I stand to lose mine, more than you."

"You still don't believe me?" said Egmont, appalled.

"If I were . . . imprudent . . . craven enough to start hoping now . . ."

"Is that what you are telling yourself?" said Egmont without violence. "What have you been doing these two years? You're not going to pretend you've been looking on passively. . . ."

"Yes, I have," said Pélion sadly. "That surprises you? Seems out of character? But you haven't heard her!"

"Pascale?"

"Yes, when she talks of you. Or when she recites your poems. Don't be surprised if I've come to hate you."

"And you've never tried to . . ."

"To haul you from your pedestal? Yes, once," said Pélion and he uttered a wry laugh. "Only once. She made me give up all desire to start again."

They remained there without moving, side by side, their heads against the stone, looking up at the sky above the houses opposite. Egmont asked softly:

"Why are you telling me this?"

Pélion shrugged.

"Which of us started? We must unravel this now to the end of the coil, I can see that."

"No," said Egmont. "At the end of the coil there'll still be the guts, and the marrow and the brain. Whereas one word will do."

"One word?"

"From her."

Egmont moved away from the wall as if jerking himself out of the cosiness, the warmth of a bed.

"Let's go," he said. And he added with a smile: "Chin up: it won't hurt for long."

They walked on. They no longer had far to go. Pascale lived with her father in one of the mansions in Grand Square—the former home of a grain merchant grown rich under the Restoration, and whose name could still be read engraved in soberly elegant characters between two fleurs-de-lis.

"Go up," said Egmont. "They'll have finished lunch by now."

Pélion kept standing on the curbstone, staring up at the first-floor windows, which were high and narrow behind their wrought-iron balconies. He went on staring. He could not have stirred a finger.

Egmont, at this moment, felt an unwonted inner calm. He considered Pélion dispassionately, with an almost amused curiosity. What was the good of having this straight, firm nose, a trifle heavy, perhaps, but manly, and this rather too willful chin . . . Not handsome, all in all. In fact, why should Pascale . . . He was gripped by panic: am I going to start all over again?

"It's not for your sake, good lord, nor for mine!" He ground out the words into Pélion's ear with restrained fierceness. "How many days, months, years will you go on letting her torture herself? Do you love her so faintheartedly that—"

"I am going," said Pélion. He had turned crimson. "You are right. It won't hurt for long: the time of the drop. Just as well to get it over now."

He crossed the cobbled roadway in three strides, and the pavement in three more. He pushed the half-open door. There he turned round.

"You'll wait for us of course, won't you?" he shouted.

Egmont remained motionless on the edge of the square, a black figure on the other shore, standing out against the dusty shimmer of the asphalt and the sun-drenched house fronts. He did not answer, nor did he move. He seemed riveted to the pavement for all eternity.

No sooner had Pascale grasped his drift than she brushed like a scared butterfly against all the furniture in her room, as if she had forgotten where to look for the door, the window.

"It's impossible!" she kept repeating. "Impossible! We must explain to him . . ."

She was as pale as the napkin which she had kept in her hand when she rose from the table, then thrown onto a chair in a corner. Pélion gazed at her silently, leaning in the shadow against a Breughel print, fastened to the wall with drawing pins. He tried hard to think of nothing. Her pallor was hardly greater than his.

"Of course I love you," she said. "Are you so blind . . ." She moved a chair in order to pass, but to go where? She put it back in its place. "It would be too easy if I didn't," she said. She wrung her hands. "But what of him? I could never . . . You must make him come up. Why did he stay downstairs? Tell him at once. . ." She looked at him with distracted eyes. "You know that I'll marry him." She took her temples in her hands: "How can I . . . what did you say?"

"I didn't say anything," murmured Pélion tonelessly.

She went to the window, looked out.

"Where is he?" she said in the same agitated tone. "I don't see him."

"Just across the road," said Pélion. "On the edge of the square."

"I don't see him," she repeated. "There's no one," and again she seemed to search for the door without finding it. She knocked a lamp over, picked it up.

Pélion was at the window with one bound, looked out himself. Egmont's figure had seemed so deeply engraved in the back of his eyes that he could not understand how it could have been erased. Grand Square looked extraordinarily empty.

"He's gone," he murmured. He felt bewildered, almost shaken. By the time he had turned round, he heard the entrance door slam.

Pascale burst out into the square, into the sun, and was blinded. She shaded her eyes with her fingers. Go where, rush where? She wheeled round, listened, but not a sound at this hour of day; she was frantic, searched for a sign, an inspiration. The Cathedral lane . . . that leads to his flat . . . yes . . . She flung herself into it.

At first she saw nothing in the dazzling fireworks that hid the darkness from her like some infernal curtain. But up there—at the top of the steps, that figure, Egmont. No, it wasn't. Yes, it was. She opened her mouth to shout. But—shout what? Panic seized her. She had always called him by his surname. Once again she clasped her head between her hands, and two tears welled up and perhaps a sob, and for the first time—the very first—the boldness of a Christian name . . . so often whispered to herself, in bygone days, long, long ago.

"Daniel! . . ."

Up there, Egmont was counting: six hundred and twelve, six hundred and thirteen, six hundred and fourteen . . . He was counting step by step. He counted so as not to think, not to feel either his heart or his head.

"Come back, Daniel, please!" implored the palpitating voice.

Pascale could see that Egmont had heard her: that halt, that hesitation. . . . But Egmont slowly went on mounting the steps; he had lost count, he was murmuring: "An Ave Maria, a Pater Noster . . . Hail Mary . . . why don't I still remember my prayers? . . ."

"I don't want this!" cried, entreated Pascale. "Come back!" she cried. And her fingers burrowed into her hair in despair.

Up there the small dark figures melted more and more into the shadows, at the foot of the silent, towering, black and red cathedral, but then, just before vanishing, it turned round—Pascale saw an arm raised and tilting back in a winglike movement, and the figure mounted the last steps backward, so slowly, my God, so slowly. . . . At last it was swallowed up, perhaps in the darkness of the porch, perhaps in the side streets that wound down and lost themselves in the maze of the sleepy old city. . . .

Only then did Pascale realize that she had been in Pélion's arms for the last minute and that together they were staring up at the flickering, translucent ghost of a vanished figure on the last steps of a lonely lane.

Chapter Eight

I felt more at peace, muses Pélion, with wry irony. The various officials of the Chaulieu trade unions are holding a night meeting, and Pélion finds it hard to keep his mind off his private troubles. Yes, everything, in a way, had been plain sailing as long as he had accepted, once for all, that he was an unrequited lover. This settled beyond argument, it left your mind free for work. Whereas look at the muddle now! The kid says: "Of course I love you" but can't make up her mind to push Egmont off his pedestal, and this Svengali bows himself out with such a flourish that the girl no longer knows whether she loves me or not. . . .

"Anything wrong?"

"No, no . . ."

"You seem a bit off color."

"Tired, perhaps."

"Hello, Bob, everything all right?"

"Sure, hello. Albert not with you?"

"No. Why?"

"Howdy, chum."

"Howdy, howdy. You're sure he's been told?"

"Albert? Well, I suppose so. Why, there he is."

There they are, practically all, and the meeting opens. The chairman—a truck driver from Moulins de la Chaulx—outlines the situation and the business in hand. This meeting at district level (he says) of officers and agents of the various federations has been called on the initiative of the progressive CGT union. They wish to thank the other unions—the Socialist FO and the Christian CFTC—for their response, but even more for showing they've understood that the wage discrimination introduced by Coubez is more than a threat just to the CGT; that it represents the first stage of a maneuver against trade unionism as a whole; if this maneuver were to succeed, it would jeopardize both the rights of the trade unions and the gains of the working class, and not alone in Chaulieu, but perhaps all over the country before long. That's why it has been considered necessary and pressing to settle a common line of conduct. The enthusiastic display of unity shown at this morning's rally is a point in our favor. It must be turned to account while the iron's hot, we are all agreed on that. We've still to agree on how to do it so as to inform the works committee concerned, who've agreed to act accordingly. The meeting is open for discussion.

The boys of the CGT promptly propose a twenty-four-hour strike by way of warning.

An FO member points out that things aren't as easy as all that. The CGT comrades at Coubez run no risk of losing anything by such a show of force, they've no chance of a bonus anyhow; but what about the others? They'll be scared of missing the bonus if they come out on strike. There'll probably be some opposition and certainly a good many defections.

If we're scared, say the former, we are done for from the start. What do you propose?

First of all, just to send a deputation from the works committee to the management: "Bonus for all, or we get cross."

What does that mean, we get cross?

Well, strike.

So if they turn it down, you'll decide to strike?

Thereupon a pause of hesitation. A CFTC man says that they're in too much of hurry. Why talk of a strike right away? Send the deputation first. It'll be time to decide what to do next when the outcome is known.

If that's as far as we mean to go tonight, remarks one fellow, it wasn't worth while making such a fuss about this meeting. As the chairman has said: We are here to decide on a common line of action. That means we all know it's a cinch that the bosses will turn us down: else there'd obviously be no need for a common line. So if we aren't going to decide on one, what the hell are we here for?

Pélion asks to speak.

He is well liked, Pélion, even by the opponents of his party. His zest and loyalty—when he might so cosily stay out of it all and run his own small workshop—have won him general regard and affection. Besides, though he's young, his advice is often sound: he can see things more clearly because his own interests aren't involved in these local affairs. He's got nothing to gain or lose by them. That enables a fellow to see straight and keep cool.

"Give it 'em, Bob!" flings a bantering voice—it's Albert.

And Bob says that before going any further, there are a certain number of things to make sure of.

First, we'd have to make sure that we are all quite agreed. We should make sure that there were no double thoughts in anyone's head. Maybe the FO and CFTC mates had some idea at the back of their minds that it might be a pity, after all, to miss this opportunity? That their taking a common stand with the CGT against the differential wage increase would enable the CGT to maintain its position at the next elections, whereas they themselves could pick up some votes if they let matters take their course? So we'd have to be sure, to begin with, that this little game was out of their thoughts. That they weren't saying to themselves: "Let's send that deputation to clear our conscience, and if it fails, well, after all, we'd be damn silly to insist."

An FO man gets up to answer. He says with a grin that in the beginning they'd certainly felt tempted to think on those lines. Particularly as, at first sight, the case had a sort of family likeness to the Renault factory deal. But looking at it more closely, you'd have to be crazy to swallow the bait. We're already fighting all together against regional wage distinctions, we're not going to see them set up right in our own ranks. Despite all our differences, it's clear that if we let down the CGT today, tomorrow it'll be our turn, and before you can say Jack Robinson, the bosses will enforce a single union and make sure that it eats out of their hand. Our friend Bob can put his mind at rest. You can count on us. We'll fight shoulder to shoulder. But if you want to fight, you must be sure of your troops. We are not yet sure enough of ours. There is no other motive behind our caution.

Pélion thanks him. He says, if that's so, things must be faced squarely: if you are afraid that your men may get cold feet when it comes to a strike call, then we mustn't send the deputation. So before sending it, make sure that your men can be relied upon. If you daren't count on them, it can only mean you are afraid they haven't grasped the full gravity of what's at stake. So what's needed, in the first place, is to make them understand. Then we must think of the fellows at Coubez who may quite likely fear that they'll be left to fight a lone battle, if it lasts for some time. So, in the second place, the issue must also be explained to the men working at the other plants in Chaulieu and the neighborhood. When all the boys have truly understood what it is all about and what exactly they're threatened with, and when the Coubez lads know that the others approve and, if necessary, will back them up, then we can forge ahead.

That's why he proposes: first, to lie low till the Sunday morning meeting and, second, that that meeting should not be confined to the Coubez works alone. It should be a mass meeting to rouse and inform opinion. The morning's victory and the general move toward unity that is stirring among workers at the moment should guarantee its success.

This proposal pleases everyone, the cautious for its reassurance, and the bold for its encouragement, and so it is adopted. To-morrow is Wednesday, there is more time than needed to round up the men. Pélion adds that it would be a good thing if the Sunday meeting were presided over by some prominent person. He may already venture to say that Professor Mirambeau, for example, if they were to ask him . . . Cheers and applause make it unnecessary for him to go on.

It is midnight when the meeting closes. For the whole debate was not as brief—nor as clear—as it appears in this summary. As usual, they all got entangled in words, repeated themselves, strayed from their subject, got angry. As usual, hoary feuds and rankling grievances cropped up ten times over and side-tracked the train of argument. And as usual, too, it took over three hours to decide what could have been settled in ten minutes. But coming out into the warm night and the sleepy streets of Chaulieu, everyone feels happy and exhilarated.

A little later, Pélion was walking down the Cours Berthollet, together with Albert and some others. Suddenly, the hoot of fire engines rang out somewhere behind them.

"Golly," said Albert. "A fire."

"So long," said a youngster excitedly. "I've got to push off."

"You're a fireman?"

"Signed up last month."

"I wouldn't care to be a fireman," said Albert. "Getting hauled out of bed in the middle of the night without any warning would twist me stomach."

However hardened a skeptic may be, he is sure to harbor some vestiges of man's ancestral fears and catch himself dimly dreading at times the invisible eye of the Grand Inquisitor. Throughout his childhood, Egmont was haunted by the suspicion that his parents might have the artful gift of seeing through walls: even shut up in the secrecy of his own nursery, he could never feel sure that he really escaped all supervision.

So when, in that mild May night, with his heart still bruised from the wrench he had inflicted on it, Egmont woke up with a start and understood that his house was on fire, his first thought, his first question, in the face of such a sequence of misfortunes, was addressed to the God denied by his philosophy: "What have I done to You, what do You want of me?" There is always some Job sleeping within us ready to call Someone to account. We instinctively refuse to believe that a succession of disasters may be solely due to coincidence: they *must* have a meaning. It's up to us to discover what is concealed behind such a relentless onslaught.

Spring was damp and warm this year; no doubt there had been some condensation at the column of icy water coming from the pump; it had slowly impregnated the electric wires on the wall.

They must have been getting hotter and hotter for a long while before setting fire to the rafter above, half eaten away by dry rot. But once they did, the wood burned like tinder and soon the whole floor was ablaze.

If Egmont had slept with closed shutters, he would have waked amid the flames. It is strange how little noise a fire makes in its early stages. He thought he had merely been roused from sleep by the first glow of dawn. But, if so, the sun would have risen in the west for once . . . and those flickering, trembling shadows? "A fire," he thought. "But not here," he still wanted to believe, and he did not move. For a short moment only: there was no other house in the wood but his. He flung himself out of bed, raced to the fire extinguisher and, a moment later, he was on the spot, spraying the flames methodically and coolly till the extinguisher was empty. Disarmed, and surrounded by burning debris that fell from the ceiling, he then retreated at a run.

He was aware that his bare feet were stepping on fallen sparks and getting burned, but he hardly heeded it at the moment. Still in his pajamas, he first ran to rouse Virgil in the left wing but found the passage door bolted. He had to run out into the garden, round the building, and shout through the window to wake him up. Then he rushed back to the telephone to summon help. A sleepy voice made him repeat three times. "Corambière . . . oh, I see . . . the fire brigade? You haven't got their number, have you?" He forced himself to reply calmly that even if there had been a telephone directory at hand, it would hardly be of use: all the light-fuses were blown already. "Oh . . ." said the displeased voice, "then how do you expect me to call them?" "Use your head!" shouted Egmont into the receiver and hung up, unable to control his rage any longer. What to do next? Even supposing the firemen ever came, they'd only get there in time to drown the embers. What should he save first? His files or his animals? And which animals, anyhow? There, one ought to be able to sit down coolly in a corner with paper and pencil and calmly draw up an order of priorities. But the fire was there, behind the door, and thirty mottled tongues already darted furtively through the chinks. Egmont thereupon began to seize objects at random, filling his arms with everything within his reach, and carrying them out into the garden. The lawn soon seemed peopled with a fantastic sort of exodus, a russet disarray of quadrupeds, gazelle, hyena, hedgehog, weasel, squirrel, field mouse, rampant, couchant, issuant, and then Egmont told himself that the first floor would be in flames before the ground floor, so he stopped rescuing the mammals and took the outer stairs to the upper story.

He tried to run but his course was slowed down. Something was holding him back. However, his thoughts were racing ahead too fast to give him a chance to detect the cause. He crossed the first room and the second; the door of the central hall had already collapsed, the flames were licking the shelves. A jar with its snake exploded under his eyes. The alcohol spread over the floor and covered it with a blue carpet that slowly crawled along. Egmont cast a despairing glance at the shelves and closed the door: that would keep the fire out of the other room for a little longer. He began to empty the shelves. But each time it meant descending and mounting twenty steps and this took him longer each time, as if he were in a nightmare. So he resumed the salvage of the downstairs rooms, accompanied now by old Virgil who, however, seemed to apply himself more to the carpets, linen, and bedding. The telephone rang; so it still worked? "I cannot find Corambière," he heard. "Do you want me to call the Chaulieu brigade?" "Call the marines if you like, I don't care a damn!" yelled Egmont, beside himself, and he grabbed a bear cub and a leopard. He went and flung them out, came back, ran out, came back, but, good lord, he no longer made any progress. He dumped one more load of rodents and tardigrades on the grass and passed his hand over his brow. I'll go and rest for half a minute, he thought. The roof of the right wing came crashing down in a shower of sparks, and the fire stove the door in as if smashing it with its shoulder, and swept into the central part. Finished. Nothing more to be done. The telephone rang again. It rang and rang with such preposterous obstinacy that Egmont could not help laughing. Like a movie, he thought. Virgil stopped before him, a last batch of blankets in his arms, and gaped at him wide-eyed.

"You should lie down," he said pointing to the mattress on the ground.

"Lie down?" wondered Egmont.

"Look at you: you're bent double," said Virgil. "And you're moaning like old Jeremy."

Thereupon Egmont noticed that his burned feet were bleeding, that he was crooking his knees and hopping from one foot to the other like a hen on a hot griddle.

And only then did he become aware, with startling suddenness, that he was suffering like hell.

PART TWO *Vertigo*

Chapter Nine

Is it astonishing that a man of Egmont's mental stature should at first behave so like an "addlepate," to use Cloots's expression? He was surprised, of course, that for almost half an hour his body had been well enough aware of its suffering to dance and hop about, to produce moans with its lungs and mouth and to crook its toes, without him—Egmont—knowing anything about it the whole time. But he merely thought: A funny thing, absent-mindedness, and, contenting himself with this comment, went to lie down on the mattress, whence he watched the remains of his "manor house" go up in flames.

For two or three days his thoughts on the subject went no further. Not because the final disaster had crushed him. On the contrary, the very surfeit of misfortunes that had befallen him, coupled with the fact that he was helplessly tied to his bed on the grass, somehow lightened both his grief and his agitation, and he could watch with a calm only slightly tinged with melancholy, the final metamorphosis of his collection into smoke. He believed himself ruined, and materially and morally in such a plight, whichever way you looked at it, that he said to himself: "There's nothing more I can do. Up to the others now to do as they please with my life." The Chaulieu firemen, as he had foreseen, arrived an hour later to drown the smoldering ashes and, in the morning, on the dewy lawn, surrounded by his motionless animals, he received, like a woman in childbed, visits of sympathy from his neighbors and even from his friends in Chaulieu, who had already been mysteriously informed.

Among the very first to come was Olga, whom he had not seen for many months. She was pale and, despite her laughter and ostensible high spirits, deeply upset. "My poor boy, what *have* you been up to now! Let me see those feet of yours." She examined them and, as she had brought her doctor's bag with her, cleaned and dressed the burns and bandaged them. In the meantime a barn had been found in which to store what little had been saved. Olga carried the patient away in her car, and Egmont soon found himself back among the iridescent phials and the baroque vine stocks, just as when he and Olga had lived together. Friends, insurance agents, and experts relayed each other at his bedside during the days that followed, leaving him little time for meditation. His feet no longer hurt if he did not move; and as he did not care to think of either the past or the future, he let himself be lulled into a mental idleness that was, in some ways, little short of delicious.

He was apprehensive, though, of seeing Pascale again. But she did not turn up. Her father told Egmont, among other minor events, that the girl was going to spend a few weeks with an aunt in Provence. "She has sent you this note," he said, handing him a folded sheet tucked into an envelope.

I cannot come to see you. Really I can't. I'm going away. If you love me, wish me some clarity of feeling. At present my heart bursts with unhappiness, remorse, and questions. I'm thinking of you all the time. Please don't hate Robert. The gentleness within that big frame caught me by surprise. Must I hurt all those I

love? Why must life be so difficult at the very beginning? I'm
not yet eighteen, and already . . .

Forget me. No, don't. I no longer know. Good-by. Forgive me.
                                                              P.

Egmont had waited to be alone before reading the note. He
now read it, folded it again, put it on his bedside table. An unac-
customed calm. It must surely be hurting him, though. But when
pain leaves no mark on one's feelings, when the visceral anguish
remains silent, what is there left of suffering? It's like my burned
feet, he thought. I did not feel them. My body suffered, yes. But
can one, in those circumstances, say . . .

Closter Cloots came in. It did not take them long to get round
to the question of the unfelt burns, this mystery of mute or felt
pain.

"And you're prepared to stand for all this?" Cloots said suddenly.

"All what?"

"This hush-hush business. Good lord, they are your feet, after
all. This hand is mine," he said, lifting and waving it like a pup-
pet, "and I know less of what's going on in it at this moment
than . . . than, y'see . . . in the tail of a comet or a spiral nebula.
That's what I won't stand."

"There doesn't seem to be much you can stand," sighed Egmont, thinking of himself, "when it comes to man's condition."

"And I don't say a quarter of what I think of it. If my book
showed life on Anabiosis as it really is, nobody could bear to read
it."

He gazed at Egmont with eyes in which the latter thought he
detected, with surprise, a glint of tragedy. Yet the slight lopsided
smile, with its usual tinge of irony, had not vanished, but stoutly
persisted.

"I'd show them life in a camp compared to which Buchenwald was just a picnic. A camp in which, on the eve of croaking, the prisoners, far from rising in revolt, persecute, double-cross, exploit, and fight each other, tear one another to pieces, set fire to the other chaps' barracks or blow them up with hand grenades, all under the impassive eyes of the *Jungfraus,* those deaf and dumb executioners. You would see kids croaking without reason, without knowing why, while some fat morons who'll croak themselves the year after step over the dead bodies of their father and mother in their scramble to corner the roller-skate market or get themselves into the Academy. For they have an Academy, titles, medals, what-you-will. If a fellow who's got to croak when he's six doesn't become a commander at the age of five he worries himself dyspeptic. He runs round the camp slinging mud at his oldest pal who is already in the gas chamber, and the pal drags himself to the window to shout abuse back at him, and then they both croak, and that's the end of it. But that doesn't prevent all the others from doing likewise. Sure enough, there are a few chaps, here and there, toiling day and night, like Mirambeau, to try to understand something about their fix and attempt to get out of it. But they don't interest the big shots who pay their keep, unless they find new bombs, always bigger and better bombs, with which to blow up the others, and, if they refuse, they get chucked into the bottom of a pit where they're fed on toads and ground glass. And then everybody croaks without there being any need of bombs. So if it weren't for those research fellows and a few inmates who, with dogged courage, try to redress this infernal idiocy, who wouldn't want to see the island blow up sky high with its inhabitants?"

He hadn't once said "y'see," but had ground out the word

"croak" with venom over and over again. He fell silent, looked at Egmont, broke into a short, embarrassed laugh.

"Here I'm getting lyrical," he said. "But there'll be nothing lyrical about my book. On the contrary, I'd like to give it a rather clinical style."

"I wonder whether what infuriates you isn't man's folly rather than his condition."

"Why? They're on a par. Man's wickedness is the direct outcome of his condition. In fact, that's what I would so much like people to understand! Everything springs from our ignorance, y'see, this revolting ignorance, my ignorance of this hand," and he raised it again, "of life, and death, and the expanding galaxies, and this whole bag of tricks of an illusionist who won't explain how he does 'em. We have to put up with it or die of it, and that's the truth. Put up with it in blind stupidity that leads straight to the hydrogen bomb, the massacre of the Jews, to Auschwitz or Hiroshima—or else keep groping in anger until we die. Isn't that true?"

"I didn't imagine you were such an out-and-out rebel," murmured Egmont.

Cloots said nothing at first. But Egmont thought he saw again, despite the faint smile, the same tragic light in the eyes fixed upon him.

"Perhaps," said Cloots, "that's because you don't know . . ."

He broke off, seemed to waver. He said under his breath:

"Maybe I have good reason for understanding my Anabiosians better than most people."

"Why?" said Egmont, and he sensed a catastrophe.

"I don't like to talk of it," answered Cloots with some hesitation. "Especially not to my friends, because . . . y'see, I like to be on easy, relaxed terms with them, no awkwardness. But with you . . . anyhow, I've said too much already," he admitted with a shrug. He dropped his voice even lower: "I shan't make old bones."

"What are you saying?"

"The doc himself thinks I don't know, but I know enough about medicine to have no illusion. My goose is cooked. I can expect another year or two at most—if all goes well. Not a week longer."

"Come, come . . ." started Egmont.

"Don't bother," said Cloots with that smile, the irony of which had now assumed a cruel meaning. "For almost fifteen years I've lived with only one kidney, y'see: t.b. And now this one's got it too. I've seen the analyses and the X-ray photos. Looks rather like Irish lace already. Less neat, though. Y'see? And since you've been a medical man yourself . . ."

"But you look so well!"

"Yeah . . . the rest looks well. The medico said to me quite overjoyed: 'You've got a liver to last you a hundred years!' That's a great comfort. I'll bequeath it to Mirambeau, who'll feed it in a glass jar. It'll be a way of outliving myself."

It seemed to Egmont that everything around him—the sunny sky beyond the window, the polished cosiness of the furniture in the golden light, the snug leather-backed books, the gleaming phials—had all suddenly changed. As if the room had turned into the gloomy cell of some inexorable prison. Yes, everything was changed, but less so, much less so, than that man sitting at his bedside looking at him with a grin. Yet it was the same old Cloots with the same little mustache over the same crooked smile. And yet we know perfectly well that every man must die some day. And didn't I see them die by the hundreds in my hospital days? And who knows but that I myself may be dead before him. Why, then, is everything changed just because we learn . . . what? Egmont asked himself. That a friend is ill, is doomed? No, he thought, it's knowing the due date, the time limit for the execution: yes, that's it, once the date is fixed, it becomes an execution. "Closter Cloots, your reprieve has been rejected." The guillotine stands waiting in the dawn of a livid day.

He made an effort to pull himself together.

"You forget that there are cures which—" he started.

"Work miracles? Is that it? If I have to rely on those . . ."

I refuse his death! thought Egmont, despite himself. I refuse it! His impotence filled him with a sort of nausea. It wasn't their friendship so much that made him suffer as the fact that he was talking like this, chatting quietly, with this condemned man whom no one could wrest from the executioner.

That night he had a curious dream. There was a war on. He was going along a road planted with tall poplars, with the weariness, the sluggishness that he always felt in his dreams nowadays. He was alone, but all around, in the woods, in the hollow of the valleys, beyond the vast hillside, thousands of eyes were following him invisibly. The army was there, camouflaged, silent, motionless, but on his shoulders he felt the weight of the Apocalypse. For he was instructed to move that army. And he felt powerless to do so, horribly, painfully incompetent. He marched on, but who was going to follow him, why should anyone? He sweated thick drops despite the bitter cold. He marched on but the huge army stayed where it was, invisible and enormous, hidden in the woods on the hillside rolling away to the horizon.

He was still dreaming as he woke. A difficult, slow awakening. He now knew that he was in his bed, yet the problem remained.

He still had to move this gigantic mass which probably wasn't an army, but was what? This something and that army remained mixed up for a long time, but gradually it was no longer an army but a leg. He now knew that it was his leg he had to move, but a huge, shapeless, monstrous leg, a dim, dark leviathan of a leg which covered the bed, the room, the town. . . . How can you move it if you yourself are a tiny, solitary creature, lost and drowned in the dizzy vastness of a boundless leg? He fell asleep and woke up again several times before recovering full consciousness, and then it seemed to him as if he had suddenly swollen to a colossal size whereas his leg had dwindled to proportions that amazed him by their meagerness. . . .

It was not a fortuitous dream—his leg was numb, and he moved it with difficulty. He touched it; there was hardly any sensation, and his finger left an imprint on the skin. Not much swollen, but the foot itself showed a marked edema.

He told Olga of it when she came back from hospital in the evening.

"One of your sores must have got infected," she said. "Have you been up to any nonsense?"

"I haven't left this couch."

Sitting on it, with her back turned to him, she was examining the swollen foot, prodding it attentively. Egmont looked at the nape of her neck, he saw a fly strolling over it unhurriedly. The fly trotted down to her shoulder, up again, followed the line of her hair. From time to time Olga twitched one shoulder slightly, but this left the fly indifferent. When her examination was over, she got up and remained in thought for a moment. At last she drove away the importunate fly with an absent-minded wave of her hand.

"When did you notice it?" asked Egmont.

106

"Notice what?"

"That fly on your neck."

"What fly? Oh . . ." she said, her thoughts elsewhere. "Well, just now, I believe."

"There you are," said Egmont in a singular tone of voice.

Olga rummaged in her medicine chest. She pulled out some cotton wool, spirit and ointment.

"What's so interesting about that fly?" she asked, shaking the bottle with the cotton wool pressed against its neck.

"It's been traipsing all over you for the last ten minutes," said Egmont.

"I had other fish to fry," said Olga.

"Did you feel it?" he persisted.

"I don't know. No, I don't think I did."

She started cleansing the wound with spirit. Egmont pulled a face but he said:

"Oh, yes you did. You twitched your shoulders all the time."

"Did I?" said Olga. "I didn't realize. What are you driving at?" she said, throwing the cotton wool away. She pressed the tube of ointment between finger and thumb.

"When I scorched myself, I traipsed around for twenty minutes without feeling anything, either. Was I in pain or wasn't I?"

"If you felt nothing, you were obviously not in pain."

"Ask Virgil: I was in a hell of a pain. The proof is that he saw me walking bent double like a jackknife and heard me groan like a woman in labor."

"All right then, so you were in pain," said Olga obligingly. "The word doesn't mean anything, it's a question of the cortex, you know that," she added, spreading the ointment on the sole of his foot.

"Cortex be damned! I'm talking of Virgil: who was right, he

107

or I? If he had to bear witness in court, he'd swear on the Bible that I was suffering horribly from my burns. In all honesty, I would have to testify to the contrary. Whom should the judge believe?"

And as Olga did not say anything: "Pass me your dictionary, the *Littré*," he demanded. "On the third shelf," he added with a grin as she could not find it.

Olga handed it to him and went into the bathroom to wash her hands.

"PAIN," Egmont read aloud, *"an abnormal, unpleasant impression received by a part of living matter and perceived by the brain.* And perceived by the brain!" he triumphed. "Well? What do you say?"

He felt in a strangely buoyant mood, a mood he had long forgotten. . . . Was it Olga's presence, or his recapturing, in this room, with her, the atmosphere of former days? Or because he was again about to feel an interest in something? A new, genuine, unhoped-for interest, with that unmistakable thrill of excitement . . .

"Once more, what are you driving at?" said Olga through the partition amid the noise of taps and pipes.

She had to wait a moment for the reply.

"Don't laugh at me," said Egmont, "I am asking myself if, of all animals in creation, man may not be the only one to feel pain."

"The only one to what?"

"Feel pain. To suffer."

Olga reappeared in the doorway, wiping her hands.

"I don't follow: what do you mean?"

"What I said. I'm wondering if Descartes was as stupid as we're made to believe."

"Descartes!?"

"Yes, when he asserted that animals don't suffer. Don't you remember? Being without a soul, they are mere machines. Automata. If a dog howls when you hit him, it's because his lungs act as a pair of bellows, that's all. It seemed to us incredible that a man like Descartes could seriously have thought such bunkum."

"And now you wonder whether he wasn't right?"

"I wonder whether we weren't dithering fools not even to grasp what he meant."

"In that case I am still a dithering fool."

"You know Closter Cloots?"

"Anabiosis?" said Olga with a laugh.

"Definitely," growled Egmont. "I was the only one in town who *didn't* know about it. What do you think?"

"Of Cloots?"

"Of Anabiosis."

"I don't remember much about it any more. A good many commonplaces, I believe."

"Precisely. That's what is so striking. Such obvious old truths that you don't see them any more. To come back to Descartes—I wailed and limped but I didn't feel anything. Consequently, it is possible to wail and limp without having any sensation. Point one."

"It remains the exception."

"Maybe, but to think it's possible . . ."

"I'm telling you again, old chap, that you are about to rediscover America. Have you forgotten Piéron's lectures on the cortex and the thalamus?"

"And I'm telling you again, damn your thalamus. Anyway, what does it explain? That an impression 'received by a part of living matter,' as my *Littré* says, doesn't necessarily have to travel up to the brain, if it happens to find the line engaged, for the thalamus to be able to release its defense mechanism or produce cries of pain. That's exactly what I said! For me, for Man, this remains an exception, agreed. But suppose it were a general rule with animals?"

Olga looked at him thoughtfully, stroking her lips with one finger. At last she murmured: "Well, well . . ."

"Ah, you see," said Egmont. "It's worth looking into, isn't it?"

"Maybe it is," said Olga, still thoughtfully. "What's made you think of it? I thought the only beasts you were interested in were stuffed."

"I'm not stuffed myself," said Egmont. "I've read masses of things about it. All Pavlov's experiments to begin with. And those of Cannon on dogs whose brains had been removed, everything bar the thalamus. Well, they go on behaving as if they suffered. When you pinch their ears, they look at you pleadingly, they moan, and try to bite you. And what about the frog? Cut off its head, then pour a drop of acid on one of its feet: not only will it shake it, but rub it again and again with the other foot. Well, for half an hour I was just like that frog: circuit disconnected. True, I had every outward appearance of pain: Virgil saw me groan and limp. An animal with scorched feet must surely suffer, poor thing, mustn't it? Descartes answers: 'Eyewash,' and I produce my evidence in support. It's disturbing all the same, isn't it?"

"Yes . . . It is rather. . . ."

"Anyhow, you know, I'm not the first to think of it. There's a whole British school of thought supporting this point of view, following in the wake of Lovatt Evans and old Lister. But if it's true, do you realize what it adds up to? It implicates the entire creation!"

"How you go on!"

"I mean it: the entire creation. We thought that pain was universal. We were sharing it with all that is alive. It was the common lot, it was bearable. But what if *nothing* suffered in the Universe, no one—save us?"

This time Olga said nothing. She was still stroking her lip musingly.

"You understand," said Egmont with a sort of sudden excitement, "if I am right, then Cloots is right, too, and we should have to look at everything with different eyes. You understand," he repeated, "pain had only one justification: that of protecting our organism. Alarm bell, reflexes, et cetera. A justification already hard enough to swallow when it comes to such useless pains as those which precede death—cancer, tetanus; and just the most horrible pains are the most pointless ones, too. Doubly pointless if, as Mirambeau upholds, the body ages deliberately so as to die, to make room. Then why protect this doomed body by means of pain? But if on top of that, this whole mechanism, all these alarm bells, can perfectly well be set in motion without involving me in this mess, me, you see, the conscious, organized citizen Daniel Roux, as was the case during that half-hour; if they can get moving without wantonly inflicting real pain, *felt* pain on me; then this pain, this perfectly redundant pain . . . what is there left to justify it, I ask you? It is a wanton sadism, pure and simple, a disgusting cruelty, an unutterably shabby trick!"

"Don't get so het up," said Olga, with a laugh. She sat down on his bed. "Now wait. Let's go over that half-hour of yours again. You felt nothing. Right. Whereupon you went on walking, running, grazing your burned feet. If you had felt the pain, you'd have stopped sooner, and your foot wouldn't be in the mess it is in now."

"I told myself all this too, but it is not quite true," said Egmont.

"I wouldn't have stopped sooner. I would have gone on running as I did until I couldn't any more."

"Very well, big boy, very well, that's what I'm saying. The moment came when you jolly well had to stop. Now, you still had masses of things to save. But you couldn't budge. But you didn't know you were in pain. But you wanted to run. But you couldn't. But you didn't know you were in pain. . . . How much longer could this little game have gone on? You can see that in the long run you evidently had to become conscious of your pain."

Egmont bounced in his bed.

"There you are!" he cried. "There you are! You're putting your finger on it! That's the very point, that's it, that's it."

"Don't toss about so much," said Olga.

"But do you realize what you've just been *saying?*" he went on, unable to restrain his excitement. "You have quite simply said this: pain and human consciousness are one and the same thing! Consciousness is pain!"

"What *are* you raving about?"

"That is the proof of the pudding!" he persisted, prodding his knee with his forefinger.

"What proof?"

"Of this whole infamous business!" he shouted. "It looks as if someone had said to us: 'You want knowledge? Here it is. But here's something to go with it: pain. Take it or leave it. We don't sell separately.' Do you understand?"

"No."

"B-buttermilk!" exploded Egmont. "Never mind. *I* understand myself."

"But there's nothing I'd like better than to understand too," said Olga with a husky giggle. "It's not my fault if I'm a bit dense."

112

Egmont shook his head and shoulders impatiently.

"Look," he protested, "suppose Descartes was right. Now here's a rabbit that would like to run but it has hurt its feet. But as this fact stops at the thalamus and doesn't go up to the brain, he doesn't know, he doesn't feel that his foot hurts. Right. So he wants to run, but the thalamus says 'stop,' he stays put, he wants to run, but the thalamus says 'stop,' he stays put, wants to run, and so forth. That may last for hours, a rabbit brain doesn't ask itself questions, so there's no need for the rabbit to know that he's got a pain in his foot. He stays where he is, that's all. The thalamus is enough. You've followed so far?"

"Maybe."

"Well, that's a blessing. Where, then, is the difference between the rabbit and myself? It's that I want to know, I need to know, in the long run, why I can't budge. And only because I *want to know*, the thalamus is obliged to make up its mind and say to the brain: 'It's on account of your feet.' And at that moment I feel the pain. Otherwise I could have stayed like the rabbit and never known the sensation of pain in my foot. So my getting conscious means suffering, and suffering means getting conscious. Six of one, half a dozen of the other. You still follow?"

"Roughly."

"Now, whether Descartes is right or not, I don't know and I don't care, because if my rabbit suffers, it's to the extent to which it, too, has attained a small degree of consciousness. And so there remains this colossal racket, that knowledge, great or small, has to be paid at the price of physical suffering. Of conscious and felt pain. So I say: If this really is the listed price, well, then, I am entitled to ask: Is knowledge really worth this price? The monstrous suffering on Anabiosis, cold, hunger, sickness, fear, agony, this exorbitant suffering that encompasses the globe, this inexhaustible abomination, all this for our ridiculous, little heap of knowledge? Great God, isn't that paying it a thousand times, a million times too dearly?"

"Even if it were too dearly paid," said Olga, "what can you do to change it—now? The price has been paid a damn long time ago."

Egmont stared at her for a long while without answering. He blinked once or twice, pursing his mouth a little. And then he repeated slowly:

"What can I do to change it? . . . I don't know yet," he admitted. "But good lord," he said more violently, drumming the mattress with his fist, "I won't be pushed around like this any more!"

Chapter Ten

The next day Olga brought back all the scraps of papers that had been retrieved from the ruins. They were few, and more or less illegible. She examined the sore foot with a worried air. And while renewing the dressing, she said:

"How's your theory coming on? Thought some more about it?"

"My theory?"

"Consciousness equals pain, and the rest of it."

Egmont rooted among his papers on the bed. He passed Olga a singed and crumpled page of an old notebook. On it she read, copied out in Egmont's hand: *"When the body's ailment permeates the mind, what misery everywhere. . . . How I suffer to exist! Thought is surely the most hateful property of the human animal. It is us and against us, an unavailing power and luminous impotence. . . . In such moments, solitude is at least a manner of freedom. Ah, let us suffer pain. . . ."*

"Who is this by?" she asked.

"I can't remember. Valéry in his illness, or someone else. Funny to have found it again—don't you think?"

Olga was probing his ankle and his leg, wrinkling her nose imperceptibly. A pit remained long after the pressure of her finger was removed.

"That doesn't hurt you?"

"No."

"No pain anywhere?"

The transparent gray eyes seemed to stop seeing Olga for a second though remaining fixed on her, and then surfaced again.

"You see!" he said with a smile.

"What?"

"I had to switch my attention elsewhere to know whether I had a pain or not. My groin hurts a little. I did not even know it ten seconds ago. And now," he added, boyishly amused, "now I notice that something's also itching in my throat. And that I have just the merest headache. And that my bottom's in a jelly. And that, on the whole, I feel rather chilly. Would you mind pulling the blanket up?"

"Does your groin hurt much?"

"No, not very. I say, Olga," he started.

"Yes?" she said, her mind elsewhere.

"D'you still have those books, you know . . . the Osty one on paranormal functions, and the other, about yogi? Not the one on philosophy, but on practicing yoga. You know what I mean?"

"The Greterey?"

"That's the one, I think. All about breathing exercises and practicing concentration, you know. I once started them, but then . . ."

He waved his hand with a rueful smile.

"I'll try to find it again," said Olga. "What do you want to look up? It's still that bee in your bonnet?"

"It's this question of attention," said Egmont. "The more I think of it, the more I come to believe that Man has somewhere come an awful cropper. Suffering means paying attention. You saw just now, didn't you?"

"I told you already, it's nothing new."

"No, but what inference has been drawn from it?" asked Egmont.

"From what?"

"From knowing that pain does not exist without attention? And, you see, the more I think about it, the more I also feel convinced that beasts suffer very little, merely to the degree that they are able to attend. So why shouldn't we do likewise? Why shouldn't we fix our attention elsewhere to such an extent that there is none left to suffer?"

"Where, elsewhere?" asked Olga, arranging a thick swathe of cotton wool around the sick foot.

"That's what I want to find out," said Egmont thoughtfully.

Olga next day unearthed the promised books, and found Egmont deep in conversation with a stranger.

"That's done," he said after the other had left. "I've sold the remains of my shack."

Olga raised her eyebrows in amazement.

"But only three days ago you still wanted to rebuild with the insurance money."

"I've changed my mind," said Egmont, throwing himself back into the pillow.

"But where'll you go afterward?"

"After what?"

"When you're on your feet again?"

"We haven't got there yet," said Egmont, tossing his head to make a hollow.

Olga stared at him perturbed.

"You don't feel well?" she said and placed her hand on his forehead with motherly concern.

Egmont grasped her hand and kept it gently in his. His gray-eyed gaze seemed absorbed in the ceiling.

"Of course I do," he said soothingly. "I feel all right. Quite all right. I'm as sound as a bell."

"What do you mean then?" she asked, and suddenly she puckered her eyebrows, narrowed her eyes. "What are you plotting?"

He smiled. She said impulsively:

"Now look here, son, no monkey business, if you please! Once you're well again, you can do as you like. But not before, understand?"

"You'd better attend to my paw," said Egmont, slipping his foot out of the sheets.

"What's the matter, does it hurt?" she said, bending over it.

"Not at all."

"And the groin?" she asked, carefully unwinding the gauze.

"Same as yesterday."

"This really doesn't hurt?" she insisted with sudden concern as she touched his foot. "And this doesn't either?"

Egmont shook his head. He picked up the Greterey book and brandished it.

"You've never tried this?" he asked.

"Tried what?"

"What he says."

"Turning yogi?" said Olga with a smile, but she did not raise her eyes from Egmont's foot, which she twisted in different directions, prodding it with insistence.

"Without turning yogi you might at least have had a shot at those exercises," said Egmont, flicking over the pages.

"I did actually, when I was a girl."

"You never told me," said Egmont, gazing at her seriously.

"There was nothing to tell."

"Nothing? It didn't work?"

"What do you mean, work? I could never forget my carcass, if that's what you want to know."

"You kept it up for some time?"

"I don't remember. I was very young, you know, I didn't apply myself to it with much method or persistence. No, I can't have gone on for long, I must have got fed up pretty quickly."

"You really can't remember having any results?"

"Well, yes, vaguely. Vague results, I mean. For some time I used it mainly to go to sleep. For that it worked all right."

"But not for achieving real . . . real . . . 'detachment'?"

Egmont suddenly saw something like a wave of emotion pass over Olga's face. She half opened her lips.

"That's funny," she said slowly, "now that you ask . . ."

Her eyes became dreamy.

"Yes," she said, "I do remember . . . something. And even . . ." She uttered a deep-throated laugh, a brief, birdlike laugh of surprise that Egmont used to love so. "And even, come to think of it," she said, "I believe it's after that I stopped. I must have been vaguely frightened."

Strangely enough, she seemed to Egmont to look absolutely delighted. As if she'd run into an old school friend at a street corner: Why, it's you!

"I suddenly remember quite well," she said. "I was staying at the Concordia at the time, you remember, the students' hostel behind the Panthéon. And almost every evening . . ."

She went and snuggled deep in the armchair at the far end of the room, in the semidarkness only feebly lit by the distant bedside lamp. Egmont had to thrust his head out of bed.

"Do you also remember the pub in the rue Delambre?" she said. "Crowds of medicals used to go there. I dined there almost every night. Well, one Sunday," she said, "you see, I remember it: a dismal Sunday, one of those damp, depressing Sundays that ooze through even the most tightly closed windows . . . Oh dear," she said in a whisper, and she seemed to sink once more into the ghost of that fathomless ennui. "Nothing better to do, you know. Take to drink, or else . . . Well, I took to those exercises all that day. Rhythmic breathing. And then the rhythm of the heart gradually follows. . . ."

It seemed to Egmont that her voice was growing soft and languid.

"A sort of adagio, you know. Everything slowing down, and then . . . You had to stroke your hand and wrist rhythmically with one finger, from the tip of your hand to the crook of your elbow . . . for a long, long time, and slowly. . . . Extraordinary how well I remember," she said in surprise, stroking her forearm with a gentle, slow movement. "And yet . . ."

She closed her eyes, and said even more softly:

"And yet, what I do remember, is just this blotting out . . . the walls of the room receding. The sounds slowly fading away . . . There was a girl practicing for eight hours a day on a wheezy piano. . . . I no longer heard her. I heard . . ."

She opened her eyes for a moment, met Egmont's glance tilted at her sideways. She closed them again.

". . . a sort of murmur, you know. Like passing near a chapel in which people are intoning psalms . . . with a muffled organ background . . . you know? And your whole attention, your consciousness, slowly dwindles, shrinks like a diaphragm, concentrates on a single spot of contact, on your hand, your wrist, which have become enormous, illimitable . . . which turn into a sort of vast meadow, an immense plain faintly stirred by a breeze. . . ."

120

She stopped. The little birdlike laugh rose again from her throat.

"I had never got beyond that," she murmured, "beyond forgetting the meadow too. . . . And that day I didn't either. Perhaps I wasn't really keen to, you know. As if there were some rather frightening threshold to cross . . . It was late. I got up, went out, walked up the rue Vauquelin in this odd state of mind, in order to go and dine in the rue Delambre. . . . I knew the way by heart, as you can imagine. For fun I kept up the rhythm, breathing and walking, just to see. At one moment I closed my eyes, I was in the rue des Feuillantines. . . ."

Egmont thought he saw her grow pale. But her lips smiled beneath her closed eyes.

"The moment after," she said, "I was on the embankment of the Seine, beyond the Quai aux Fleurs."

She opened her eyes again, fixing a sightless, dream-laden stare on Egmont.

"Between those two moments, I know nothing. Where I lost my way I don't know either. How I crossed the streets, the squares, why I chose the right or the left is a mystery. . . ."

She said, a little more audibly:

"Imagine, I was holding a chocolate bar in my hand! Had I bought it? Or stolen it? I was biting into it lustily, that's all I know: I was ravenous. I had mislaid my own person for over an hour, you see. And I have not the least recollection where it may have gone all the while. Yes, I have!" she cried suddenly, and her hand darted forward as if to save something from falling. "Yes," she repeated with a no less sudden gentleness: "whenever it crossed my mind again . . . very seldom, you know . . . it was always linked with the notion . . . the image . . . of a delicious bath in southern seas, among those aquatic trees—what do you call them?—with a tangle of roots. . . ."

"Mangroves?"

"Yes, perhaps . . . Maybe that's what I dreamed of while I was walking. But I can't be at all sure. Maybe I dreamed it much later, I no longer know. There you are," she said in a low voice, "that was the first time that . . . I crossed that threshold without meaning to. The last time, too. I never dared begin again."

After a long silence, Egmont eventually said:

"Why have you never told me this?"

"I haven't thought of it for almost fifteen years," said Olga. "Tonight is the first time."

She said no more. But Egmont saw her slowly rubbing her wrist and hand with one finger, with a blissful smile as if she were looking at some childhood photographs. He would have liked to question her, but he kept silent. He watched her for some time without saying anything, then silently turned the bed-side lamp away so that Olga was even more deeply in the shadow. The silence lasted. And out of the silence and the shadow rose a softly droning murmur:

"A gray sea . . . warm and pale, with pink reflections . . . the trunks of the mangroves are dark, a deep red, is that what they are like?" asked Olga in a childlike voice.

"No, I rather believe they are gray," said Egmont, lowering his own voice to a whisper.

"They are the color of sandalwood, of logwood," said Olga after a moment. She said even more inaudibly: "I am swimming among their roots. Such a lot of roots . . ."

"You can see the sky?"

"No. I don't think there is any. Or else it is black."

"Do they breathe?" said Egmont.

122

"Who?"

"The mangroves?"

". . . No," said Olga hesitantly, "I believe they palpitate a little, if that's what you mean. Like . . ."

She broke off.

"Well?"

"Like the pulse in my wrist," she said in a very small voice.

They both remained silent for some time.

"You are swimming alone?"

"Yes, alone. And naked. It's delicious," she whispered.

"Quite alone?"

"No. There are sponges, millepores, sea anemones. . . . I don't really see them, but I feel them gliding past . . . along my body. . . ."

"Like fish?"

"No . . . much softer . . ."

She was so utterly still, her finger had ceased its slow, moving caress, and Egmont saw her breathe with such slow suspense that he awaited each fresh intake with a pang of anxiety. But he dared not move a finger. Olga's lips stirred.

"Do you think it's a dream? Or . . ."

Egmont could hardly hear her. Long, long afterward Olga opened her eyes. She shivered, took a deep breath, smiled. She gazed at her friend without speaking, and he returned the gaze and the smile. At last she said:

"That's funny, don't you think? That it should have come over me again. Like this . . . without warning . . ."

"Not quite without warning," said Egmont gently. He hesitated before venturing: "Did you feel happy?"

She murmured:

"Happy and scared, as I used to feel."

She added in a smiling whisper:

"Very happy. A little scared."

Egmont saw her get up and slowly walk over to the looking glass. He admired her for remaining so beautiful. The half-light wiped out the wrinkles at the corners of the mouth and the slight looseness around the chin. Olga's glance moved from her own image and met Egmont's in the glass. Her lids fluttered.

She came to his bedside and clasped his temples in both her hands. She murmured: "You swear you aren't in pain?" He shook his head vigorously.

She smiled as she bent down toward him. Her mouth trembled a little.

Chapter Eleven

Pélion and Mirambeau advanced toward the platform, more or less elbowing their way. The hall hired for the meeting was a former tramway depot which, becoming too small and inconvenient with the advent of trolley-buses, had been turned into an exhibition hall. Under its vaulted roof it resounded with a muffled drone: that of a thousand private conversations merging with the roar of the machines from the adjacent power station.

The platform—a few planks thrown over steel girders behind a skirt of red bunting—was already practically full. Mirambeau was welcomed with warmth and deference. But he caused some disappointment by declining the honor of the chairmanship with unshakable firmness. "I'll talk to them when you deem it advisable. But it's not for me to conduct, even symbolically, proceedings of this type with which I am too unconversant."

They did not venture to insist, but this raised another problem which was discussed with Pélion in undertones. Should they immediately announce the presence of the famous scientist? Or keep the news in reserve to galvanize the audience at the right moment? It was agreed that they would bide their time, and the chair was taken by an old trade unionist, white-haired and weather-beaten. He invited Mirambeau to sit on his right, and Pélion on his left. There was a burst of applause: Pélion, as he sat down, shook the hand of his other neighbor, a delegate of the Christian unions, and the handshake was greeted as a symbol.

The atmosphere was convivial, the hall crammed to bursting. The ardor roused by the St. Gregory's Day rally had not yet cooled off; it was aglow in the vibrant audience. Pélion noticed, with surprise and satisfaction, the presence of a number of North Afs among them. Usually they didn't come: completely unorganized, they kept apart, unsure and diffident, perhaps even harboring a doleful mistrust.

Mirambeau gazed at this working-class crowd which he had never before approached. Confronted with those attentive faces, deeply lined as soon as they were past their youth, he felt a surge of affection which was gradually mingled with apprehension: "What am I doing here?" he began to wonder. He felt out of place, indiscreet in a way, unwanted. He was not one of them, however much he might support them. Would he even know how to talk to them? I'm sure to say a lot of nonsense, make myself ridiculous, perhaps even odious.

Like a defensive reflex, the memory of a film that had delighted his young years came once again to his rescue. In moments of self-doubt, it was indeed to Charlie Chaplin that Mirambeau would turn for help. It happened whenever he had to stand up to some "expert," armed with no more than his common sense; whenever he poked his nose into politics under the supercilious stare of some deputy or minister. . . .

A poor chap brings his alarm clock to sell to Charlie. Charlie shakes it soundly, puts it to his ear like a stethoscope, prizes it open with a can opener in a professional, self-confident fashion, guts it like a chicken, scatters the cogwheels on the counter. The poor chap goggles but daren't open his mouth: an expert, you know. . . . And after Charlie has magisterially examined every piece under his magnifying glass, dumped the lot pell-mell back into the case, shaken it against his ear once more, and at last returned it to his stunned customer with a disdainful pout as if to say "Nothing doing," the poor wretch shambles off with his alarm clock in a hash, dumb with dismay—and awe. And Charlie nonchalantly wipes the palms of his hands and passes on to other business—just like our French generals and ministers after Dienbienphu. . . .

Under a minister's eye, therefore, Mirambeau thinks of Charlie and he promptly stops feeling overawed. And tonight, too, he thought of him, as he listened to the first orator, Pélion's neighbor, and it restored his self-confidence. The fellow spoke without apparently managing to grip the attention of his fidgety, chattering audience. He read from a piece of paper in a flat voice which did not dominate the surflike roll of murmurs. Although he did not seem aware of this measure of indifference, Mirambeau now suffered for him. He breathed deeply when the speaker finished. And then, to his surprise, there was an outbreak of applause. The friendliness of this popular audience touched him and reassured him completely.

Pélion rose to speak. Mirambeau responded to the warmth of the rich, deep Burgundy voice. How he rolled his words! Mirambeau was amused by the youngster's already consummate art as a public speaker. Far from raising his voice to capture attention, he uttered the first words almost in a half-tone, establishing at one stroke a churchlike silence. He spoke smilingly and his words smiled too. A shot of banter tickled the audience, pricking their self-conceit while provoking their grins. And the listener found himself caught in a flow of such simple notions, such familiar images, that they sank into his mind like a butter knife, meeting no resistance. The effect was exhilarating.

And then, step by step, the tone changed. He smiled less. The ideas became harder, more penetrating. He sketched a picture of former times—of the prehistory of trade unionism. He showed how it had been possible then to lead the isolated workers by the nose, how easy it had been to exploit their misery, to set them against each other and maintain them in slavery. In a voice that grew in power, he reminded them of recent gains, of the strength of a united front, but also of the hope that always flourished in the heart of their adversaries, of splitting this front, of breaking it. So far this hope had relied mainly on threats, the specter of unemployment, fear of dismissal and starvation. But now, he cried, new tactics are to be tried out: the lure of money. Let your mates down and you'll be able to run a midget car, own a refrigerator, a TV set. . . . "Yes, let your mates down," he burst out violently, "let them down and in two years' time you won't need a refrigerator, I tell you—you'll all be out in the cold yourselves!"

There were shouts of "Unity!" while Pélion, with jerky fingers combed his rebellious hair. But they weren't as unanimous as Mirambeau would have wished. Not that applause was lacking. These people were fond of Pélion, they showed it, they felt he was right—but to be expected to go without! It's hard having to miss a bonus at the end of the month. With all those debts piling up . . . They had already done some rough figuring, made their little plans, and big ones too. In the space of a year—twelve bonuses—you might afford new linoleum, the old one's cracking everywhere, buy a rabbit coat for the lassie who's getting on for eight now, and, why not, with two or three pay envelopes, get a second-hand motor bike. . . .

Yet they shouted "U-ni-ty! . . . U-ni-ty!" in rhythmical chorus.

But a good many of them didn't shout—or with faint voices. Ducking their heads a little, as if waiting for the storm to pass. And even among those who shouted, how many would remain steadfast once they were face to face with the missus, the carping, uncomprehending housewife?

Mirambeau's eyes met Pélion's and he thought he understood, from a gesture by the chairman, that they were now asking him to speak. But no, someone rose from the audience, spreading both arms to request silence. Pélion darted another glance at Mirambeau which the latter could not make out, a slight nod as if saying: "Never mind . . . let's get this over." Mirambeau wasn't long in understanding.

It was the counterattack, and from the word go it reeked of provocation. By the time the platform realized it and the chairman tried to intervene to stop the troublemaker, it was already too late.

Everything proceeded now like clockwork. A shaken fist, a hoisted chair, a scuffle and uproar. And through all the doors poured the police, as if at a given signal. One squad was already swarming along the wall toward the platform, while the crowd in the hall seemed to disintegrate, to scatter in turmoil and confusion, like tapioca in water as it came to the boil.

Mirambeau's companions, standing motionless on their stage, gazed at the police squad streaming up in the pandemonium. That's the prefect and his minions getting their own back, thought the old scientist. They didn't waste much time. He wondered whether they would dare to have a direct go at him. Instigating public disorder, he thought with amusement. If they want to, they have got their charge cut and dried. . . . He caught himself wishing like a youngster that they would grab him by the neck, just for the fun of it. No. They'll pounce on Pélion again, he told himself with concern. He's a better target than any of us. He turned toward him, just in time to see Pélion being dragged away by two comrades in lumber-jackets. He felt himself taken by the arm. "Follow us," a young fellow said to him with a grin, and added shyly ". . . Professor," to show he knew whom he was dealing with. He jumped down lightly from the boards and held his two fists out to the burly man. Mirambeau found himself on the ground with not too much effort. "You licked those cops all right the other day—that was a snorter!" said the young lad dragging him toward the end of the shed. Among the welter of emotions that were stirring in him, Mirambeau felt a warm wave of pleasure. "I'll go first," said the lad and squeezed through an iron trap into a tangle of pipes and drains. I'll never get through . . . thought Mirambeau, but he clattered down the iron ladder with a nimbleness that surprised and amused him. For a few minutes they dashed through a low, labyrinthine vault, long and sinuous, and crammed with cables, hose pipes, and electric wires. You had to bend double as you ran, so as not to bump into obstacles. In front of an iron door Pélion and his companions had come to a stop. One of them turned an enormous key in an enormous lock. "One of the trolley boys," said Mirambeau's young guide. They stepped through the door. Another iron ladder which, this time, had to be climbed. This was a longer and more breath-taking business. They emerged in the machine room. The dynamos whirred like a monstrous hive. Pélion and Mirambeau were led past the first two, and had to edge between the wall and the huge marble switchboard, covered with gauges, dials, and switches. "Wait here for a moment, someone'll come and fetch you. Don't move meanwhile, you never know . . . So long, and good luck!" The lads in the lumber-jackets shook their hands with smiles that brimmed over with affection. "You had those cops in a frazzle all right," they too said to Mirambeau, and their grins showed what they thought of it. They exchanged winks of connivance with the fat man, shaking hands all round. "A real snorter!" repeated the young guide, flicking his fingers loosely from the wrist, as if they'd been pinched in a door, and they went away.

"Where will you go?" asked Mirambeau.

"Not straight home, anyway. They must be waiting for me," said Pélion, looking worried.

"They'd put you back in jail?"

Pélion had been sentenced to three months not long before, for interfering with the freedom to work.

"They wouldn't stand on ceremony," he said.

"But they have no charge against you!"

"Oh, they'd just keep me inside for five or six days, time enough to keep me from talking. I'll lie low at the paper mills," he said uncertainly.

"A bit out of the way, isn't it? Come on, I'll take you along."

"Where to?"

"You'll see."

Two fellows in blue boiler suits came to fetch them. They led them out into the open air. A hired car was waiting outside the gate. The two friends dived into it and the chauffeur drove off straight ahead. Only when he had turned round behind the cheese market did he inquire at last where he was to go. Mirambeau gave his home address.

When the men arrived at the Coubez plant on Monday morning, they found the following notice put up:

The Management have decided that the 7% bonus on the gross wages of all employees eligible by their records, which was origi-

131

nally to be introduced at the end of each month, will be paid to the beneficiaries on a weekly basis and come into effect as from the end of this week. Any disturbance in normal working, wherever it may occur, will naturally entail the immediate cancellation of this free and voluntary offer, which will not be renewed.

The members of the shop committee read this notice over and over again, and every reading increased their dismay. What devilish cleverness! Could the high hopes aroused by the rally and the mass meeting have been more adroitly—and more brutally—scotched? Would their brittle unity withstand this blow? Was not any attempt on the part of the CGT lads now doomed to come up against the other fellows' fear and hostility, thus causing bitterness and rancor to drive an ever deeper wedge between the divided workers?

"I've always had a grouse against Monday," said Albert in a disheartened tone. "It's a lousy day for luck."

Chapter Twelve

Egmont stuck his foot out of bed, put it on the blanket. Olga was still asleep. The skin at the base of his big toe had turned a grayish color. The toe itself did not look normal. Egmont remained in thought.

He dared not wake Olga. But she began to stir. He felt relieved. For a moment she seemed startled to find herself there, then she laughed and kissed him on both cheeks.

"I should marry again," she said. "It's lovely to have someone to hug. And to feel such snuggly warmth against you."

Then, as he did not say anything:

"How's your foot?"

"I've had an odd dream," said Egmont.

"What, again?" said Olga with surprise.

"I wonder," said Egmont with a grin, "if I haven't missed my vocation: another army tale."

"I love army tales," said Olga. "I used to be crazy about Esparbès and Courteline. I don't know why, but I just doted on both of 'em."

"My dream wasn't a bit like either, I'm afraid. It was more like a Chirico painting touched up by Salvador Dali. I was standing at the water's edge. A turbulent river down which floated the bodies of dead horses. Hundreds of them. They piled up on the banks. So much so that the banks gradually caved in. And the water carried everything away. There was an awful stench of rotting carrion."

"Personally, I prefer Esparbès," said Olga.

"Matter of taste," said Egmont. "Mind you, I didn't like it much either. I tried to find a path to get away from the sight and the stench, but there was no end to it, the field was covered with those carcasses and with smoke, because there were cavalry charges in furious progress amid clouds of dust. It was a horrible melee. I hid behind a crumbling wall, gasping and shaking, and the fear slowly woke me. In my half-sleep I recognized the battlefield perfectly well: it was the big toe of my right foot. An outsize toe, just like my leg the other night: a toe as big as Mont-Saint-Michel, as Vesuvius. And then the same amazement, on really waking up, to find it so small and me so big. I am telling you all this because I've just had a peep at my toe. It doesn't look pretty."

"Show me."

Egmont saw her face darken while she examined it.

"You're right," she said. "It doesn't look pretty."

She got up, wrapped Egmont's dressing gown around her lovely, naked body, and began to dial a telephone number.

"You're calling someone in?"

"Yes, sonny, I'm ringing Vauthiers."

"The surgeon?"

"I'd rather like to have his opinion."

"I say, as bad as all that?"

But someone had answered at the other end. Olga asked Vauthiers to drop in, if possible, that same day. She put down the receiver and smiled:

"Better nip this sort of thing in the bud."

"But it isn't an abscess, is it? It would hurt if it were."

134

"It doesn't look like an abscess."

Egmont gulped and asked:

"Gangrene?"

"Don't start worrying your pretty head," said Olga. "It may be nothing at all."

She took his head between her cool, rounded arms, pressed it against her chest. Egmont's lips tasted the rising of one breast, bit at it. She let him, kissed his hair. Then she moved away, disappeared into the bathroom. When she emerged from it, fully dressed, the patient had not moved. He seemed asleep. She came closer. She saw his eyes were open. She murmured in a drawl: "Dan . . . iel?"

Sometimes, at the bottom of a pool, a bubble forms. You see it form and swell, detach itself, and rise faster and faster until it bursts on the surface.

It was something like this that Olga saw forming in Egmont's eyes. Not a bubble: a look. As if, at the call of his name, a look had formed at the back of his eye and had come to burst on the surface. Egmont turned this look on Olga and said: "Yes?"

"What's the matter?" she asked. "Were you asleep?"

"I don't know. No."

"Where were you?"

"Not far," said Egmont in an almost toneless voice, and he added in the same low voice: "Not very far."

Olga gripped him by the shoulder and shook him. Her face was stern, almost angry.

"Don't start those idiotic pranks of yours!" she commanded. "Do you hear? First of all, give me that book back. Where did you put it?"

"What color were your mangroves? What shade did you say they were?"

Olga turned crimson. She stared at him reproachfully.

"That isn't fair. You're taking advantage of my bad example to . . ."

Egmont kissed the palm of her hand and insisted coaxingly:
"What color?"

"No, Daniel. I'm not game. Pink. Or blue. I no longer know. Now let me go. I have tons of patients to visit this morning. I'll be here tonight at six, to see Vauthiers. Give me that book," she repeated.

"Take it back if you want to," said Egmont, without ceasing to smile, and he opened the drawer of his bedside table. "Actually, I should be able to do without it by now. . . . Otherwise I'll ask Virgil when he drops in to go and get me another copy. And I'll read it on the sly."

"Daniel," begged Olga. "Promise me . . ."

"Don't count on it, old girl."

"You're merely going to make our task more difficult."

"That we'll see."

"Can't you wait a week before starting this childish nonsense?"

"This is too good an opportunity."

"What opportunity? Daniel, you scare me."

"A little scared, and very happy," mimicked Egmont ironically, in Olga's voice.

"But I was young and in good shape, and, anyhow, the scare was good and real enough to make me stop that silly game. Daniel, you'll promise me . . ."

"Hurry up. Your patients are waiting."

"No, Daniel, I demand—"

"It's almost nine."

"What are you saying?"

"Almost nine o'clock."

"That's impossible!"

"Ten minutes to, to be precise."

She swayed irresolutely from one foot to the other, and then flung "Pig!" at him, kissed him hurriedly on the mouth as if biting him, betwixt laughter and rage. Ten seconds later the entrance door slammed. Egmont heard a clattering sprint down the stairs. Then everything fell silent. With a relaxed sigh he let his head drop back on the pillow. His lips were curved in a half-smile of peaceful expectation.

Olga returned with Vauthiers. Egmont received them wide-awake, looking so well-behaved, patient, and ostentatiously meek that she found him enigmatic. But wasn't it merely that she had expected to find him enigmatic? She mentally sniffed the disquieting atmosphere in the hushed, hermetically closed room, she scented some mysterious endeavor, as if shreds of it still clung to the dark folds of the curtains, the weird contortions of the gnarled old vine stocks, the gleaming phials in the subdued light. . . .

The surgeon meanwhile was examining the sick foot. He then withdrew with Olga for some time. Ever since she had shown such concern, Egmont had prepared himself for the worst. Hence he was not surprised when Olga reappeared behind Vauthiers, to find her looking very pale.

"We're taking you to the clinic," she said in a voice she imagined sounded natural.

"Just a moment," said Egmont calmly, and he turned his eyes on the surgeon. "What is it, Professor? An ablation?"

Vauthiers bowed his head:

"It is wiser not to waste time. The spot of gangrene is minute, but it goes deep and the position's awkward."

Egmont said quietly:

"You'll remove the toe?"

Vauthiers coughed a little before explaining:

"We may possibly find it necessary . . . for a section around the toe . . ."

"You'll remove the foot?"

"No, no!" protested Vauthiers hastily. "It hasn't gone as far as that, thank goodness! For the time being, I think I'll remove this," he explained, drawing with his fingernail on Egmont's foot the restricted seat of the ablation.

"May I put a question to you, Professor?"

Vauthiers made a gesture of assent.

"Suppose that for one reason or another it were necessary to postpone the operation. How much time can you give me before the whole foot goes the same way?"

"It is hard to say with accuracy, I'm afraid. It depends on the soundness of the tissues, and yours seem to have suffered somewhat. Then again, we cannot overlook . . . you are still young, we may be allowed to presume that the touch of gangrene is the direct outcome of your accident . . . still, we aren't entitled to discount in advance the possibility of a more disturbing origin. It may be a very slow process, but it would in my view be foolhardy to wait for more than eight or ten days."

"Professor, I have very serious reasons for waiting at least those ten days."

"I must insist that we should not wait if your reasons are not very, very serious."

"They are extremely serious, Professor."

The surgeon bowed. He turned toward Olga.

"I don't think," he said, "that the risk is very substantial, after all. The patient belongs to the fraternity," he said with a smile, "and besides, you will be here. You'll see the patient every day?"

"Twice, more likely," she said, casting a black look at Egmont and tightening her lips over her suppressed rage.

The surgeon took his leave. Olga accompanied him to the door, then came back to Egmont's side to let her anger burst.

"Extremely serious reasons! Are you making a fool of him—and of me?"

"You're not being sensible," said Egmont.

"Well! Of all the nerve!"

"Look here, Vauthiers himself agreed: where's the risk?"

"You know so well where it is that you said it yourself: you may lose your foot."

"Not at all, since you'll be here. Listen," he suggested, "let's strike a bargain."

Olga narrowed her eyes and looked at him askance.

"What are you cooking now?"

"Vauthiers gives me ten days: just give me five. Only half, you see, I am not greedy. All right?"

But she clenched her fists, stamped her foot.

"But why, for heaven's sake, you beastly little . . . worm? Why just now? What do you want to do?"

Egmont coughed, embarrassed. Once or twice his finger seemed to follow the trace of a tear from his eye down to his chin, before he declared:

"I hope to go on a long trip."

"Get that out of your mind!" she exploded. "You can't even leave your bed!"

"Oh, my foot and I," said Egmont, "won't budge from here. But I . . . but you . . . well, don't count much on my conversation. You see?"

"Ah!" said Olga, "so that's it . . ." And suddenly she burst out again: "And you can't wait? Five days! It's madness!" she cried.

"The time it takes to see," said Egmont with the mulish expression of an obstinate child.

"But to see what?"

"Look here, Olga, it's too soon to say. I can't tell you. It would seem so . . . Look here," he said again, "I think I caught a glimpse of quite extraordinary things. I can feel them here, within my reach. One step further, one small step, that's all. Do help me instead of hindering me. What are five days to you? Don't you want to help me?"

"I'm doing nothing but help!" protested Olga, tucking in a corner of the blanket that had come undone. "What more do you want? I've got my patients, old boy, you aren't the only one!"

"I know, and that isn't what I meant. When I say help me, I don't mean look after me. It means that you'd simply have to . . . I don't know what's going to happen," he said, gazing at the back of his limp, lined hand and spreading his fingers as if to detect some anomaly there. "It may happen . . . I don't know," he said, raising his eyes to Olga, "that I am . . . not back for lunch, for instance. Nor for dinner. So you'd have to make do without me. Suppose we asked Virgil to come. You could, between you, look after my carcass. As if, in a way . . . as if I'd gone dotty. You understand?"

"I understand only too well," she said sulkily, and sat down on the bed. "Except one thing, the same old thing: Why now, why before the operation?"

Egmont seemed very busy pulling the top of his sheet over the blanket, flattening it out and smoothing it. He said without raising his head:

"Because I need proof, that's why."

"Proof?"

"That these aren't mere dreams. The warm seas and the rest.

The army in the hills, the cavalry charges, the dead horses. You used to be afraid because—though you may be as rationalist as a pragmatic horse-doctor—you still felt there was something . . . something real, something actual, something carnal. . . . I want to take a serious look at things down there, you understand," he said with quiet gravity.

Olga murmured after him, musingly:

"A serious look at things . . . Are you really serious?" she said.

He nodded his head several times, gazing at her placidly. She got up, took a few steps across the room. She stopped to contemplate a twisted vine stock which resembled some maimed centaur. She took it in her hands and said without turning round:

"How far have you already been? To what depth?"

"I don't know . . . I thought I recognized your mangroves from afar. Something, anyhow, that looked like them. A tangle of branches and roots. A murmur, a pulsation . . . and a tropical moisture . . ."

Olga, with her back still to him, was stroking the centaur's trunk with her finger tip. She said:

"You surely don't imagine, though . . ." she hesitated, "that it was anything but a dream?"

"Of course not," said Egmont, "a . . . sort of dream." But he added, his voice trailing: "For the time being."

She only turned her head to glance at him over her shoulder.

"What are you hoping for?" she asked.

"To get out of the dream. To see the things themselves. Good lord," he suddenly said, "why shouldn't one be able to? Osty's book gives tons of examples of what he calls internal autoscopy. So why not I?"

"But beyond that?" said Olga without answering, her head bent once more over the tortured centaur.

"Beyond?"

"Suppose you succeed, what then?"

"Nothing," said Egmont. "What a question."

Olga replaced the centaur stock among its fellows, came back and sat on the bed beside Egmont. She looked hard at him for some time.

"This isn't . . ." she started, but seemed afraid to go on. She took his hand, lowered her eyes. She ended, playing with one of his fingers: ". . . a way for you to quit this world?"

Egmont at first did not reply. Then he sighed:

"No risk of that for the moment, worse luck: the slightest noise, the slightest touch calls me back, like a diver who's only got to let himself float to the top. I'd have to find leaden shoes. . . ."

"Don't go too far, all the same," she murmured.

"If anyone heard us," said Egmont gaily, "they'd take us for a couple of old English spinsters talking of haunted houses."

"If it were a question of haunted houses," said Olga, "I'd let you poke and pry to your heart's content. But you know as well as I do that these aren't phantasies. It's a very carnal domain, as you say, a quite concrete matter of nervous connections, unusual links, I admit, but perfectly feasible ones, between various systems, perhaps between certain neurones and the organic tissue. . . . I don't count Osty, who's a bit of a humbug, but there are others. Even a top man like Lapicque takes these things very seriously. That's just what frightens me."

"I don't see why it should. On the contrary, it's rather reassuring. Since it remains so physical, so carnal, what do you expect can happen to me?"

"I don't know, said Olga. "I distrust the body."

She looked at Egmont, wrinkling one nostril.

"Because you've been a doctor, you think . . . you think you're venturing into known country, into friendly territory. . . ." She wagged her head. "Friendly . . . remains to be seen. A so-called bosom friend who always left you on his doorstep, without ever allowing you in, would you say he really was a friend? What'll he do the day you make up your mind to slip into his home by stealth?"

She drew a sinuous line on the sheet with her fingernail.

"The body, the *soma,* doesn't trust us, and with good cause: if we were in charge of our kidneys, our heart, what tricks mightn't we play, purposely or not? A stoppage or a bungle, and we're dead. No wonder the *soma* keeps us at arm's length. And a damn long arm it is too," she said, and her tone was at once dreamy and sarcastic. "How much has Man come to know about his own body, his partner, in the five hundred thousand years that he's been trying to penetrate to its mysterious life? Biology, medicine—it all amounts to what? Some anatomical butchering and those vague aerial photographs that the most powerful microscopes provide. But what really happens down there, in those forests, those valleys, those cities and factories? What about the customs and rites, the joys and pains of their inhabitants? No admittance. Any landing to find out strictly prohibited. If you trespass it's espionage. I don't like the idea. That's all."

"I don't see the difference," said Egmont.

"What difference?"

"Everything's espionage: what's Mirambeau doing other than spying?"

"But he stays *here,*" said Olga.

"That's exactly what I'm asking you to do," said Egmont. "To stay here, in my place. To watch out while I'm . . . Listen, please!" he said, to stop Olga from interrupting him. "To quit this world, you said? No more than a week ago I might have answered yes, I don't deny it. I would have left it without regret, this impossible world, had an opportunity come along. But I honestly believe this isn't so any more. That it's outdated—outstripped. Curiosity has got hold of me again: scientific fervor. My anger backs it up, that's possible. And other, mixed feelings. But what stirs me now, what's driving me on, is already the explorer's giddiness. I have only had two or three paltry tries so far, a cautious and swift reconnaissance on the other side of the water—and already I see myself traveling up the Amazon, venturing boldly among the savage tribes. . . . Am I only deluding myself, shall I be able to land at all, shan't I be thrown back into the sea at the first step? Well, I don't think so. I think, you see, that I've managed to get a foothold on the shore without meeting any opposition; that I might have penetrated further, had I only wanted to. I *think* so, no more. But that's already enough to have roused in me a passion that I thought was dead: the passion for knowledge. I won't let it subside," he said with sudden excitement, "die out again, yield myself up to my former fathomless boredom. I couldn't bear it. Oh God, as if it were a question of my toe, or even my foot! It's my whole life that's at stake, don't you understand?"

"Nevertheless," said Olga, "don't go and lose it in order to save it."

Chapter Thirteen

Olga was musing as she drove in her midget car to a dinner party at the other end of the town. That argument with Daniel! A hardheaded woman—what did the beast call me? A pragmatic horse-doctor. The little beast! Fancy letting herself be dragged on to such . . . irrational ground! She wavered between a desire to laugh and to shiver. My word, she thought, I took him seriously, I argued, I fought. What came over me? It's just a new fad of his, nothing more: first the vine stocks, then the phials, yesterday those stuffed beasts, now this whim. . . . He'll tire of it before he's gone ten steps. Leave him alone and think of other things.

But she did not succeed. Always a fast driver, she drove on her nerves, without looking. At the corner of the Avenue Thiers she almost knocked down a cyclist with his whole load of evening papers. She kept on muttering: "The beast." She thought: He has an answer to everything. She remembered their former squabbles. No argument ever found him at a loss: he'd think up a reply on the spur of the moment. And it was never utter bull.

She left the car in the drive, absently leaving the headlights on. Only then did it occur to her that she had forgotten to change.

Never mind, too late now, let's hope the other women haven't dressed up to the nines, or I shall look a draggletail.

It was a lively dinner party. A couple of lawyers, some more doctors of course. A running crossfire of table talk. Everybody more or less shouted to make himself heard. Olga's mind frequently strayed and what she then heard was a crazy hubbub, a hotchpotch of syllables, a wild bubble-and-squeak capped by the women's voices and their shrill laughter. From time to time Olga recovered herself, tried to listen to a breezy young man opposite who was telling the story of a famous confidence trick. At these moments the man's words suddenly stood out from the jumble of voices, relegating all the others to a sort of nondescript background which she no longer even perceived.

This is even more fantastic than Daniel's story with his burned feet, she thought suddenly. The little beast is right. I'll have to look rather more closely into this attention business. The most incredible things happen right next to us without our even noticing them. Just because they are so ordinary. Who was talking of that not so long ago? Oh, yes, that crackpot Cloots, at Mirambeau's. It seems to be in the air, definitely. Why has it never struck me before? she wondered, listening to the zoolike din around the table, which was glittering with glasses and atinkle with spoons. It's really amazing what's going on in my ear. It receives everything higgledy-piggledy like a garbage can—the words, sounds, noises all merge and mingle. If one tried to make a tape recording of this hash, nothing could be heard but an inextricable jumble, a real Irish stew, nobody could manage to pick out a single recognizable word. Yet it's this hash that is sent pell-mell up to my brain. And there I make my selection. Every second, without a moment's thought or hesitation, I unravel this Gordian knot of sound vibrations. And I pick out the thread I need, not its neighbor, no, always the right one—and the surplus, this hotchpotch of sounds, I don't even hear it. Such a splitting up of sensations is little short of miraculous. Walking on burned feet without knowing it is nothing in comparison!

She tried, for fun, to listen to the fellow opposite, to stop listening, to listen again. It was just like a telephone line with intermittent fade-outs.

". . . and said to the jeweler: 'I'm afraid I can't write on account of my arm, would you mind writing for me?' The jeweler natu—"

What a stew, a real bouillabaisse, thought Olga. That's funny, that's precisely what we are having at this moment. A jolly good one too. What's in it? Can I pick out, the way one does when listening, the separate flavor of, say, hogfish? Cut out all the other flavors by an act of thought? It's more difficult, still it is possible . . . yes, there's the hogfish flavor . . . and there's the taste of mussels . . . good, and there's the saffron . . . Had they added cognac to it? No . . . more like an apple brandy.

She noticed that her eyes were wide open, her spoon suspended in mid-air. Whatever for? Why, of course, to play up to the fellow facing her, in a courteous pretense of listening to his story:

". . . his wife was waiting for him, all aflutter. 'Well, darling, what's the big surprise?' The jeweler looked blank. 'But your note?' said his wife. 'The one that woman brought: "Hand her the money, it's for a surprise." ' The jeweler gasped: 'Great Scott! you didn't give her—' "

Olga stopped listening: and howling banshees promptly filled the dining room. Fantastic. She cocked an ear to her right:

". . . yes, in general," a somewhat apoplectic man in his fifties was shouting, "but on the Trunk Road 303, if you go via Jossigny—"

Click, wide aperture: the howling banshees.

Click, to the left, a student of Vauthiers':

". . . no right! Absolutely none. Look here, imagine opening the abdomen of just anyone who—"

Click, wide aperture: the howling banshees. Click, her vis-à-vis again:

". . . the bird flown of course. The poor, paralytic millionaire had skedaddled with the five-thousand-dollar sparkler. Not bad, eh?"

I've come in at the right moment, thought Olga. She was laughing, anyway. She noticed she was laughing uproariously as if she had followed the story from beginning to end. Actually, one part of her *had* followed it, without her even knowing—exactly like Daniel with his burned feet.

The beast, she thought. The salad was being served. Absentmindedly she put it on her meat by mistake. We are inexcusable, she mused, thinking of the medical profession. The layman is one thing, but we! She saw a lady opposite daintily depositing her salad leaves in her small crescent-shaped plate, without interrupting her lively chatter. Damn! thought Olga. She furtively transferred a few leaves from one plate to the other. I always get it wrong. The fact is I rather like my salad to soak in the gravy. . . . "Pardon?" she said aloud, bending toward her neighbor who was asking: "Are you, too, crazy about Gérard Philipe?" "Can't sleep for it," said Olga with a laugh. She thought: What an ass. What was I thinking about? Oh yes—about doctors. But the ass went on talking to her about CinemaScope. She nodded her head while munching some excellent meat, which must be wild sucking boar. She tried not to lose the thread of her thoughts entirely. She tied it, lost it, retied it. Meanwhile she was answering her neighbor, or at times a friend addressing her across the table. And then she returned to her ruminations. To think that, night and day, we are poring over organisms that have got out of order without their owners knowing the first thing about it, she thought. Her neighbor was explaining: "It's like this Chambertin," he said raising his glass, "suppose it suddenly went pastel blue, you'd hesitate to drink it, wouldn't you? And you'd fancy it didn't taste the same. Well, the cinema in color . . ." But she was not listening. Actually that's precisely why we exist, she thought, the existence of us doctors is the patent proof of this divorce between people and their organism, this fundamental, total, and inexplicable divorce. . . . We ought to be obsessed by it: why should there be need of a physician to tell people what's happening inside their own bodies —instead of it being the other way round? Why don't they know, why this divorce? What's the purpose? What does it mean? Everybody was getting up in a general hubbub. Her neighbor was talking to her about Lollobrigida. "You've read the Kinsey report? Sixty-eight per cent of American males pet their wife's breasts, evidence of an advanced degree of sexual civilization. I must be particularly civilized, because Lollobrigida's—" Olga nodded politely, with an attentive smile. They followed the others into the drawing room. Mirambeau provides the answer, I expect, she thought. We must be kept away from the cellular administration, or else, if we could intervene and settle the length of life ourselves, we'd play havoc with the normal sequence of generations. But in that case Daniel is right, she thought, he's right a hundred times. I've no right to stop him. What he's trying to do is not the fruit of a sudden impulse, a scatterbrained whim. She remembered his words: "I want to take a serious look down there." She thought: Where'll he get to? Perhaps nowhere, probably not far anyway. What he'll bring back from his expedition will doubtless be . . . of precious little use. But it's fascinating all the same. Exploring is one thing, putting it to use is quite another. The scholars may expound the Lascaux cave paintings, but if it hadn't been for a couple of kids venturing into those caves, the scholars would have had nothing *to* tell. "Why, of course," she said to the man next to her who asked her to excuse him: just a word with the Judge over there. Her eyes searched for her colleague Burgeaud, the neurologist. She found his razor-shaven skull in front of a small painting by Trouillebert, which he was examining close up.

"Do you mind explaining?" she said to him when she had joined him. "I'm a bit out of touch. It comes from living too much in other people's ovaries. What exactly happens in the encephalon when one listens, for instance? How does the selection operate?"

She had dragged him off to a couch by a window opening onto the night. She stretched out on it, with her back propped against the wall. Burgeaud also installed his interminable body on it in zigzags.

"By shubtraction," he said slurringly—he hardly opened his lazy lips when speaking. "By massive inhibition. You put the whole brain to shleep—except one narrow, watchful sector. That's why my students doze off during my classes: if this listening sector gets a wee bit tired in its turn, if it relaxes even for a second, all the rest being lulled already, hey presto, you see, everything's asleep. So the ones who doze off are actually my best pupils, those who were lishtening most attentively. The others didn't inhibit anything, they were woolgathering, and they go on woolgathering. This isn't a paradox," he said, because Olga was laughing.

One never knew with Burgeaud whether he was serious or not. He never smiled. Olga knew, however, that his classes were considered huge fun, and that no one ever slept during them.

"But this doesn't answer my question," she said. "Mental inhibition, all right, but how does this waking sector manage to select among the hotchpotch of a dozen simultaneous cross-talks?"

"You've never gone in for eshpionage? Still, I expect you know what they call a cipher stencil?"

"A sheet with holes?"

"That's it," said Burgeaud. "A sheet with holes. Someone sends you a cooking recipe. Calf's head à la Mock Turtle. You place your stencil over it, and you read in the holes: '*Three-German-factories-clandestinely-manufacture-hydrogen-bombs.*'"

"I don't quite see how one can make those words figure in a recipe for calf's head, even à la Mock Turtle, but let's skip that. What—"

"It may not be easy, but it's probably true."

"That they manufacture H-bombs? No . . ."

"If it isn't, it soon will be. But I'm straying from the subject. Where are you stuck?"

"The stencil. It's perfect, but how do the holes come to be open, how do they close?"

"How do you expect?" said Burgeaud, thrusting his little finger deep into his ear, and shaking it sluggishly. "Conditioned refleckshes," he concluded.

"That's getting to be a bit of a cream puff," remarked Olga.

"Any general principle gets to be a cream puff. Newton's apple, Planck's quantum." He whisked his finger more energetically. "Thank God there's that in life," he said with relish.

"Why? What?"

"These sensual pleasures," he said, finishing his voluptuous ear scratching. "When everything has boiled down to a primary principle, that'll be the cream puff of puffs."

"Are they so universal?"

"Itching ears?"

"Conditioned reflexes."

"But, my dear gal," said Burgeaud, coiling up even more tightly on the couch to stare at her. "Our whole life, our minds are nothing else!"

"One of us two definitely lags behind. Would you mind amplifying a bit? I'm listening."

"Are you so sleepy?"

"No, I'm one of those pupils who are poor listeners. Never mind, I get the gist of it. Go ahead."

"It starts with Noah's ark, you know."

"The ark?"

"Once upon a time there was a little protozoan in an aquarium. A single cell, with pseudopods. They kept flashing a light at him because he doesn't like that. Nor do you: you drop your eyelids; *he* takes to his pseudopods. Each time he touches one side that's a bit rougher than the others, the light's flashed and he decamps. The eleventh time, no light: he decamps all the same. This is the basic property of all living matter, this ability to be trained. Absolutely basic. Right. You asleep?"

"Not yet. I like to listen with my eyes closed."

"That's what they all say, even one hefty wench who can't doze off without snoring the house down. Which fortunately wakes her up. Where was I?"

"The protozoan."

"Right. Let us now take a neurone of the encephalon. Train it to contact one particular neighbor neurone in preference to any other, according to the message received. A shunting point, in short. From synapse to synapse, from switch point to switch point, the train is sent from Paris to Lyons rather than to Lille or Bordeaux. Send the same message ten times over. The eleventh time, the first switch will start off all the others: the routine has been established. That's memory. Right. Now, as these reflex circuits multiply—you aren't asleep?"

"You take yourself for a hypnotist."

"Is that a challenge? All right, you've asked for it. Thus, as they go on multiplying, by thousands, by millions—there are nine billion neurones in the human brain, the number of possible combinations would have more noughts than would reach to the moon—so, progressively as they intersect, command, and stimulate each other, the mind develops. Hence those sudden flashes of illumination: two tracks or more produce a fuse. Hence also this certitude: Homo sapiens is a social product. If the reflex circuits are not established in the very earliest childhood, under the constant influence of environment, if, in brief, you don't get the canvas pattern on which the tapestry can then be embroidered, the mind doesn't form. In proof: the little girl who got lost and grew up among wolves. At the age of eight she's found again. It's already too late: the pattern has formed, it's a wolf pattern. No longer any chance of embroidering our arabesques on it, her mind is and will remain a wolf's mind. Kipling led us up the garden path completely. Counterproof: the baby who was taken away from a distant tribe of savages, a tribe that hadn't yet got beyond the Stone Age, because for thousands of years they'd been too isolated, reduced as they were to a mere few hundred individuals; the adult pattern is too rudimentary, impossible to teach them anything, not even the causal link between love-making and childbirth. The baby girl is taken to France when a few months old: today she's a graduate of biology—"

"And has married her professor."

Burgeaud's body seemed to unfold like a carpenter's rule.

"If you know all this, why let me make a fool of myself?"

"I don't know a thing, I only know this marriage caused some stir. He's the cousin of a girl friend of mine. Sit down—I mean, lie down. Go on, I'm interested. All this is news to me. Is it a long time since neurologists have generally admitted this mechanism?"

"Oh," said Burgeaud, "generally admitted . . . that's a pretty big word. We haven't yet been treated as dolts, parricides, or, more kindly, as renegades. That's already a lot."

"There is some reluctance to overcome?"

"You must understand, my dear, that the inference to be drawn is that the individual is only an illusion. This does not please the individuals, which is pardonable. Nobody enjoys much to see himshelf reduced to the shtatus of an illusion. There aren't many people as yet modest enough to admit readily that our precious individual mind is, by its conshtitution, a collective product. Everything goes to show it though: the multiplicity and diversity of mental fabrics according to different societies and civilizations; the permanence of myths and religions, of simple thought patterns; all that these patterns have in common, and again, above all, their mutual imperviousness—all these are the obvious conshequence, the irrefutable evidence of this mechanism at work. The brain of even a genius is only a privileged meeting place, a relay post on the Great Highway, a market town. Descartes, Einstein are the names of crossroads. Each individual discovery remains a product of the entire human race."

"Could one reach down?"

"What?"

She laughed:

"Sorry, I think I stopped listening toward the end. What I would like to know: the level of those switches, how far down can it reach? Are there any physiological reasons to prevent the formation of strictly peripheral circuits? Couldn't conscious contacts develop between the mind and the body, the psyche and the *soma*. I'm thinking of Osty, of yogis. Can one hope to go further than they?"

"Further?"

"Deeper down. To rock bottom, contact the substratum of the protoplasm."

"I wonder," said Burgeaud, "if that question has the slightest meaning."

"I've read things by Lapicque about it. He's not a dreamer, is he?"

"Lapicque!" cried Burgeaud. "Good lord, no. Why?"

"He firmly believes in the existence of a cellular consciousness, an elementary consciousness, which our own merely integrates at top level. In short, he believes in those 'little lives' dear to the Hindus. If that's true, then what's happening in one direction ought to be feasible in the opposite one, and it should be possible to establish some contact, shouldn't it?"

"There are a good many irreversible phenomena in the world, you know. Starting with that negligible one called time."

"But actually, it's rather in this mind-body direction that things do happen, isn't it? I mean, sadness excites the tear glands, it isn't the tears that make me sad?"

"How do you know? James claimed the converse: we experience fear because we tremble."

"I thought that theory had been exploded ages ago."

"In its paradoxical form, yes. But it still applies—once again—to the field of conditioned reflexes: it is hard to know, if you take fear and trembling, which of the two starts which."

"That's what I said! You see that the connections work in both directions: from the physical to the mental, and vice versa. Well?"

"Pooh-pooh," said Burgeaud, "the relations of the mind with the body are shlender in that direction. A condemned man at the foot of the scaffold knows he'll be dead in three seconds. But what do his kidneys do during those three seconds? They filter. His glands? They secrete. His red corpuscles? They swap their oxygen, the white ones go ahunting for bacilli, the whole metabolism continues as calmly as if nothing were the matter, as if our fellow had another thirty years to live. The knife drops and the *soma* still hasn't grasped a thing. It understands only when the first vertebrae snap."

"That's really staggering, it's true," admitted Olga under her breath.

"Mark you," said Burgeaud, "the heart will beat faster, the bowels will writhe or evacuate, but that's still pretty close to the sphere of consciousness. Sometimes, though, at the post-mortem, you can see that some deeper organ has reacted too: one kidney's blocked—not the other; or else the adrenal gland seems to have suddenly discharged. Did they know something? Hard to say. But, after all, it is not imposhible."

"Well, if it isn't impossible, then it may after all be possible to establish contact some day?"

But Burgeaud raised his two hands with a pout of mildly sardonic ignorance.

Chapter Fourteen

S it down," said Pélion. "I'd like to call Mirambeau. This will interest him."

Albert sat down on the edge of an old Louis XV armchair, which was too large and too deep for him, and looked around. What a lot of books! Fine things, books are, but there's something overpowering about them; there are too many.

"Hallo," said Mirambeau.

Albert rose with a start and stammered a greeting.

"All right," said Pélion, "tell us what happened."

Albert had come to report to him on the previous night's shop committee meeting at the Coubez works, after the morning's blow.

"You did well not to show up," said Albert. "The whole area was lousy with cops. I believe the bosses were scared of a sit-down strike. What mugs!" he said. "Not the bosses: us. Real mugs. We don't seize our chance when the bosses have the jitters."

He sighed.

"The trouble is there's not enough unity," he said. "Always the same thing. We got nowhere again last night. And yet if you'd seen the chins wagging in the sheds all day! That's what put the wind up to the management. No need for it, really!"

He shook his head despondently.

"The mutts! A bunch of jellyfish. It's this, and that. And the missus! And the kids! And the gas bill! Balls!"

"Start at the beginning," said Pélion.

Albert pulled a face. Easy for Bob to talk. Tell things in their proper order! That's what's so hard. He breathed deeply to lay in a store.

"All right," he said. "Well, first there was Ernest and me telling 'em: 'Now us, we call our fellows out. So will you, if you aren't yellowbellies.' So the other bloke says—I don't like that guy," he remarked, wrinkling his nose, which made him look like a mandrill.

"What guy?" said Pélion, perplexed.

Albert passed his hand over his neck. His sleeve gaped at the armhole.

"Blest if I remember his name!" he grumbled. "You know the fellow: cheeks like coffee and milk, you know, with the skin all crinkly on top like when the coffee gets cold. You know," he repeated, "he stands for the independent union, a little runt of a fellow. Hell, you know him inside out," he said impatiently.

"Never mind. Name'll come back. What did he do?"

"If you ask me," said Albert, "that guy is in cahoots with the bosses. Emilien, that's his name!" he flung triumphantly. "Emilien Faulme. He says that . . ."

"Oh, Faulme, him," said Pélion. "Albert's right," he turned to Mirambeau, "he pretends he's an anarchist, but there's a general feeling he's on all sorts of people's payroll."

"Anarchist or no, he's a dangerous guy. Gosh, how he can talk! One moment it all seems above board, and the next, by God, the lads are all upside down."

"Yes," said Pélion, "pity I wasn't there."

"You'd have shut him up, but we couldn't keep upsides with

him. You know, a sort of way of making out that it's us who aren't doing enough. . . ."

"Hoary old dodge," said Pélion.

"Maybe it is, but it comes off every time. And there was us finding our traps shut. Call a strike? he says. All right with me, he says. Laying off fits me fine. But what for, exactly? Because it all depends, after all, he says. If it's to refuse the dough of those Coubez gents, you can count me out. Because if that's why we're going to strike, he says, well then I'm asking you, is this what we've been elected for? Did we really get the votes to say to the bosses 'thank you kindly, but we don't want your money?' Because me, he says, I see it all different. The way I see it, he says, we should grab it, on the contrary, and double quick too, he says, even if it isn't handed all round at the start. We should grab it and come back right away and ask for more. That's what we ought to do, he says, because the way I see it, he says, what we should be out for is bigger and better pay packets, that's what the boys voted us in for, and not for saying to the bosses 'keep your brass,' and those who say we should lay off and refuse the Coubez dough, well I say, he says, they are meddling in politics, they are, and not defending our interests at all. That's what I say, he says, so after that we couldn't very well go on insisting or what would we have looked like?"

He had reeled off his piece in one breath, working himself up gradually as he remembered all those specious arguments, which he knew well enough to be specious without being able to put his finger on the right spot to expose them. And he nervously passed his big hand over his brow, his badly shaved cheeks, his neck above the crumpled, rather grimy collar.

"But it's not a question of refusing the money!" said Mirambeau after a short pause.

"Course not," said Pélion. "It's that twirp Faulme who got

them tied up in knots. The cops know what they're doing," he said with a grin to Mirambeau, "in keeping fellows like that on their payroll. Well, Mr. Mirambeau, this means work for us," he sighed, stretching out his arms as if roused from sleep.

"Work? What work?"

"Decision on Sunday, I suppose?" said Pélion, turning to Albert.

"Yes. There'll be oodles of talks till then, interunion, intershop. I don't know how it'll all end."

"Mr. Mirambeau, here we go on a seven-day walking tour," said Pélion, chuckling soundlessly.

"Where do you want to take me?" said the old scientist, on his guard.

"House to house every night, after hours," said Pélion. "We'll have to win them over, one by one. Explain, argue, persuade."

"And you mean to take me along?" protested Mirambeau, flinging up his short arms in indignation.

"Mr. Mirambeau, once you start a thing, you've got to see it through. . . ."

And he explained, firmly and patiently—as he was to do later with the others—all the difficulties they'd be up against. The men they'd have to convince during those few days were not workers so much as heads of families; what they would have to cope with was not so much wrong ideas as the housewives' lack of understanding, the men's weakening in face of their undernourished kids. Pélion also knew that he was too young, that he would soon be hated for tampering with their livelihood. Whereas Mirambeau would impress them all.

The old scientist struggled for all he was worth. No, no, and no; what about my work? "Come along once at least," begged Pélion. "Just once, so that people'll see you." As usual, Mirambeau

160

eventually gave in, but firmly resolved that he would not relapse. He had reckoned without the slums.

Poverty, for Mirambeau, had so far been synonymous with going without. More than once, it is true, he had said to himself that a collier's wife cooped up in her mining village was less happy than a Berber nomad with nothing but a camel and a gun to his name. But he had not gone as far as thinking that she was actually more wretched. Yet at first his visit with Pélion to the workers' district of Chaulieu had surprised him rather favorably. The sloping streets were clean, despite the gray slush between the paving stones and the refuse floating in the rushing gutters. The houses, built of solid concrete blocks, though black and dismal, were not yet dilapidated, though the premature cracks that gaped between woodwork and masonry betrayed the jerry-builder. It was not immediately apparent how little thought had been given to affording pleasure to the eye—not the least ornament, the slightest molding, the tiniest fancy scroll on this sullen bareness. Rain had left its mark in grimy trails. The whole street seemed to have wept long sooty tears of endless mourning.

As if protesting timidly, there were flowers growing in some windows. Ghosts of flowers: a russet stem, three flaccid leaves that moldered on their stems. Alone, high up in an attic, a single tulip still uttered a survivor's cry, which only rendered more leaden the surrounding drabness. Gradually, Mirambeau's eye was caught, here and there, by a scar, a festering sore, a makeshift dressing: a piece of cardboard replaced a windowpane, a sheet of rusty iron blocked the top of a door, a length of wire held a drainpipe in place. Through an open window could be glimpsed a stained mattress scattering its intestines over an iron bedstead. Between unhinged shutters flapped limp underwear—discolored shirts, frayed flannel vests, old, threadbare handkerchiefs. Some sulky mongrels, belly-deep in dirt, would lift a joyless leg against the walls. A vague smell of urine prevailed everywhere.

Pélion and Mirambeau walked along in silence. There were few men in the streets, it was the evening shopping hour, the women crossed from one pavement to the other, carrying baskets and string bags. They were, on the whole, simply but neatly dressed. However, looking more closely, you discovered that there was hardly a face without some blemish. The scar of a harelip ran across a mouth that might otherwise have been charming. You admired a woman's profile, her eyes, but the full face showed the other eye protruding in a divergent squint. Or else a birthmark furtively lapped one side of the nose. Or again, a patch of skin near the ear had deepened to a disturbing bronze.

Mirambeau did not dare look around as much as he would have liked, torn as he was between a shuddering curiosity and tact born of respect. He saw people frequently turning round after them. Pélion responded to the smiles and the hands waved in greeting. The older man felt some shy, surprised gazes fixed upon him; he knew he had been recognized. This made him feel at once pleased and embarrassed. His pleasure was not mere conceit, petty vainglory, but rather the joy of finding himself accepted, admitted, even adopted—as if his reputation as a scientist served as a sort of passport to this country of the poor. . . . His discomfort sprang from a doubt as to whether such a passport was really good enough to wipe out the injustice of fate.

He saw at a window a woman of indefinable age talking to another across the street. Her lank hair, falling in graceless strands, looked almost moth-eaten. The woman opposite supported her flabby, shapeless, voluminous breasts on the window bar. A purple swelling spread from her throat to her arm and disappeared in her black bodice, which was discolored and acid-stained at the armpits. They crossed a dark passage which exhaled a smell of sewers; a little boy was squatting on a doorstep, idly teasing a cockroach which he turned over on its back with the tip of an old knife, letting it wriggle. His pleasure in this game seemed vague and spiritless, without real enjoyment, and he hardly watched with his tired eyes set in dark haloes, like blobs of chewed quid, that reached to his cheeks. He never stopped sniffing and kept doggedly scratching a lean, wan thigh.

Two little girls stopped talking at their approach. One already had deep lines on her young forehead, the other opened pale lips over decayed teeth. Out of the corners of their eyes, they cast sly glances after the two men. Beyond them a cellar opened its black maw from which was wafted a dank odor of stale wine and latrines.

Pélion crossed the street, and Mirambeau followed him. They went into one of the houses. It was like entering a cave that was clammy with the rancid chill of night. At the end of the passage a staircase twisted between two walls on which the paint blistered with saltpeter rot. The banister was so greasy that their hands instantly recoiled from it. They knocked on a door with a cracked panel and heard the shuffling of old slippers. The door was opened by a badly shaved man, his limp, crumpled cotton shirt open to show shaggy tufts on his hollow chest. The noise of children's scurrying feet receded behind him.

The long, bony face, with its fine network of wrinkles despite its youth, bore a surly expression. This changed, however, into a toothless grin of dumb surprise. The man seemed to fumble painfully for three simple words of welcome: "Do come in," promptly followed by halting explanations in a flat, formless mumble. While opening doors, pulling chairs forward, pushing the table aside, he excused his poor welcome by disjointed references to his wife being out shopping, his own incompetence in the household. Three glasses, however, at once appeared filled with a reddish liquor on which floated a few cherries. Mirambeau's eyes wandered over the linoleum, polished to a shine but worn threadbare where most trodden—by the door, in front of the rickety deal sideboard, on which a sham cut-glass bowl vainly tried to sparkle. The wallpaper must have been pink a good many years ago. The window curtains, in imitation Irish lace, had been carefully mended over and over again. Everything proclaimed painstaking cleanliness which had not quite managed, though, to dissipate a faint but persistent, insinuating smell.

Pélion talked, explained. The man listened with a strained look on his face, as if he struggled to grasp each word in turn. He opened his mouth a little, now and then scratched his skull beneath his hair. From time to time he threw a glance at Mirambeau, a somewhat questioning glance. And Mirambeau slowly nodded his head to mark his approval, but he was not listening. He was thinking: Hope . . . He looked around and thought: Poverty doesn't mean the lack of this or that. It means the absence of hope. Tomorrow will be like today. In ten years, in thirty. They know it. They'll die in it. It's a sort of eternity. A sort of hell. From the man near him emanated a dubious smell, of a body not washed often enough, of skin turning a little sour with the underwear, of clothes gradually impregnated with the whiff of stale fried oil. How can he visualize his future? wondered Mirambeau. How can he picture happiness? With a lot of luck and privations, he'll own a shoddy refrigerator in five years' time, an old crock of a car in ten: what then? What will have changed? He'll still be up to his belly in this horrible slum, without a hope of ever getting out. In the small, clean, dismal dining room he felt the weight of the neighborhood bearing heavily down on him. I'm not well off, thought Mirambeau, I'm not much better dressed than he, I've little more comfort around me. But just this type of poverty is what I find so humiliating. And it concerns me personally, he thought, and he wondered why. He imagined himself in the man's place. Equal chances at the start, my foot! he thought. I'm not even talking of the obstacles in his way: obliged to leave school too early, to earn his living when he's fourteen . . . but merely of the fact that the substructure of intelligence, except by an exceedingly rare fluke, simply cannot come into being in brains formed in a street like this. It cannot develop fully, I mean. What a loss, good lord! How many little Mozarts . . . Can the human species really bear to be deprived of so much stillborn intelligence, so many stifled, miscarried minds? As if one didn't first need the *tools* to think with! Crimes against the spirit! Can there be a greater crime than to strangle millions of minds at birth? If I'd been born in this house, I should at this moment be listening to Pélion, scratching my skull, taking his words in painfully and incompletely, I should be brooding over all the money that's needed for rent, coal. . . . What funds of energy they must have summoned, a little chap like Albert, like the brighter among his chums, to develop their brains despite this handicap; to turn them into sounder tools than those of our college cock sparrows! But how many of them bring it off? Most of them have to fall back on pluck and common sense to fill the gaping holes in their minds. How can they extricate themselves? he mused. Preposterous to imagine that they could do it, each on his own. There are millions of them, in the world, stuck in these slums as on flypaper. They can only help themselves by pulling together. The others know it too. Great Scott! thought Mirambeau, it's evidently nice as can be to study, as I do, the conditions of cellular survival—but for whom? For these people whom one prevents from being full-fledged men, for people reduced to the state of a feeding-machine? First help them to get out of this mire. Help them at least as Pélion does, not to sink deeper into it. . . .

Pélion was still explaining. The man nodded. His head approved, but his heart visibly wasn't in it. Mirambeau listened, waited for Pélion to finish, then rose and touched the man's shoulder:

"Think it over," he said. "We're not so sure we're right. . . ."

Pélion turned round, perturbed. A light shone in the man's eye —he was a schoolboy let off his homework.

"You'll see it all right," went on Mirambeau. "Remember just this: Don't let your mates down, ever. Because if you do, it's you who'll find yourself all alone. When you don't know what to do, it's an easy rule to remember. You can't go wrong."

Pélion, too, had risen. He was still puckering one eyebrow. Mirambeau kept the other's hesitating hand clasped in his. His heavy gaze held the faltering one by its authority. He smiled a long smile, and repeated:

"You can't ever go wrong. Just remember. It's easy."

He did not drop the other's hand until the man managed to smile in turn and to articulate:

"Yes, Mr. Mirambeau."

It was such a pathetic effort that Mirambeau felt like caressing his crumpled face as he would a child's. He merely clasped the other's hand a little more firmly and felt a firm grasp in response. He grinned more broadly, screwed up his eyes, motioned a little "yes" of connivance. The face before him was now beaming all over.

They left the house, and went into the neighboring one.

166

Chapter Fifteen

"No, no, no, no . . ." muttered Olga as she arranged the iron cradle around the sick foot to keep off the weight of the blankets.

"No what?" said Egmont anxiously. He was always afraid lest Olga went back on her word and had him dispatched to the clinic.

"I'm saying no to myself," she confessed. "I'm getting potty too. It must be contagious. I can no longer think of anything but that business of yours. I hardly slept a wink last night; this can't go on."

"You promised . . ." started Egmont, on the alert.

"I wouldn't care a hang for what I promised, but it's worse," she said, sitting down at the foot of the bed. She gripped his knee through the sheet and tenderly rocked it to and fro. She bent over him: "You may possibly have me sitting over you more than you bargained for!"

Her breath always smells of tangerines, thought Egmont, but his face remained so apprehensive that Olga burst out giggling. She declared:

"I shan't budge from here."

"Naturally, it's your home," said Egmont, surprised.

"I shall not budge from this room," she explained. "Day or night. I won't leave you alone any more."

"Yet I can hardly run away!" Egmont pointed out, motioning with a smile to the humped blanket over his foot.

"I don't know anything about *that*," said Olga.

They looked at each other in silence for a moment, until Egmont turned his head away, though he did not cease to smile.

"Day and night, you said?" he asked at length.

"Those were my very words," she announced.

"What about your patients, the hospital? How did you fix that?"

"We're near the end of May. I rang up young Crozatier. He was to be my locum during the August holidays. He'll take over from tomorrow. He swears he doesn't mind."

Egmont sank back on his pillow and gazed at her through half-closed eyes for a while.

"In order to help me, really?" he said at last in a very dubious tone of voice.

"Scientific curiosity," said Olga.

"What?"

"I said I'm going to stay here and watch you out of scientific curiosity."

"Oh . . ." murmured Egmont, a trifle disappointed.

"You'd rather I did it for your beautiful eyes?"

"I don't know," he said. "No . . ."

"Weren't you the one to talk the other day of the passion for knowledge?"

"Yes . . ." said Egmont uncertainly.

"It's petered out already?" she marveled.

He jerked one shoulder.

"It's stronger than ever."

168

"Well, then?"

"Nothing," he said, without taking his half-closed eyes off her.

They observed each other for a few seconds, and then Olga suddenly took Egmont in her arms and started kissing him fiercely on his cheek, his throat, kneading his shoulder blades. The image of Pascale rose furtively to mingle with these embraces: Am I going to forget her, in turn, so quickly? he thought with caustic irony and a hint of self-disgust. But he let himself be kissed with the breath-taking pleasure of a swimmer rolling in the cooling waves of a summer sea. They separated at last, out of breath and laughing.

"Filling the larder for the winter," said Olga. "And now, when do you start?"

"Well, I . . ." murmured Egmont, taken aback.

"What?"

"Now *you're* getting impatient? You're actually egging me on?"

"I am a sensible woman," said Olga. "You've asked me for five days. I have granted them. Almost two have gone already. If you spend the next three days doing nothing either, I'll have given you all this time for nothing, while your toe is getting worse."

"Who told you I'd done nothing?"

Surprise left her speechless.

"I plunged pretty far down last night," said Egmont almost apologetically, with a shade of irony.

"Without me!" she flared up.

"Oh," he said, "at night . . . 'to sleep, to dream—no more . . .' No danger."

Olga seemed to waver. Was she going to make a scene? And then she said with bristling curiosity: "Go on, tell."

Egmont's face clouded over.

"It's difficult," he confessed. "On waking, everything fades more or less; you know how it is. But . . ." he rubbed two fingers against his thumb as if rolling a bread pellet: ". . . I've already brought back a kind of proof."

He lifted the sheets, turned back his pajama trouser. Below the knee, at the level of the shinbone, a slight bluish swelling strained the skin. Olga looked at it closely, and raised her head:

"You knocked against something? Or pinched yourself?"

"I never got out of bed for a minute."

He stroked the small blue disk with a certain tenderness.

"I made it grow myself," he murmured, and added: "By way of evidence." He said again: "Evidence of my passage."

"Your passage? Where?"

"Into my leg," he said. "I wandered around in it all night. I recognized it at once. You know, the army in the hills."

"Your leg, your leg . . ." said Olga. "A dream is a rather hazy thing to go by."

"Was it really a dream?" mused Egmont absently. "I'm afraid," he went on slowly, "I'm afraid that all I'll see will for some time yet seem rather dreamlike. It can hardly be otherwise, can it?"

"I don't know. What do you mean?"

"Ah," said Egmont, "that's hard to explain."

He pondered and, groping for words, said:

"Let's say you land in the Gobi Desert. And there you find . . . something you've never seen before, neither animal, vegetable, nor mineral. No name. First thing you'll say to yourself is: 'It looks like'—a tree, a rock, a tortoise, something that exists, evidently. Or else . . . look, you remember the example of the blind man? Someone wants to describe blood to him. It's red, they say. What's that: red? It's the color of fire. What's fire? You scorch his finger. 'Ah, so that's what blood is like,' says the blind man. . . . Now, how do you want me myself to visualize things that are so alien to my mental structure as . . . as the private life of a cell, of blood plasma, of goodness knows what . . . their customs, their preoccupations? . . . Perhaps that'll come later, but in the meantime I'm obliged to transpose. Don't you think so?"

"Yes," admitted Olga musingly. "Sounds reasonable."

She thought of the little girl brought up among wolves: our brains, she thought, are impervious to tracks too alien to their formation; they'd have to be laid in childhood, she thought, while Egmont resumed:

"I obviously can't start—can I?—by having a pleasant chat with a red corpuscle, or a nerve cell. Even if I do manage to . . . climb down, to plunge to their level. What I'm going to say may sound rather silly, but I feel it very strongly: I did climb down to their level. I made contact with them, established relations. . . . Perhaps, at one moment, I even saw and understood things. But here and now, on waking, what do you expect to remain? It's all transformed, necessarily, into images comprehensible in *our* language. . . . I have to translate. . . ."

He sighed:

"No good having illusions: for a long time to come all I'll remember will be mere translations. . . ."

Thereupon he seemed to sink into a deep reverie. In the end, Olga said:

"What about your dream last night?"

Egmont did not answer at once. He had thrown himself back on his pillow. With half-closed lids, his forehead creased in a frown, he soon said softly:

"You wouldn't like to draw the curtains?"

"Quite close?" said Olga, by the window.

"No . . . or else draw them but switch on the little lamp."

The room, plunged into nothingness at first, re-emerged to life in the soft, warm, very gentle glow. A room partitioned into light and shadows, a night fractioned into strata of silence within the shelter of the four self-enclosing walls.

Soundlessly Olga let her sandals slip and soundlessly lay down by Egmont's side. She took his hand. They remained like that for a while, breathing slowly and in unison.

Egmont did not move, he stared up at the ceiling as if to discover some sign, some inspiration there. When he spoke, his voice was so muted that Olga was not sure she had caught the first words.

". . . everything seemed under water, a flooded hill country," he said in that muffled voice, which seemed as hushed as the shuttered room. "Calm, grayish, very muddy water swamping the fields. That's what paralyzed the army, I suppose. The troops stayed encamped in the hills, numb and inert."

He paused for a moment, and she said: "And you?"

Egmont hesitated for a while.

"I was gliding down the valley"—he halted—"in a boat, or on a raft," he said uncertainly. "Drifting without effort down the even stream . . ." He stopped again. "There were crowds and crowds of boats," he murmured.

"Fishermen?"

She felt him shrug his shoulders slowly.

"I no longer know. Perhaps. Yes . . ." he resumed, "I believe they were pulling vague, sticky things out of the water. The boats were full of the stuff. They came and went all around me."

"Were you fishing too?"

"No. I couldn't get near them—yet more than once," he continued just as haltingly, "my boat bumped into one of the others, remained stuck to it for a moment, but . . . it was rather that no one seemed to pay any heed to it. The canoes were full of a sort of, I remember now, a sort of rotting and transparent seaweed. But I did not dislike the smell, though it was rather sickly sweet, with a whiff of garlic."

"You couldn't talk to them?"

"To whom? I did not see anyone, I told you—anyway, not that I remember. Besides, it didn't happen like that. . . . I was keeping an eye on the hills, on account of the commotion up there. How can I explain: a sort of teeming swarm, a constant to and fro—like an ordnance column, you know, files of soldiers with trucks and carts. . . . You see what I mean? From a distance, it looked, yes, it looked just like those tiny rows of ants along a wall in spring. And I even remember thinking: I'm having ants in my legs!"

Egmont gave a short laugh.

"This amused me a lot. And you would have found I was pretty proud of myself. Not only to be down there, but to know it, to have grasped that I was there. And to be thinking too that my leg was probably hurting me. Yet knowing that all this was going on somewhere else. Whereas I, the real me, was down there with my consciousness, my attention. I said to myself: 'Unless this, too, is only a dream.' That idea rather pricked my pride. And I wanted to make sure."

His tone of voice changed.

"After that everything becomes a bit muddled. . . . I must have forgotten certain things or else . . . or else they happened on a different plane. I no longer know. I only remember"—he broke off as if stumbling over a step—"well," he groped, "something like . . . like having taken command of one of those supply columns . . . getting them somehow to pile up stocks . . . right

. . . right on the hill. I don't remember clearly any more what notions guided me. They seem so confused now I can no longer grasp them. But at the time, down there, I knew very well what I wanted and what I was doing. And I even exulted beforehand. I was thinking: If it's still there tomorrow morning, just imagine what a success! Well, old girl, it *was* there."

He gave another, light laugh.

"And it still is, as you see. I didn't hesitate for a moment. Odd, isn't it? I made straightway for the right spot under my pajamas. Didn't hesitate a second," he repeated in a tone of voice that had suddenly gone dreamy, and tinged with surprised wonder.

Olga wavered for a moment before saying:

"It may not be such foolproof evidence, you know."

She felt Egmont's hand twitch slightly in hers. She quickly added:

"I'd rather see you nurse a disappointment than a delusion. That thing of yours doesn't prove anything yet."

And as Egmont kept silent:

"We mustn't mistake the effect for the cause," she said. "It's an old pitfall. Like those sprightly old codgers who assert that love-making keeps them green, whereas actually it's their persistent greenness that enables them still to make love. . . . You may very well have dreamed all that *because* this little bruise was in the making. Your dream was its reflection, not its origin. At least that seems to me more credible. Remember your dream about the battle: even had you played the role of Bonaparte, the dream would still have been the result of your gangrene, not its cause. I don't want to hurt your feelings but . . . you don't mind?" she said.

Egmont did not answer. Olga saw him close his eyes for a long time. Then he smiled and said:

174

"And Therese Neumann?"

"Who?"

"Therese Neumann, the German woman who, on every Good Friday for the last twenty-seven years, has been able to produce the stigmata of Christ's Passion. She doesn't know how she does it, whereas I'm beginning to have an inkling of how it's done, that's the only difference. All right," he said, "I'll try to start all over again. Just a try," he repeated and he still smiled. "That's all I can do, of course. No government guarantee. Can you be patient?"

"Not on the whole. But this time I shall, you bet!"

"All right then, make yourself comfortable," he said, "and watch my leg. There, at the same spot."

Olga pressed Egmont's hand, which she still held in hers, to mark her agreement. He hollowed out his pillow with his head to be more at ease. He fixed his eyes on the moldings of the ceiling. Olga soon heard him breathe with an increasingly slow and regular rhythm. Her heart was throbbing with anguished delight.

For quite a long time, of course, there was nothing for Olga to watch. Her cheek pressed against her own pillow, she gazed at Egmont's profile which stood out calm and relaxed and firmly cut under the graying temples. She suddenly thought: I'm about to fall in love with him all over again, and she felt such a glad, warm tide surging through her that she gave herself a good scolding: Watch out, old minx, don't again start taking for love what's only your desire to feel it. You're past the age of self-deception. She mused: The fact is, he's really knocking me over this time. I never felt much at home with the writing brotherhood: they scare me and yet I can't take them quite seriously. But who but a poet would dare in all seriousness to attempt such a venture? It's perfectly harebrained, agreed—yet quite lucid as well, cogent, and methodical, and preposterous, and raving mad; in short, it's stunning. She also thought, with her eyes still on the peaceful profile: And he's damn handsome too, the brute.

Egmont's breath had become so faint that Olga had to prick her ears to catch it. It seemed to her that his face was sagging, growing pale, and she became worried. She seized his wrist to feel his pulse. It beat slowly but regularly and very clearly. Reassured, she kept still and tried hard not to think. Whereupon her mind wandered off in a half-sleep. Indeterminate spans of time elapsed. At intervals, she'd open a heavy eye, glance at his leg. Nothing was happening. She fell completely asleep.

She woke suddenly with the impression of having been called. The room was silent, motionless, like the form stretched out at her side. An almost unbearable stillness. She bent over the bare leg. Was it an illusion? It seemed to her that the swelling had gone down a little.

From then on her eyes no longer left the bluish disk. Her heart throbbed (foolishly, she thought to herself). She felt an irrepressible, childish thrill of excitement. And when, at last, the disk visibly started to grow pale, her whole body shook with nervousness, with itching expectation, with real spasms of impatience; she clenched her fingers convulsively before her mouth, gnawed at her nails. She controlled herself with difficulty, forcing herself to remain calmly attentive as the minutes passed. At some moments she told herself she had been mistaken, the slender disk had not altered. But then the change seemed to gather pace, the growing pallor became so obvious and, comparatively, so swift that any doubt would have been absurd. And when at last, after some time, almost an hour, which had seemed horribly long yet strangely brief, the remaining redness faded under her eyes like rings of moisture on an overhot iron, she stood there, her

176

heart tense but fast-beating, staring at the skin which had become pure and clean over the shinbone, exactly like the skin all around.

Breathlessly, Olga fastened a greedy glance on Egmont's insentient face. A tenantless, fascinating face! What a stupendous absence! She wondered: *Where* is he? She found it hard to resist an urge to shake him, pinch his arm or his ear. But a sort of fear held her back. She waved the palm of her hand before his eyes which had constantly remained half open, but was unable to draw a glint from them. Where is he? thought Olga with rising anguish. She was no longer a doctor. She no longer reasoned as a hardheaded woman, in sensible, rational terms. Where is he? she thought, and she imagined him roaming through those vast hills which he had described to her, lapped by muddy waters and inhabited by an invisible army. . . .

She felt Egmont's hand quiver in her own. A very short quiver, a faint tremor. A swift wave rippled the skin of his face, his chest rose with a deeper breath. The lips opened more widely. In the depth of his eyes a bubble formed, the bubble of a look that Olga had seen there once before, forming and detaching itself and bursting on the surface.

Without moving his head, Egmont murmured: "Did you see?" But he did not dare look at Olga. She felt lifted up by an unexpected gust, as if a tidal wave was surging from her toes to her head, and she found herself shivering on Egmont's chest. "What's the matter? But what's up, little one?" Egmont asked her in amazement. He had propped himself up on an elbow and was stroking her hair. Olga shook her head, sniffed: "Nothing, it's nothing," and mingled a rather shamefaced laugh with her sobs. At last she managed to control herself, wiped her eyes, her face, laughed more outright, making fun of herself.

"I haven't the foggiest notion what's the matter," she stuttered.

"It just came over me, all of a sudden. Damn your eyes, I never thought you'd give me such thrills!"

Egmont smiled at her in some perplexity, not knowing how to respond. He dared not match his mood to hers—lest he were snubbed again as so often before.

But Olga gently ruffled his hair, murmuring: "Little beast, little beast." She had such a young smile, such a sparkle in her eyes, that Egmont let himself be lulled by their warmth. He repeated more confidently this time:

"So you saw?"

"I saw, I saw it all," answered Olga, shaking his head by the hair. "Beast," she repeated, "you've knocked me all of a heap. Tell now, tell," she demanded without letting him go.

But once again Egmont's face darkened.

"It can hardly be told," he muttered as if to himself. "It's all slipped through my fingers. Isn't it maddening? As if, in order to get back I was obliged to . . . to drop everything, to throw all my luggage overboard, the way one drops the ballast in a balloon. . . ."

"It wasn't the same country?" asked Olga, sliding down onto the pillow.

"Oh yes . . . it was . . . the same hills with water all around. . . . But afterward I went further, or . . . deeper. I no longer know. I passed through woods, through thick, endless forests— Ah," he said, and his eyes flashed, "the mangroves! Yes, it was them, this time I'm sure, I recognized them. Their roots plunged, shaggy and tangled, into the warm water. . . ."

"You were bathing?" she murmured.

"No, I think I . . ."

He passed his hand over his brow, with slow, painful perplexity.

"And I was not in a boat, either. It was all—" his voice became uncertain, indistinct "—all packed with amphibians, or what seemed like masses of them anyway, thick living masses, slow and heavy. . . ." He groped, he seemed like a blindfolded child. "What was I myself? Was I one of those sluggish masses too? At all events, I moved heavily among them, just like them. . . ." He murmured again, almost reluctantly: "They obeyed me. . . ."

It was hardly more than a whisper. Olga, snuggling next to him, alongside him, stared up at the shadowy ceiling, as he did. She merely held his hand and pressed it.

"They pulsated too, your mangroves?" she asked in the same low tone.

"Perhaps . . . I no longer see them clearly. . . . I wonder whether it wasn't rather . . ."

He broke off, remained silent and attentive, as if listening, and finally said:

". . . rather as if they were sucking the water by their roots. As if they were swelling with it. It made a noise of . . . of a distant cascade, you know? When one is still far away and wonders: What's making that noise?"

"And then?" whispered Olga. "What did you do?" she asked.

"That's what escapes me, you see," said Egmont, and his voice was sad, dispirited. And suddenly he said loudly: "I wasn't there!" Like a flash of illumination. "No," he said, "I wasn't there. I was . . . I was . . . ah," he groaned, "how can I make you understand?"

He tossed about and Olga felt her friend's fingers twitch with impatience in her hand.

"Like the pilot of a submarine, you know, who sees a picture on the screen of his periscope. Do you understand?" he asked with what sounded like anguish. "All this, all those . . . those amphibians, this vegetation . . . I saw them, if you like, but as if through . . . through a relay, you see? But I only had to think, to think hard enough to— Oh," he said with sudden tiredness, "it's too difficult."

And he closed his eyes. Olga saw the skin of his face sag a little, age mysteriously. . . . She cried:

"Don't you feel well?"

Egmont answered with a wan smile, lightly shook his head:

"I'm all right . . . don't worry. . . ."

He turned his hand over on its back to grasp Olga's hand. He kept it in silence for a while, tightening and loosening the grip of his fingers as a mark of affection. At last he murmured in a still weary, mushy voice:

"Strange how exhausting it is . . . Not so much going there, as remembering afterward."

"Yes . . ." said Olga. "You see: it's contraband all right. The Customs confiscate the lot."

"It's unbelievable," said Egmont. He stopped and said in the same weary tone: "Inconceivable." He shook his head: "Why this iron curtain between us and ourselves? What do they want to hide from us?"

"Oh," said Olga, "nothing at all probably. No doubt we are held to be idiots, clumsy fatheads who can't be entrusted with the priceless chinaware. . . . Unless, on the contrary, they fear the use we might make of our power once we knew how to wield it."

"And that doesn't revolt you? Good heavens!" said Egmont fiercely. "And you are a doctor!"

"Well," said Olga thoughtfully, "I believe that the simple fact of being a doctor is already a revolt. In actual fact, each gesture a doctor makes is blasphemy. As is each prayer," she added even more pensively.

180

"I used to know you as a believer," said Egmont gently. "Have you lost your faith?"

"Less than ever. It has evolved, that's all. I believe that this revolt is God's will."

"Against him?"

"Perhaps. I believe He abhors submission. I believe that the way He looks at us is like a lioness looks at her cubs, when she excites them against her to develop their muscles. I believe that this unbearable human ignorance compels us, century by century, to develop our mind. We are still far from grown up, that's all."

Egmont pondered over this and said:

"That's too good to be true. For my part, I believe it's purely and simply a matter of obscurantism. I could have brought back trunks full of papers, notes, documents!" he cried. "But nothing. It's all taken away. That's the practice of book burners, the policy of the Dark Ages! A people that knows too much becomes unruly, and what's wanted is our obedience. That's all they want!"

He pressed his lips, shook his head, repeated:

"Crass obscurantism. At heart, what I'm really after is just this: to make sure once for all."

"If you can," said Olga slowly.

"Why couldn't I?"

"What are you going to find? A life within a life, like those Russian dolls, one inside the other."

"There's always a last doll."

"Because human hands can't make anything smaller. Otherwise there'd be no end."

Egmont exploded soundlessly, like a badly inflated paper bag.

"Hell! I don't care. I'll find at least a refuge there."

Olga gripped his hand.

"The way you said that . . . What makes you so unhappy? A refuge! Against whom, against what?"

"Against everything . . ." said Egmont. "Against me. Against the others. Against things. Against God."

Olga caressed his forehead with a gentle hand.

"You count me with the rest?"

Egmont took her in his arms.

"No, little one, no!"

He hesitated, blinked, and murmured:

"If you had cared to keep me, perhaps I would have. . . . But you didn't want to. Is it too late?"

"I don't know any more," said Olga, slowly passing her hand over her neck. "Keep you? It rather tempts me afresh, but I don't know if"—she blew a light kiss on his lips—"if it's love or fright, the urge to protect you, to stop you from getting into too much mischief. . . ."

They remained silent, and then Egmont said haltingly:

"In any case, you know, it is too late. . . . No other way is open to me any more. All are closed, blocked up. Mischief . . . perhaps. But as matters stand now, what else *could* I do?"

"You could love me," said Olga.

Chapter Sixteen

When Pélion reached the Coubez works the following Sunday morning, he found the military in charge. The gates were closed. In the yard, the C.R.S., munching sandwiches, were camped around their pyramids of piled arms. Outside the gate, the approaches were guarded by a squad posted along the walls, with tommy-guns wedged under their armpits.

Mirambeau, acting as a scout for Pélion, watched silently from the corner of the rue Grenette. Pélion took him by the arm.

"Let's clear off," he said.

"Where to?"

"Emergency stand-by's at the Corn Market," said Pélion, falling back instinctively into the old Resistance jargon. "We must get there before the cops."

They were not the only ones. The Avenue Sancerre was full of scurrying groups.

"They've found some Italians, apparently," said Pélion. "Or some Poles. They're to be carted in trucks from Poitiers or Châteauroux, at the same time as the North Afs from Saint-Vaize. They've been promised full rates, bonus and all. . . . Cripes!" jeered Pélion, boiling over, "this really beats the band: first time

I've seen a boss trying to force people to accept his money at the point of a gun. . . ."

"It shows that in the employer-worker relationship money is primarily a pretext."

"That's a good one!" laughed Pélion. "You couldn't lend me some pretext, could you? . . . My father used to say: Money doesn't make you happy, but no money makes you jumpy. . . . A pretext indeed!" he protested.

"What I mean is that it is, first of all, a pretext for domination: poverty gives tyranny a leg up. It's a method of government."

"It was," Pélion corrected him.

"Exactly. The powers that be are beginning to understand that it's a risky method. That's what I find disquieting."

They reached the Corn Market. In front of the building a group of men were milling about. One of them rushed forward on seeing Pélion.

"Hurry home," he said to Pélion. "Your windows were smashed last night. Paving stones."

Pélion turned toward Mirambeau, as if to take him as a witness.

"Now I ask you," he said.

He had gone pale. But he merely said:

"Where's my mother?"

"It's her that wants you. Go straight there."

"No," said Pélion. "She's all right?"

"Nothing wrong with *her* . . ."

"Go there yourself then, and tell her—"

"She wants to see you, I'm telling you. She wants to see you at once."

The drooping mustache, turning rusty at the ends, was quivering over the thick, moist lips. The man's hands opened and closed.

Pélion grew even paler, looked at Mirambeau, gripped the man's wrists.

"What's up? You're keeping something back. Is she hurt?"

"Who?"

"My mother."

"No, I've told you so! She's okay. She wants—"

"What's happened then?"

The man's eyelids twitched pitiably.

"Go and see for yourself," he said.

"In Heaven's name, will you tell me what's wrong?"

"Oh, to hell then: they threw some grenades too."

"Into my workshop?"

"Yes. Plastic. Didn't you hear the firemen last night?"

"No. Everything blown up?"

"Well . . ."

"Everything blown up?"

"More or less."

Pélion released him. He remained, with arms hanging limply, for a few seconds. The other put a hand on his shoulder.

"Don't take it too hard," he said gently.

"No," said Pélion, but he did not move.

Mirambeau took his arm.

"Better go home, my boy."

"Think so?" said Pélion tonelessly.

"Do you want me to try to take your place here? I'll do my best."

But the young man shook his head with a brave smile.

"Don't mind my saying so, Mr. Mirambeau, but you just couldn't. Too many things you've got to know about as matters stand now."

This was so true that insistence seemed pointless.

"In that case, I'll go along with you. Come on."

But Pélion remained rooted to the pavement. He looked at the Corn Market. The groups were swelling.

"How are they going to manage without me?" he said almost to himself.

"You aren't irreplaceable after all!"

He glanced at Mirambeau.

"Nobody is, to be sure. But just today . . . They'll feel so much like giving in. Fernand will be so alone."

"Fernand?"

"The local CGT secretary. Whereas I . . . why, they know I've no personal ax to grind. They know I've nothing to gain—" his voice broke on a sort of half-laugh or a sob: "This proves it. . . ."

Yes, this proves it, thought Mirambeau. And, by God, that's what one should rub in. . . .

"Look here," he said out loud. "Let me speak to them. I won't talk through my hat."

"What will you tell them?"

Mirambeau hesitated. It seemed a trifle callous to turn a friend's misfortune to account, even if it was for a . . .

"Those grenades hurled at your place haven't finished their job yet," he suggested cautiously.

Pélion did not understand.

"They'll find them bouncing back on themselves like a boomerang," said Mirambeau.

Pélion puckered his brow. He murmured: "Who will?"

"Those who're out to stop you talking," said Mirambeau. "Leave it to me," he insisted.

There was a silence. A rather long one.

"Go and get Fernand," said Pélion eventually to the fellow who

186

had listened to them with eyes bulging with attention. "He'll introduce you," he said to Mirambeau. "They don't all know you yet."

The man was already off. His nailed boots were heard flying over the cobblestones.

"What will you tell them?" asked Pélion again. He was still very pale, his ears, his strong lips remained wan, transparent; the skin around his eyes had turned blue. But those eyes were looking at Mirambeau with steady penetration.

"I'll make them see that this bomb wasn't meant for you: it was meant for all of them, it was flung right in their faces."

"Yes," said Pélion, "it was, but they weren't at the receiving end. And you have to persuade them to come out on strike, and then you have to persuade them to organize pickets, and then you have to persuade them to stop the other fellows getting out of those trucks, and maybe go and fight the cops, and maybe lose their jobs, and maybe go to jail. Whereas if they give in now, they'll get their raise, and things will merely look bad for some of their CGT mates. You feel up to persuading them of all this?"

Mirambeau suddenly felt like a tiny tot trying to spit like dad. He shook himself. It would really be the limit if I couldn't manage what this young fellow can.

He had a sudden brain wave.

"Is that all the trust you put in their heart and gumption?"

He saw Pélion flush and grin.

"You're trying to make me angry. . . . You're right, Mr. Mirambeau, it's a good trick. I lost grip. Good lord," he said, "you're right to give me a slating. You're right," he repeated, "tell them about the grenades. After all, that'll shake them up—and I won't feel so alone. The thought of being all alone amid the rubble got me down. That's true, you know. . . . I just can't stand that sort of loneliness. Whether I'm in luck or out of it, or in a fight. *My* rubble knocked me over, *ours* bucks me up," he said, almost with a laugh. "We'll tighten our ranks—our ranks and our fists. I suspected something like this would happen one day, it had to start some time. It proves we're holding the right end of the stick. And that they're scared of me. They've got a good memory. It was I, you know, who upset their shock-troop stunt in the Post Office strike. No wonder they're out gunning for me. And the prefect by the same stroke missed his promotion to Rouen. That's the sort of thing they aren't likely to forget either. All right, then, if they want a fight— Here's Fernand. I feel quite bucked up, Mr. Mirambeau. Fernand," he said, "come here, I want to introduce you. My, what a face you pull! Anything wrong?"

The face of the man addressed as Fernand, already long by nature, seemed indeed to have lengthened beyond its natural limits. He looked at Pélion with eyes brimming over with condolences. He made you feel you were at a funeral.

"Come on," Pélion told him, thumping his back, "snap out of it. This won't kill you."

Fernand's rather flaccid lips began to open in a partly surprised, partly reassured smile, while by a sort of inertia the lugubrious look still remained in his eyes.

"Mr. Mirambeau will be the first to speak," said Pélion. "Just say a few words to introduce him. A few words only," he stressed, "but from the heart, you know. Remind them what sort of man he is: Resistance, Fellow of the Institute. See? And let him speak right away. Above all, don't spin it out."

"I understand," said Fernand. He studied the tubby man with a profoundly thoughtful mien. His eyes had lost their load of condolence, had swapped it for an equivalent load of motherly concern, anxiety, and kindliness. Mirambeau, under this scrutiny, felt himself growing as fragile as porcelain, as dainty as a bird of paradise.

"You'll look after him," said Pélion.

"Don't worry," said Fernand, without taking his eyes off Mirambeau, and his solicitous nanny's gaze was already wrapping him in cotton wool and napkins.

"Right. I'm off then," said Pélion. "Don't be too long," he said to them. "Mustn't give the cops a chance to come and break up this meeting too."

"The prefecture knows about it?" asked Mirambeau.

"Didn't you see the C.R.S.?"

"I mean about our falling back on the Corn Market?"

"You may be sure they've got their narks. That's why we have to be quick. So long," he said. "Good luck. Will you drop in at my place when it's over?" he asked Mirambeau diffidently.

"What do you think? Of course I will."

Pélion grinned and strode off.

"Shall we go?" said Fernand, turning round. His eyes no longer spilled consolation or concern. They brimmed with Spartan calm.

Mirambeau had never imagined that so spindly a body could contain such a booming sound box. With one word he obtained silence. The meaning of Pélion's advice became clear as you heard the little man launch out in an improvised torrent which rolled its tumultuous waters like the Orinoco rapids. Would he indeed be able to stop? And once he did? Mirambeau doubted whether he, in turn, would be able to get a hearing—anyone speaking after Fernand would seem like a eunuch piping.

He was not given much time to worry. Fernand stopped abruptly, and cheers and applause broke loose. Standing, they applauded the name of the old scientist. Mirambeau raised one hand, without a smile or a greeting, the way one stops a car, with so grave an expression on his face that an immediate silence ensued.

"I've come to bring you bad news," he started. "Disgraceful news."

Mirambeau was not yet used to this type of audience, even less to speaking without notes. His voice shook a little with apprehension. He told himself that this added a pathetic note to his words. He raised his voice. But the ordeal, as usual, remained painful. In his mind, each word seemed to be followed by a black void which it would be impossible to fill. And yet other words came, keeping the void at bay. The fascination of this void prevented his listening to himself, his seeing the faces before him. He proceeded in a sort of frantic rush, tripping, catching himself up, falling headlong, mounting to a sudden gallop. At some words to which he himself had given scant attention the audience would break into applause. Or again into shouts of indignation. Mirambeau let himself be carried on the wave. From time to time, one of his own sentences would strike fully on his awareness, and he would think to himself: Why, that's not too bad! . . . He heard:

"Who do you think will foot the bill for this shameful outrage? You'll see, it will be our friend Pélion. You'll see all the trouble he will have with the police, he the victim, while the criminals will be left in peace. Yet they're known, you may be pretty sure. They're known, but they'll get off scot-free and even enjoy protection, while Robert Pélion will get such a grilling as to make him yelp for mercy!"

Quite true, too, what I'm saying, he thought. And while he was speaking he kept worrying about the lad. I must go to see him as quickly as possible, he thought. They may well have the nerve to run him in. We'll have to protest, collect signatures . . . he reflected as he explained to the audience that the grenades flung into Pélion's workshop proved that not only Coubez but the whole gang behind them had one uppermost fear: to see the strike spread. He exhorted them: "That's why you mustn't give in. Don't let the others jockey you!" while he was thinking of how to form a Chaulieu watch committee. I'll go to see Egmont, he thought. His feet must be all right after all this time. . . . He heard himself shout: "Show them you've understood what they're after. Let your answer be so strong and swift that they'll see you can never be divided! Down with the splitters, long live unity, that's the message I bring you from Pélion, from the shambles of his bomb-wrecked workshop. Your union leaders are agreed, I believe. It's their turn to speak, and I cry with you: Cheers for Pélion! Trust Pélion! And down with the bomb throwers!"

While the hall burst into applause and Pélion's name rang out under the high glass vault, ricocheting from wall to wall amid the clapping of hands, Mirambeau saw Fernand thrust forward, heard him overrule the din with his mighty voice. He did not listen to him. He heard behind his back the alternating murmurs of an argument in subdued voices which, however, he guessed to be agitated. He felt horribly empty: powerless to do any more. He had no idea what this crowd would do in the end, even less did he know whether the union leaders were indeed agreed. He wondered whether he had not put a bull-like hoof amid the china-ware. His inexperience lay heavily on his stomach. He felt an urge to go away.

He noticed that the speaker was no longer Fernand but a small, podgy man who kept flexing his knees and shaking his fists. But Mirambeau did not succeed in following his words. He suddenly became aware of Fernand's gaze resting on him once again with its full load of concern and gentle sorrow.

"They'll do it," said Fernand. "It's in the bag."

"What?"

"The strike. They'll do it. But that's only the beginning. After that comes the holding on." He looked at the audience which was responding to the orator's trusty slogans with the traditional shouts and applause. Everything now seemed to be proceeding in accordance with a well-tried set of rules. Fernand's heavy, woeful eyes were brimming over with anxious tenderness: "Holding on, that's always what's toughest."

Mirambeau found Pélion surrounded by fallen plaster, amid his broken looms and gutted cupboards. The ceiling hung in shreds like the sails of a Chinese junk. Two gendarmes were taking notes. They asked the elderly scientist what he had come for. "To see my friend," he said curtly, and they did not pursue their inquiry, the red rosette on its gold ribbon in his lapel serving him as a pass.

One look from Pélion told him all he needed to know: say nothing. Mirambeau perched one haunch on the corner of an oak side table which still seemed fairly steady. He suddenly had a shock: there was a human head at his knee level.

It took him a few seconds to realize that someone was emerging through a trap from the basement. A few more seconds to guess that the head in question sat on the shoulders of a police officer.

He saw a red, shiny skull with a few strands of hair plastered across it. Then he heard a voice proceeding from it:

"Nothing left down there, either. Smells awful: burned bales of wool."

He hoisted himself up to the floor with an effort, dusted his clothes with a handkerchief.

"Someone must have felt pretty safe to go and plant the dynamite right in the cellar, eh?"

He was talking to Pélion, who raised his hand and let it drop.

"I gather you weren't at home last night—quite by chance. Is that so?"

"I have already told you," sighed Pélion.

"Funny coincidence, though, isn't it? And why weren't you at home?"

"I have a girl friend," said Pélion with a bland smile.

"Are you trying to be funny?"

"What an idea, Inspector. What did *you* do back in your twenties?"

The skull flushed crimson.

"I warn you, young fellow, if that's the way you take it, you're in for trouble."

"You don't mean it? Surely you're going to catch my assailant by the ear and bring him back here! Provided, that is, you look for him elsewhere than in my basement. And provided you hurry a little."

The inspector seemed undecided as to what he was going to do. He clenched his mighty jaws once or twice, and then rapped out insolently:

"I expect you're insured?"

"Yes."

"Quite so. Show me your books."

Pélion motioned to the debris with a wide wave of his hand.

"Help yourself, if you please."

"They are destroyed, no doubt? I thought as much."

"Who said so? You may find what remains of them, with luck."

"I'd be surprised."

"So would I."

The inspector, his legs planted wide, drew himself up in front of Pélion.

"I warn you that things may take an ugly turn."

"Who for?"

"You, young fellow."

"I am sorry, Inspector." Pélion no longer smiled. He had got up. "I must ask you to leave," he said.

"What?"

"I am asking you to leave. You're not here to conduct an inquiry about me, let alone against me. You're confusing the victim with the culprits."

"That's precisely what remains to be proved."

"I've already grasped what *you* are instructed to prove, Inspector: the converse of what stares you in the eye. Let's not talk of justice, since no question of it even arises, but what exactly do you hope for? What does the prefecture hope? That you'll catch me making a fool of myself? You're wasting your time. And you're going to make me lose my temper. Because these workshops, Inspector, were my own. Six years of unremitting toil, smashed to pieces in one minute by a band of thugs. For you know very well, Inspector, that you're on a battlefield here, and what's at stake. There'll be many of us fighting this battle, make no mistake. You didn't by any chance expect to win the day without even a fight?"

"I don't understand a word of what you're saying. I am doing my job, my boy, and that's all. I shall not leave here before I've finished."

"Right," said Pélion. He was standing on the crumbling doorstep. "In that case I shall leave." He turned to Mirambeau: "Coming?"

"Stay here!" thundered the inspector.

"What did you say?"

"I told you to stay here. You'll leave when I allow you to!"

"Am I under arrest?"

The police inspector took a step forward. The two men were facing each other with a smile. Mirambeau, too, smiled, but beneath his smile lurked visions of neck-wringing.

"You may be before long," said the inspector through clenched teeth, when he found himself under Pélion's nose.

"But not yet, am I?"

They turned their backs on him.

Outside, an apricot-colored sun was floating in the mist of spring. The bells were calling the faithful to the ten o'clock mass on this Ascension Day. Behind the high walls of the Augustine cloister sparkled the snow of flowering apple trees. Pélion and Mirambeau passed black-clad gentlemen with their ladies, full of gravity and clear of conscience, on their way to confess the Kingdom of God and His justice.

PART THREE   *The Last Solitude*

Chapter Seventeen

A tray of patties and hors d'oeuvres balanced on his arm, Virgil would first put his ear to the door. If he heard no sound, he would not dare go in. He would return to the kitchen to wait, then start out again. He would thus travel back and forth two or three times until a murmur of voices encouraged him to knock. Ever since he had seen Egmont lying still and insensible in the permanently darkened room, with its soft light on the strange phials and eery vine stocks, and that queer woman doctor motionless in an armchair or at times even stretched out on the bed beside the unconscious body, he felt a clammy anguish whenever he intruded into this oppressive sanctuary. He had listened to Egmont's explanations with respectful surprise, without quite grasping them, but his inborn tact and discretion precluded his asking questions or raising objections. However, he had tacitly decided to send for another doctor as a last resort, should Olga one day go too far in her eccentric compliance.

For the past fortnight—ever since that first success with the disappearance of the small bruise on his leg—Egmont's attempts had advanced with almost frightening leaps and bounds. It seemed as if each lock, once forced, opened a door that he could thereafter pass through at will. He "dived" and "surfaced" with the ease of a sponge fisher, yet the booty he brought up from the depths remained scant. He constantly butted against the same obstacle: the Customs, as Olga called it, which impounded all recollections. The only ones that still managed to slip through were those that had passed the gate, by surprise perhaps, on the early occasions: the hills, the mangroves, the swamps alive with weeds and amphibians—but even these memories, these dream-images, merely filled Egmont with anger: they were no more than petrified, fossilized disguises, dim allusions to a remote, inexpressible reality.

"I have gone so much further . . ." he whispered bitterly, in a vain effort to break through the Customs. "I have seen, shared in, so many things. . . ." At times a flash would light a transient vision: "A hermitage!" he suddenly shouted under his breath. "Caves dug into the mountainside . . . crystal rocks covered with trembling, undulating moss . . . Something's coming," he breathed, "a chant rises, an unearthly murmur, oh, I can hear it. Listen!" he said to Olga, squeezing her hand, as if she could hear it too. Olga said nothing at first, so as not to tear him from his visions. But she could not hold out for long: "And then?" she asked. But: "Oh, nothing," he would say, "it's all gone again."

Egmont's stubbornness gradually surrendered to the failure of so many futile efforts, and imperceptibly he wearied of this useless striving after recollection. He no longer tried so hard to transmit to Olga the perishable and deceptive yields of his exploration, which, however, absorbed him more deeply every day: ever farther and longer-lasting. But Olga herself became less pressing. Besides, Egmont had obtained almost immediately a conspicuous success in the most threatening sector: the gangrene in his toe. On one of the first days, he had "emerged" with the triumphant glee of a small boy bursting from an attic where he has discovered a secret

200

passage. Without looking at Olga, he had crushed her fingers in his clenched fist, whispering excitedly: "I've got there, Olga, I've got there."

"Where?" she asked.

His voice, in answering, was already distant and submerged: "My toe . . ." and, the moment after, Olga had had beside her no more than a vacant husk. For hours she had awaited Egmont's return with the same anxious thrill as on the day when he had obliterated the bluish disk on his leg before her eyes.

But once again his return was disappointing. He brought back nothing but mirages.

"And yet," he stammered, "I did, I did at last take part in the fight. It was horrible, exalting—but I don't remember anything," he admitted dejectedly. "If I try very hard, all that comes back is that old dream, you know, about the cavalry charge, the endless melee. What is the good of those silly pictures? What I really took part in was something so different. . . . It was a battle indeed, a fierce, interminable one, but . . ."

He almost groaned with the effort to remember. At one moment he thought he was clutching reality: "A vast expanse of crumbling cliffs, eaten away at their base by myriads of sea urchins and starfish . . . No," he corrected himself, "the cliffs themselves are a welter of starfish, huge piles of them, whereas the sea urchins—what am I talking about," he said with a scornful laugh. "Nothing like it, of course. I'm inventing those images up here. Perhaps because of the things I know, bacilli, phagocytes . . . Next time, maybe," he said, mocking his own humiliation, "I'll think up centaurs or hippocampuses. . . ."

But suddenly:

"And yet," he started, and he slowly bit his lip, "and yet . . . there is something true in it all the same, but what? I can see it again, this rout . . . this headlong flight of the hordes of sea urchins because I had brought up, infested the sea around them with other mollusks with caustic excretions. . . ." He clicked his tongue sadly. "That's not it," he repeated, discouraged. "Those mollusks were really *myself,* you know . . . as if I had summoned myself from all the horizons, rallied and reassembled myself . . . and created myself too, in some way . . . and all that from my observation post at the periscope, you see. . . . Myself," he repeated, and his voice was once again full of hesitant irony, "Who's that, myself? What a tangle! I'll never get it straight. . . ." And he shook his head with a lost-dog look in his eyes.

But one fact remained, real and verifiable: the gangrene did not spread. Yet several days passed before Olga dared speak of a regression, more long days before this regression became conspicuous. But then it did so increasingly. The time limit granted by Vauthiers had long since expired. Olga was now so little doubtful of the eventual cure that she slackened in her supervision.

During all those days, Egmont had exulted unashamedly; this victory over his flesh consoled him in his failures against an oblivion which became ever more relentless. He started to pretend that at heart he did not care at all about being thus powerless, he even went so far as to rejoice in it: "Remembrance, recollection," he said, "after all, what's the good of it? It's a luxury. A highbrow luxury." He went one better: "In fact, one's much better off without it! This frenzy for knowledge, for understanding, for remembrance, wasn't that just what I determined to shun from the very first day? We really are incorrigible," he cried, "always ready to fall headlong into the trap." He warmed to the idea: "It's the major trap, in fact. The trap of knowledge, with all that it involves. Finished!" he exclaimed. "I no longer want to *know* anything, I want the very opposite: to forget all knowledge, live my organic life, flourish like a vegetable!"

Olga smiled at first, unperturbed, joked about it:

"You want too much," she said. "To lose all awareness . . . What about washing, stretching your legs, having your lunch? You jolly well have to come back from time to time. . . ."

"Those are minor obstacles, they shouldn't be insuperable either," he replied in a dreamy tone, with a trace of impatience.

This impatience very soon made Egmont resent any presence but Olga's, which was less a presence than a complicity. But he rejected, almost violently, any intrusion into the motionless silence of the shuttered room by that outside world which he was trying to annihilate.

He left Pascale's letters unanswered. Her memory had paled and no longer racked him.

I want you to love me, she wrote, *I cannot bear the thought that you may no longer love me. We shall suffer, but what does that matter? I never thought one might come to yearn for pain with such fervor: because it means aliveness. Oh no, please do not forget me! Forgetting scares me, with its flavor of death. In this house I am surrounded by drowsy old hearts. My uncle, my aunt, my cousin. They seem happy enough. But it's the happiness of dazed fish in a muddy pond. It makes me shudder.*

> *May they come soon, the days*
> *that set our hearts ablaze!*

I long for the evening, when I can abandon myself to my tears. They rend me, but I feel alive!

Egmont marveled at his own aloofness, his victory over his own heart. Alive? Why, it's I who am alive at last! he thought. No longer this meaningless life of cramping cares and lonely minds, but a radiant, teeming, brimming, exuberant life! I exist as does a continent. I swell, I burst with existence! How meager, dull, remote, and shadowy all the rest appears henceforward. . . .

He had gradually closed his door to his friends: they brought with them from outside paltry echoes that he had almost ceased to understand and which exasperated him. A visit from Mirambeau had all but turned into a quarrel, which, although a mild quarrel full of gentleness, had left the elderly scientist in a state of utter bewilderment.

Pélion, summoned by the police two days after the explosion, had been questioned all night long. They tried to make him admit that his business had been in a bad way. Pélion pointed out that his insurance did not cover explosions. They parried by suggesting that he might be swindling his suppliers by spiriting away their wool deliveries. What had become of the wool? Why don't you come clean and admit that you sold it secretly at a cut price! "You noticed yourself," said Pélion, "that it all went up in flames." You let a few bales burn for show, where did the rest go to? And your ledgers? Vanished, dissolved into thin air! What has become of them? "You know that better than I do," said Pélion. Thereupon a punch broke two of his teeth.

However, he was released in the morning. Pélion first went to Mirambeau's to take a shower and clean up his swollen mouth.

"I wonder why they let you go," murmured Mirambeau.

"Because my books must really have been burned or else removed after the bust-up. The cops suspect I may have hidden them somewhere to call their bluff at the proper time. The day they're sure I've no trump card up my sleeve, they'll take their gloves off."

204

"But they'll never get a conviction on such trumped-up charges!" exclaimed Mirambeau.

"Maybe not. But meanwhile they'd keep me in the cooler for six months. That's all they want at the moment. I'm off," said Pélion. "No need of you," he added with a grin, "everything'll be quiet over the week end. The trucks are due on Monday."

During the first days of the strike, Antoine Coubez and his friends had indeed resorted to the well-tried gambit of alternating threats and promises in an attempt to break the workers' unity. A full pardon was promised to the "well intentioned" and rendered more attractive by special rates during the strike period. The "bad eggs" on the contrary were threatened with the sack and with eviction from their factory-owned tenements. Fernand, Mirambeau, and Albert had worked hard during that early period, which lasted just over a week. Pélion was champing at his bit at Mirambeau's, but held himself in reserve for the showdown, which was expected shortly: the arrival of almost a thousand scabs—Italians, Poles, and North Afs. Till then he meant to avoid giving the police the slightest pretext for running him in.

All this while Mirambeau had not found time to set up the watch committee he had thought of forming since the first day. It now grew urgent, since Pélion's liberty was of paramount importance for the outcome of the strike. When Saturday came round, he could take a breather and think about constituting an effective, that is to say, representative committee. He therefore drew up a short list of Chaulieu notabilities, whose reputation would be sufficient to make the prefecture think twice. He himself would go and present this warning to the prefect. He hoped that a Fellow of the Institute might carry some weight.

On Sunday morning he therefore set out to make his various calls.

Although Egmont headed the list, Mirambeau first of all climbed up to Closter Cloots', who lived but a few steps away.

He found him busy writing, immersed in his Anabiosis.

"Ah!" said Mirambeau, "so you've got down to it!"

"In the nick of time," said Cloots, smiling as usual, "if I want to get it done."

Mirambeau seemed to be unaware of Cloots's state of health, for he did not pick up the hint.

"How far have you got?" he inquired.

"To religion. They've got seventy-two different persuasions. Which, by and large, isn't much and shows the Anabiosians' lack of imagination when it comes to explaining their existence. All the more so, y'see, since they are all pretty much alike on certain points."

"Mightn't that prove on the contrary that there's something real at the root of them all?"

"There is: death. All of them offer comfort for dying. And laziness: they all preach resignation. It's so much easier to resign yourself than to fight, especially to fight without hope. Except when it comes to killing each other. Then they are suddenly in a frenzy. The mildest creeds become the most ruthless, once it's a question of forcing the others to believe in what you believe. The people least listened to are those who suggest it might be wiser, perhaps, to have a shot at the *Jungfraus* first. The most hated are those who hold that you should begin by reforming camp life, and stop killing and exploiting each other, so that, all together, they might take a clearer view of things. A number of people would be glad to see such bandits burned in the market square, as an example. Or have them bombed out of existence."

"You seem to me in an excellent frame of mind," said Mirambeau, "for what has brought me here."

He told him of Pélion and the watch committee.

"Don't count on me," said Cloots, still smiling.

Mirambeau could not help staring at him round-eyed.

"Pélion may not be a bad chap, but I detest his sectarianism. You've heard him talk of Egmont?"

"I know, I know," said Mirambeau. "But that isn't the question."

"I can't stand his chops and changes. Even last year, if you hinted a doubt of Stalin's genius, he'd have scratched your eyes out. Now he goes around calling the Father of the Peoples a son of a bitch, and heaps insults on the unbelievers. It's intolerable."

"So you'd let him go to jail?"

"I won't meddle, because I don't know what he's done or hasn't done. With Anabiosis, y'see, I know where I am. I can simplify, work in black and white. Good uns, bad uns. But in life it's different. Nobody is altogether good or bad. There are intentions to consider. You may commit a crime with the best intention. Or again do kindly deeds with evil designs. People fight to prolong social injustice because, in so doing, they consider they're defending highly prized values—a different kind of justice, y'see. And maybe they're right. Forgive me for speaking frankly, but men like us, y'see, like you and me, haven't the means of seeing straight. We should never meddle in issues of this kind. As far as I'm concerned, I've made it a rule. It's the only way of keeping a certain inner purity."

People and their coats of mail! pondered Mirambeau, once outside in the street. The more high-sounding the words, the more invulnerable they feel. Inner purity! That takes care of all the contradictions. And he won't have a single qualm when next year he'll at last be offered the top form at high school. . . . Dammit, here I go thinking along Pélion's lines, he thought, pulling a face. Bad sign, that. But for whom?

With this, he reached Egmont's place. He was surprised to see the shutters closed. What's up? he worried. Has he had a relapse? I ought to have inquired after him more often.

Virgil's attitude did not reassure him.

"He's there all right," said the old man, "but I don't know if you can see him. . . ."

"Any complications? Are his feet bad?"

"No, no . . . he's very well. Only he . . ."

"Well?"

"He sleeps a lot, you know. And when he's asleep, he must not be disturbed on any account."

The poor fellow is all mixed up, thought Mirambeau. Egmont must be more fagged out than had appeared. Some infection, no doubt, masses of antibiotics, and now he's all in.

"Go and see, though, if he won't receive me."

Virgil seemed at a loss and ill at ease. He turned a perplexed face toward the closed door of Egmont's room.

Just then the door opened unexpectedly, and through it emerged Olga in a dressing gown of sheer silk over a nightdress generously open on an attractively plump bosom. Mirambeau had to control himself so as not to burst out laughing: "So that's it . . ."

But Olga did not seem put out in the slightest. On the contrary:

"Professor Mirambeau!" she cried. "What a pleasure! You've come to see Daniel? You've picked a good moment, he's just come back, you're in luck."

"I didn't think he was getting up yet."

"Of course not. Not for a few more days."

"You said he's just come back."

"You can't understand, of course. He'll tell you, I'm sure. Come in, come in, I'll join you in a moment," she said, motioning toward the room.

"You are sure I won't be tiring him?"

"Him? He's in the pink of health. Never felt better."

Mirambeau jerked his chin in the direction of the kitchen.

"Virgil was saying that Egmont spent most of his time sleeping."

"Poor Virgil!" said Olga. "He must take Egmont and me for a couple of crackpots."

"So shall I," said Mirambeau, "if you don't stop talking in riddles."

"Why don't you go inside," said Olga. "Don't wait till he's gone again. . . . I'll be back presently," and she left him there, bemused.

He went in. The appearance of the room gripped him with astonishment. He had never been in it, even in the old days, and the sight of the shelves with their tortured vine stocks and weird phials gleaming in the half-light was unexpected enough in itself. No less so were the closed curtains at midday, the silence, the scent. He stepped close to the bed, even more deeply in the shadows than the rest of the room. Nothing moved in it. The shape of a stretched-out body dimly raised the blankets. A motionless head hollowed the pillow.

Mirambeau thought that Egmont was asleep. He therefore received with a shock of amazement the gray, dull shaft of those unseeing eyes. But the face itself surprised him even more: he had expected to read fatigue in it—whereas the features, the complexion glowed with health and vigor. He bent over him. The half-open lips let through a calm and even, but almost imperceptible, breath. The hands, flat on the sheet, were relaxed and peaceful.

The old scientist had grown as motionless, in his turn, as those husky stone warriors that guard the ancient Ming tombs. He could not tear his glance away from those unseeing eyes, which seemed to keep a fixed watch on a sleeping fly on the ceiling.

At last Olga returned. She murmured: "Oh . . . he's gone again . . ." and stood quietly by Mirambeau's side, gazing at Egmont with him. She waited for the old man to speak. But he did not say anything. He felt too awkward. How much ought I to know? he puzzled. What should I know had I troubled to get news of Egmont more often? My ignorance will betray my neglect. He therefore kept silent, embarrassed and perplexed.

Olga seemed to understand his difficulty, for she took Mirambeau gently by the hand, led him toward a small settee on which she made him sit down. She herself sat down beside him.

"He'll be furious, but never mind," she murmured.

"That you let me in?"

"He doesn't want to see anyone," said Olga. "He pretends that . . . But I let you in on purpose. He frightens me more and more, with his . . . experiments. It's only right that now and again somebody or something should tug him back into this world."

"I am completely befogged, you know," said Mirambeau rather testily, "I don't understand at all."

Olga smiled wanly: she could imagine it, she said, and slowly, in an undertone, she tried to acquaint him with the facts.

When she had finished, Mirambeau opened his eyes saucer-wide.

"This is enthralling or else completely mad," he growled.

"Come and examine his toe," said Olga. And she described the gangrene, Vauthiers' diagnosis, the unbelievable healing.

"You aren't pulling my leg?" said Mirambeau, bending over the perfectly sound toe, and Olga merely shook her head. "It would be stupendous," he gasped.

They went back to the settee. Mirambeau was pinching his drooping cheek with his short, ruddy fingers, staring hard at Olga. He started firing questions at her. Olga answered them with medical precision. Then he fell silent for a while.

"A case of hysteria," he said at last under his breath.

"Don't you believe it!" cried Olga. "You surprise me," she added more quietly. "You're surely not one of those who insist on imprisoning man in his hapless condition as if it were a strait jacket? Who deny him the right to wriggle out of it?"

"I don't do the imprisoning," said the old scientist with a smile.

"But you condone it. If you had told Voltaire that man might fly through the air in battle swifter than sound or cannon ball, he'd have laughed in your face."

"He would have been right. At that time it was neither possible nor even conceivable."

"But, in the absolute, it was both."

"The absolute? Never heard of it. Tell me in two hundred years that it has become a common practice to control one's organism, and it will mean that we shall slowly have made headway in that field as well. I am plodding hard enough at it to know what it's all about. We are miles away still. And until we get there I don't believe in fairground freaks."

"But Egmont comes and goes at will! He remains in complete control of his will power."

"Hysteria can assume most unexpected forms."

"In fact," said Olga, "that word sets your mind at rest."

"It isn't a question of my mind being at rest or not. Hysteria has been properly studied, classified. Whereas those fakir's exhibitions of yours . . ."

"And his gangrene? The healing? Has that been studied and classified?"

"A lot of similar phenomena have been: hysterical stigmata of certain religious maniacs, resorbed tumors under the stress of fear, or trauma, or what you will . . . One's never yet been able to produce anything of the sort by the sole exertion of one's reasoned volition."

"Dear Professor, we are quarreling over words. Hysteria, reason, volition, are mere labels. What matters is surely what we find beyond them, isn't it? And beyond we find what you see here," she said pointing to Egmont. "Whether we call it hysteria today or volition tomorrow, I don't mind, but you will admit that Blériot crossing the Channel and I-don't-know-who crossing the sound barrier are not two distinct phenomena: the latter was already completely contained in the former."

"Maybe, maybe," admitted Mirambeau, still kneading his cheek. "You're not altogether wrong there . . . besides, it's quite true that hysteria has become a sort of blanket word. It covers all and then some. . . . I even grant you that it may be able to assume quite unpredictable forms and appear at times to adopt the ways of reason. . . . Is the opposite possible, though—can reason adopt the ways of hysteria? Why not, after all?" he muttered, pulling at his plump throat until it drooped like a turkey's crop.

He started again after a pause.

"Have you talked to Burgeaud about it?"

"I did, but without going into details. . . . I did not mention Egmont. . . ."

"You ought to call him in."

"You think so?" said Olga reluctantly.

"Certainly," insisted Mirambeau. "I wouldn't feel too easy if I were you."

"What do you think could happen to him?"

"It's a form of hysteria, all the same, from the medical point of view. Might turn out badly."

"Many thanks for your kindly thoughts," said Egmont's voice. Mirambeau got up and went toward him with a grin.

"One should never discuss serious matters in the nursery," he said, shaking his hand. "Little pitchers have long ears."

"What did Olga tell you, actually?"

"Everything, from beginning to end. I know the lot now, I believe."

"Well, and what do you think?"

"I thought you were eavesdropping."

"No, I merely overheard your charming diagnosis. I'll tell you something: I am hysterical to just the same extent as your chicken heart, or those bits of raw meat that age or rejuvenate at a signal. Am I wrong?"

Mirambeau felt an armchair, pushed by Olga, slide under his knees and sat down. He said:

"No. That's not a foolish notion. And we'll return to it. But today I've come to talk to you of other matters."

And he briefly told him of the strike, the bomb outrage, the prison threat hanging over Pélion's head. Egmont's face hardened.

"Why should I care?"

"I know there isn't much love lost between you and Pélion. But this question doesn't concern him alone. If one lets justice be flouted . . ."

"I like Pélion a lot, that's not the point. But all this no longer interests me. Or rather, I refuse to be interested. You won't understand, I know, but that can't be helped."

"I don't see how your experiment, supposing it is one, can in the slightest degree render human problems less acute."

"It doesn't render them less acute, it obliterates them. Politics? What's that? I no longer know. It's counterfeit money. Man never stops barking up the wrong tree. He's got onto the wrong universe."

Mirambeau's hand felt for his skull.

"The wrong what?"

"Universe. He lives out there on his balcony, minding his neighbors' affairs, instead of worrying about what's going on in his own place, inside his four walls. His wife's cuckolding him, his children are killing each other, while he doesn't even care. When there's too much of a row, he sends for a doctor, but he himself doesn't step down from his balcony. Well, I've decided to step down, to go back home and put my house in order, instead of bothering about my neighbors' business."

"One doesn't exclude the other."

"I beg to differ, you can't be inside and out at the same time."

"But if you hear someone outside shouting 'Murder!' . . ."

"They're shouting 'murder' inside my home too. Millions of cells in my right toe are succumbing to the onslaught of a villainous virus. Why should I be less responsible for their well-being than for that of the people out in the street? In the light of the galaxies, the death of a million men by an atomic bomb has no greater importance than that of a million cells by gangrene."

"You don't yourself believe a word of all this rigmarole," said Mirambeau gently.

"But I don't believe a word of the converse, either," said Egmont. "On what do you expect me to base my ethics, a valid idea of good and evil, as long as I am ignorant of what I am myself, of what you are, of what we all are? What does good and evil mean for an oyster, a baobab, or the cells of my pancreas? *Primum vivere*. I am sure, absolutely sure now, of one thing: there is no

214

moral problem in the universe but one—suffering. Suppress pain and you'll suppress all problems. Without consciousness, no pain exists. *Ergo,* I suppress consciousness. It's simple and irrefutable. And henceforward I shall live in a world which we should never have left, a world where only life exists, nothing but life, where even death is life still, a mere displacement, a simple permutation. Good-by. Have a good time."

"Are you serious?" asked Mirambeau.

"As serious as a bishop. I've finished arguing over insoluble questions. 'Why do we exist?' We exist for the prosperity of the thousand billion individuals that compose our organism. Outside that certainty you will find no two persons who live for the same thing: power, or women, or music, or the supremacy of the White Man, a gorgeous automobile, the victory of Britain, salmon fishing, the conquest of Mount Everest, the neighbor's field, the love of God, a stamp collection, the French Academy, nirvana, a small bungalow in the suburbs with a wistaria, or cabbages and kings. Now to get them to agree, and stop them from pitching a thermonuclear bomb at each other's mugs with a view to imposing their mutual way of life, you would first of all have to make them agree on what Man is doing here on earth. Do you know what he's doing? I don't. Do you know what Man is? I don't. Do you know what's going on inside him? I don't. But I *shall* know. And once I know what goes on inside him, I won't be far from knowing what he is. And once I know what he is you can come and talk to me again about your watch committee."

When that Sunday at nightfall Mirambeau at last came home, tired out by all his calls, he had obtained the support of just one classical scholar, now curator at the Jacquard Museum, two professors of science at Chaulieu University, and Dutouvet, the archaeologist, Pascale's father. The other thirteen had explained to him at length the peremptory though widely divergent reasons which made it morally impossible for them to associate themselves with his endeavor. He felt depressed and profoundly weary. A watch committee of five would have no authority whatsoever.

As it happened, Pélion was arrested at Mirambeau's flat the following morning, just when he was about to go and join, outside the Coubez works, the reception party for the trucks from Châteauroux and their cargo of blacklegs.

Chapter Eighteen

Olga was racked by doubt: ought she to follow Mirambeau's advice? Should she go and see Burgeaud? Or shouldn't she? The days passed without her coming to a decision. The old scientist's visit had settled nothing. On the contrary, it seemed to have made Egmont only more impatient to have done with the outside world. Egmont himself denied that this impatience was merely the visible sign of his escape into oblivion, of his desertion.

"The very opposite is true!" he protested. "Staying out here would now be tantamount to desertion. I have spotted the enemy in his hide-out, and you expect me to withdraw on tiptoe? You'd have me say: 'Let's not meddle'? I'll have no rest now till I've forced him into the open."

"The enemy?" said Olga. "What enemy?"

"All this," he answered, kneading his chest in ironic anger. "Have you already forgotten? All this hide-and-seek business. This ghost train whose engine I'm driving without knowing anything about the passengers, what they are, what they think, what they're up to, except that when we get to the terminus they'll string me up on a lamppost. 'Look after the other trains,' says Mirambeau. 'Nothing doing,' says I, 'I'm minding my own.' For at night I wander through the corridors, hear sighs and whispers, I listen and watch, and not only listen, but more and more often I enter, intervene, share in this secret life. It's a good deal more exciting than timetables and shunting-points."

"But if other trains collide with yours, your secret life goes bust."

"That's why I've decided to put my train in a siding."

Olga argued as a matter of form. She constantly wavered between fright and fascination—more frightened every day to find herself more fascinated. But how could she have resisted the sort of felicity that Egmont brought back from the depths like a pearl fisher? His spot of gangrene had disappeared completely. "That's ancient history," he triumphed, and he grew ever more excited.

"Can you imagine the feelings of a geographer, a geologist discovering a hidden rift through which he can wander into the bowels of the earth? That's just what I feel."

"But if he remembers nothing on his return?"

"He'll tell himself that one day or other he'll be more successful. You don't see him giving up for such petty reasons?"

"I'd like to be sure he does not take to these expeditions out of misanthropy—the way he'd take to drugs or opium."

"And even supposing that entered into it as well? Are you so sure of the motives that spurred Charcot or Admiral Byrd?"

"But they brought back negotiable coin. The type of explorer who scares me is Alain Gerbault, with his profitless escape from the world."

"Have no fears on that point. Still, even Gerbault's time was not wasted: he discovered roads, currents, atmospheric passages. We don't know all the fun he had, but he had it. And I swear to you I'm having mine. I'm beginning to know the whole place so well," he said, waving his hands in gliding motion over his own body. "I wander all over it, feeling quite at home. . . . You've no idea what it feels like . . . this fantastic sensation of freedom, of power. . . . Because I'm exercising this power. Not always easily, nor too well. But however limited my power still may be, it's already marvelous. And bursting with unimaginable promise."

"If you could at least explain a little of it," complained Olga.

He shook his head.

"You must understand that it is impossible. Even more impossible than for a virtuoso to explain in detail the movements of his finger muscles when he's playing Vivaldi. He can play it, that's all. By dint of practicing and exercises. My instrument is myself and I am learning to play on it by dint of training and return trips. But explaining is a different matter!"

He tried, nevertheless:

"Look, at this moment, I am busy with my kidneys. Because I must regretfully inform you that they aren't doing so well. Something queer going on. The orders and messages don't come through properly, there's delay on the line. And traffic jams at the sluices. A certain reluctance, too, one gathers, on the part of the management to—"

He burst out laughing:

"Mind your peepers, or they'll pop out! Don't try to understand, old girl, we no longer mean the same thing when we talk of kidneys. All those dissections, and microscope slides, what do they teach us about medicine? Roughly as much as a road map can teach us about the sexual habits of the beetroot parasite. . . . A kidney . . . if you saw what a country it is! A real nightmare. Imagine—"

But he stopped himself:

"I was going to talk once more of jungles and reptiles, of

219

gorges, torrents. . . . What rubbish," he sighed. "I strike myself as some conventional Academy artist who'd try to represent nuclear energy by a saraband of nudes. . . ."

Listening to him, Olga felt like a bather in the sea buffeted by the waves. She did not wish to hold Egmont back on the brink of fresh forays, yet she would have liked to detain him. . . . She brimmed over with questions. But what was the good of questioning him since he could not bring back one sensible image? She tried hard enough to interpret Daniel's transpositions in the light of her own medical and biological knowledge, but she was soon deterred by the hopelessness of the attempt. And thus, despite her disapproval and her fears, she, too, subsided into a torpor lit, like Egmont's, by fitful visions and phantasms, which gradually got the better of her professional zeal. She abandoned herself to it more and more often, and each new abandonment weakened her resistance.

The awakening was all the more brutal. Its first warning came when Olga one day emerged with Egmont from their common lethargy in circumstances that plunged him into triumphant exultation, but filled her with a frightened joy, a medley of ecstasy and alarm. Ecstasy at having at last—at long last—joined Egmont in his enticing abyss, alarm at seeing him revel in such a total loss of self, the depth of which she now fathomed.

Olga first remembered sinking into what she had at the time believed to be slumber. But when she recognized, beyond the fleeting images of half-sleep, the mangroves of long ago, the palpitating roots, the madrepores, the warm seas swarming with sponges and coralline, all this tingling, live, luminous darkness, she knew she was no longer dreaming, but rediscovering a forgotten path to which she abandoned herself blissfully. She let herself be swept along in the fluid chaos, now lightly with a swallow's buoyancy, now with the lithe vigor of a grayling. She kept just enough self-awareness to enjoy the wonders offered to her, to savor their transient delight, to marvel at their profusion. She floated with dreamlike ease along a hill through ghosts of comfreys that vibrated with the sound of harps. She swam amid the pervasive caresses of quivering seaweeds, cradled by the softness of huge clusters of marigolds, of giant tuberoses. . . . And this shimmering swarm, was it birds or shells? No sky, but streamers, a shower of warm, transparent snow, a vast flurry shot with eddies, with calm whirlpools, and so soft that Olga felt merely the fanning of an exquisite breeze. She glided on again, and there rose the invisible murmur of a hidden brook among the grass. The grass itself was nothing but dewdrops that glistened as far as the eye could see. It swayed gently, and its undulations bore Olga toward darker, more redolent groves, stirring with mottled multitudes of sparkling moths or dragonflies.

Suddenly, as if someone had called, the shimmering flutter froze solid—with expectancy, surprise perhaps; then streamed on again, but as if directed, carrying Olga along for a while in its smooth, even flow. Gradually, though, amid the rushing sound of cascades, the stream grew turgid, rolling her toward a seething vortex, slashed with lightning, with liquid fire, with cold flames like flickering glowworms, battering her with heaving seas, with ever more boisterous breakers, till Olga was sucked into a blaze of swirling snow and refulgence, in which at last she lost herself. Cold flames and warm snow in a dazzling whirl were all that Olga's ravaged senses could grasp for a while, and then this, too, seemed to dissolve in the radiance of a fathomless night, abandoning her on the sand, spent and shaken. And she awoke, spent and shaken, to find herself on the bed, clasped in Egmont's embrace, crushed by his heaving warmth.

In the calm that follows love—the mind's drowsiness, the body's fatigue—Olga at first thought only of savoring the still present and quivering memory of this mysterious upheaval of her carnal depths. She held Egmont close, and in a surge of tenderness hugged him more tightly, but Egmont did not respond, he remained strangely listless in her arms. She moved away to look at his face. He was neither asleep nor awake: absent.

Oh God, she thought, can it be that . . . She hardly dared finish the thought. Absent as I was absent? she wondered, and felt a sort of horror. What have we done? The vision of their unconscious entwinement suddenly struck her as sacrilegious, humiliating, intolerable. Without quite knowing why, she thought of the catoblepas, Saint Anthony's monstrous tempter, the insensate brute that would unwittingly devour its own feet. They had not been two creatures entwined, but one mollusk, a polyp, a brainless monster vilely coupling with itself without even knowing it. Why this shudder, this violent repugnance? she thought. Why do I feel it a sacrilege? Because two souls have never shared so little in the blood's appetite? Ah . . . because this coupled monster is not innocence, it's the very contrary, a perfidious temptation . . . the ultimate one, the very one that Saint Anthony himself could hardly withstand—the vertiginous lure of unconsciousness, of the spirit's surrender, the refuge in nonbeing. . . . Her heart contracted: what else has Egmont been doing for the last month? she cried inwardly with growing horror. A tempted and consenting Saint Anthony, even much more than consenting, she thought, determined, avid to dissolve in that abysmal darkness . . . that monstrous submission. . . . She thought: What will he say when he returns? He

222

won't be frightened, she predicted, he'll glory in his victory, I am certain of it. . . .

She was not mistaken.

"Do you understand, do you at last understand what's happening to me?" he kept repeating in a fervent whisper. He bent his face over Olga's and gazed at her, eyes sparkling with excitement.

She dared neither acquiesce nor question him. She was afraid. Afraid lest he continue, lest he fall silent, lest he explain. But there was no stopping him. He glowed with joy:

"We have shaken ourselves free, we two: my body and I! I shall be able to pass the reins. . . . Do you understand?" he repeated. "No more need of father to drive junior to school," he laughed. "Good boy!" he said, and he patted his hip with the palm of his hand, the way one gentles a horse, "so you can love all by yourself now? And tomorrow you'll be able to eat all by yourself, and dress yourself, and go for a stroll. . . ."

"Stop it," said Olga in a fierce whisper. "Daniel, you horrify me."

And as he merely lifted his eyebrows and stared at her wordlessly—

"I beg you, I beg you, don't go any further," she implored. "Oh, I should never have yielded, in my turn, to this . . . this fascination. . . ."

"Olga, fear always lurks for us on the threshold of the unknown, it's quite natural," said Egmont gently. "But don't expect me to give in to it," he concluded more firmly.

She wrenched herself from his arms, jumped out of bed.

"No, I know that."

She turned her back, furiously tore off her nightgown. She had two charming dimples on her thighs. Egmont felt a touch of tenderness.

"I blame myself alone," she said. "I was mad. I became your accomplice instead of remaining your warder." She started dressing with frantic haste.

"Olga, where are you going?"

"I don't know. Nowhere. I'm putting on my armor, that's all."

"Against me?"

"Against this contagion, this snare. I'd lock myself up in iron armor if I could."

"You're leaving me?"

"I'm leaving you to your catoblepas. As for me, I'll watch over you here, in spite of him and in spite of you. I'll never again let go the diver's rope."

"Will it be long enough?" murmured Egmont. "Olga darling," he said suddenly, almost feverishly. "Stay down with me, come with me. You could do it once, you'll be able to again. Don't leave me alone."

"Oh darling, you, too, are afraid!"

"Yes, of course I am. A little, a very little. Too little to stop. Even if it were to cost me my reason, I wouldn't quit now. You know that I'll stay the course."

He forced himself to smile and added:

"Let those who love me follow me!"

During the ensuing days, Olga gradually recovered her calm. She soon persuaded herself that it had been a false alarm, that this single misadventure was the effect of her own weakness; her involuntary complicity, she explained to herself, had encouraged that body, ruled by its instincts alone, to assert its will, a will which, though deprived of consciousness, was not without initiative—like the will that inhabits a hedgehog, or a field mouse, the blind mole. . . .

Ah, she thought, that's it. . . . I've submitted to the embrace of a beast! It was Sodom, it was Gomorrah.

She examined this thought with surprise.

Why should that matter? she wondered. It was Egmont after all, not a bull or a donkey! Egmont? she thought. I wonder. Where does he begin, where does he end? If tomorrow, as he hopes in his madness, he can come and go, dress, eat—who will he be? Daniel or not? A man or some Pliocene gorilla? She thought of the pleasure she had tasted in the clasp of this familiar body, this rejuvenated and superb, but unconscious, somnambulant body, and she blenched. Yet, after all, she protested inwardly, why should she not be allowed to savor lust in the arms of the man she loved? But was it the man she loved who embraced her? she worried a moment later. And suppose she surrendered again? Allowed her own flesh once more to quiver with radiant delight? Would it not be like yielding to some vile perversion—some new version of the myth of Pasiphaë?

Failing to find an answer, she found at least a guide to her future conduct. I must resist, she decided. For his sake, if not for my own. It's the only way to keep him here. I mustn't forget that by resistance his very appetites will force him to regain awareness—just as the urge to run despite his burned feet eventually roused his consciousness: because the impotent thalamus had to appeal to the brain for help. In fact, she thought suddenly, isn't that the mechanism which must have provoked the birth of reason in the first men? . . . Yes, of course, I can see it quite well! The brute in face of an obstacle, frustrated and furious, and a pale "why?" mounting from the depths, opening out confusedly in the murky brain, slowly rousing it. . . . Rousing it to a rebellion which, still sluggish and groping at first, gradually becomes willed, reasoned. I really should discuss all this with Burgeaud, she concluded, but could not bring herself to send for him or look him up.

As the days passed she regained confidence; yet, looking at Egmont's uninhabited face at times, she would again feel a shock, a revulsion. Behind that tranquil brow, those cheeks, the palms of those hands, there would suddenly appear a chasm, a universe of shimmering darkness, teeming with a nocturnal, threatening life, rent by storms and tempests—and in such silence. . . . A siren-like silence, terrifying and ensnaring . . . For a second she visualized Egmont floating, roaming, groping in this black silence, and she shivered.

At other times, on the contrary, she felt a compelling nostalgia, when her memory conjured up lambent visions, ineffable realities she had shared in, and the impure sweetness of a delicious complicity. But she kept her word: she did not let herself be tempted again. I feel strong, she thought, I shall not falter.

She felt reassured, but in her heart there was a vague expectation of further trials. One evening Virgil, as was his custom, carried their dinner up to them. It seemed at every mealtime as if hunger, or merely the hour, pulled a bell in the depths to recall Egmont to the surface. He "came up" and usually ate with a healthy appetite. Olga and he grasped these opportunities to talk and talk and talk. . . . That evening, however, Egmont seemed tired, inattentive. As if his legs were still caught in some heavy clay that he could not quite shake off. He hardly answered a word to Olga's questions as she sat in her accustomed place at the foot of the bed. For a few moments they dined in silence. Only the sound of forks was heard. When Egmont had finished his slice of roast meat, Olga looked up to offer him another. She saw two glazed eyeballs, the tint of gray mist, resting on her with nail-like fastness. Egmont often had that look when he was deep in thought. He would stare thus at someone in a restaurant or a train, and the other would turn away in surprise, lose countenance, begin to fidget under this insistent eye: Egmont simply did not see him, he had hung up his gaze as one hangs up an overcoat in the cloakroom—to get rid of it.

"Another slice, Daniel?"

Olga asked it with a quaver in her voice. Did Egmont hear her? The misty stare remained nail-like, glazed with indifference. A sort of smirk, however, pulled up the lips in an inexpressive half-smile—the smile he offered to talkative bores when he wasn't listening. Olga, baffled and uneasy, remained silent, motionless. The smirk faded. But the look remained, blank and harrowing. Olga could only repeat: "Another piece of roast beef?" and the flickering smile reappeared, then a somewhat groping hand seized the plate and raised it. Olga put a slice of meat on it and said: "Here you are, darling." But another few seconds passed before Egmont set the plate down before him, with a sort of dull growl, just articulate enough to resemble human speech, not enough to be understood—and he started cutting up his meat with an absent air.

He cut it, chewed it, and swallowed it, no more greedily than usual, hardly more hastily. But he did not once raise his eyes. Olga whispered: "Egmont . . ." and all over his face the skin seemed to ripple, especially on his brow and ears; but he continued cutting his meat. She repeated more loudly, more firmly: "Egmont!" and this time he raised his head and once more fastened his dull, fixed gaze on her. She said: "Oh Danny, Danny, can you hear a little, do you understand?" but he did not speak and merely went on watching her out of lackluster eyes. A door slammed somewhere, he turned his head sharply, seemed to go on listening, then returned to his roast beef. He did not touch the vegetables.

When Olga started piling the soiled plates on the tray, he fixed the same dim, mechanical gaze on her and her every movement. As she put down the tray on a chair to open the door, she suddenly heard him cry: "Olga! Oh Olga! . . . if you . . . if you could see . . ." She turned round, found Egmont's wide-awake eyes resting on her, wide-awake, flashing and dilated, and his fingers twitched, rubbed each other with exasperated impatience. "What is it? What is it, darling?" said Olga quite close to him, and she grasped his shoulders eagerly, anxiously, full of hope and burning curiosity. Egmont's eyes signaled her a pathetic message, as if to beg her: "Oh do see! Please do!" But his lips only shook over words that would not come. "So many . . ." he stammered, "such swarms and sails . . . and trumpets . . . and this joy . . . what? No . . . so many . . ." and as if he had suddenly seen his friend move away from him, fast and far, he stretched out his arm to retain her, and his eyes grew even wider, his glance seemed slowly to sink behind the pupils, and the whole body slumped a little, soundlessly and imperceptibly. His arm slowly dropped and his gaze became button-fast again—insentient and vague.

For a long minute, Olga returned the lusterless gaze with eyes that were dimming with tears. Egmont no longer moved, seemed to wait. She picked up the tray again, walked out of the room. She heard steps and turned round. She saw that he had got up and was following her onto the landing. She cried: "No, Daniel, no!" and he stopped without taking his eyes off her. She trembled under the stress of a complex emotion: pain, fear, but also once again a sort of eager curiosity. She controlled herself and said: "Go to bed. Back to your room." She looked at him with firmness, with authority. Egmont's eyes shifted, pulling his head along sideways. She put the tray down, returned to the room, flung back the sheets. Egmont started unbuttoning his pajama jacket as if it were his coat. Olga had to stop him. He sought on his wrist the watch that wasn't there. She pushed him toward the bed, he slipped into it, and said suddenly "I'm thirsty" in a faraway tone that shook Olga. She asked: "Do you want some water?" and he dully echoed: "Water," while his hand groped for a book or his glasses on the bedside table. Finding nothing there, it remained suspended, half open, as if questioning the sky.

Olga went down into the kitchen, sorely tempted to tell Virgil. She checked this impulse, as much from a desire to safeguard her self-respect, her professional standing, as from loyalty to Egmont. She put down the tray with a smiling "good evening," filled a glass at the tap after letting the water run for a moment to freshen it, and went back. On the threshold the same mixed feelings of fear and eagerness lay waiting for her: but the pain had vanished. Instead, Olga found again the secret delight in this mysterious complicity, in which were mingled sweetness, horror, and defiance —like the spell of incest or of drugs. She entered.

The room received her with its heavy breath, its warm, padded, prison air, lit only by the feeble glow of the small lamp on the cherry-wood chest. She drew a deep gulp of this cloistered air in which hovered their dual scent. She filled her lungs with it as with an exquisite poison; and she approached. Egmont, his knees pulled up, his face to the wall, was already asleep, with the true sleep of the living.

Chapter Nineteen

Mirambeau was in a state of simmering rage. So that's what justice has come down to in my country! In the days of Dreyfus they tried at least to keep up appearances, make a show of good faith. But this cool cynicism did not even trouble to pay lip service to virtue! They all knew perfectly well where the guilty could be found, they knew that Pélion was a ruined victim. They also knew that everyone knew. But they couldn't care less.

Take this defense rigging! he thought. Bruised and dazed after his "questioning," Pélion had found, in the examining magistrate's office, a young pip-squeak of a lawyer who, as he only afterward realized, had been officially appointed to defend him. Once back in his cell and his wits collected, he lodged a protest to get a more reliable man to represent him. The CGT union had sent him one of the town's good lawyers. But the pip-squeak alleged this infringed the etiquette of the Bar, the case had to be taken to the Law Council, entailing no end of wrangling and pettifoggery, while Pélion, between two stools all this time, saw his prospects worsen every day. The police, empowered by a court order to question the accused as they pleased, seized the chance of seeing him so ill-defended to throw their weight about. Their aim was to extort a confession. They didn't care a hang whether he retracted it later in court, their main object being to prevent his release for lack of a charge that would enable them to keep him locked up.

With his eye glued to his microscope, the old scientist was fuming inwardly. As he scrutinized a minute section of one of the tissues he maintained in artificial youth, he was unable to chase from his mind visions of police grilling. Gradually his thoughts drifted. This indifference! he reflected. He recalled his own during most of his life, not so much with regard to social problems as to their living manifestations in the daily struggle. He also thought of the indifference of most people, if not toward science, at least toward the real problems, the ultimate ends of research. We pay them back in kind! he thought ironically—and what he meant by it was confused yet crystal clear: the indifference of the one lot to a world of injustice, of the other to a world of ignorance, complemented each other and merged in a sort of general indifference to the condition of man. He's not so crazy, this man Cloots, he thought, with his Anabiosis. What had he said? We put up with things. Yes, everyone invariably puts up with some thing or other. And this something is always merely one facet of the whole. He felt a pleasant flush of naïve pride at the thought that he himself, his eye to the microscope probing into the mystery of life and his mind on Pélion and all the victims of social injustice, wasn't putting up with anything.

Neither Fernand nor Pélion had wanted him to be present when the trucks arrived: it might possibly come to blows, and his place was not in a scuffle. Mirambeau could not help feeling vexed: was that the way to remember his intervention on St. Gregory's Day? However, he was reasonable enough not to object or insist. He realized the part that chance had played in his success and knew too well that history does not repeat itself.

The strike pickets had not waited for morning to take up their stations: it had been deemed wiser to post them already on Sunday night. The strike committee had met at Mirambeau's, with Pélion attending. Special care had been given to the deployment of the reserves who were to command all the roads leading to the Coubez plant. In the morning, while the police came to arrest Pélion, the C.R.S. squads moved to occupy the approaches to the factory, but they came too late: everywhere they were faced by determined groups whom, in the absence of definite orders, they did not dare to remove by force. For several hours, C.R.S. and strikers kept staring at each other grimly, with an occasional exchange of jeers and insults.

The first trucks arrived toward ten o'clock, bringing Kabyle and Mzab North Africans from Saint-Vaize. The authorities obviously banked on the strikers' reluctance to use violence against them—for fear of passing for racialists. But the strikers had been galvanized by Pélion's arrest, the news of which had spread like wildfire. With the temperature rising hourly, their hearts were set on blows and bruises by the time the first truck appeared.

It was plain that the trucks had orders to get as close to the gates as possible. But they could not advance beyond the Place des Grands-Chais where they found, confronting each other, the C.R.S., gun on arm, and the strikers, standing with their backs to the houses or sitting on the edge of the pavement.

The trucks drew up in close file on the other side of the row of lime trees, behind the backs of the C.R.S., who kept their eyes on the strikers. They were open, uncovered trucks, and the North Afs were standing in them, tightly wedged. They averted their heads in a constrained manner.

Fernand crossed the square. When he came up level with the

C.R.S., he ignored their existence. One of the cops stuck his tommy-gun barrel into his stomach, but Fernand brushed it aside with one hand, knowing full well that he would not dare to shoot. Other policemen drew closer. The strikers squatting on the curb rose slowly, those standing came unstuck from the walls they had been leaning against, and all started to advance without haste.

Fernand flung at the trucks in his stentorian voice:

"Comrades! . . ."

The cop's free hand came down hard on his mouth. Two others pinioned him. Fernand did not attempt to struggle. Something like a shiver ran through the line of the still advancing strikers. A stir over by the trucks brought them to a halt. A man had jumped down to the ground. He was small, and gesticulated. The jacket over his jutting shoulder blades was all pieces and patches. He addressed his mates in a guttural accent. A deep silence had fallen over the strikers, each one trying to understand. But he must have been talking Arab or at least pidgin French, of which they couldn't grasp a word. As if he had sensed their questions, he turned round, laughing and waving his two hands above his head in token of brotherhood. It could be seen that he was very young. And when he once more started shouting in the direction of the trucks, everyone understood his drift as if he had spoken in French.

The cops, too, had understood. Half a dozen of them got moving. A warning cry went up from all sides. Some North Afs scrambled down from the trucks, in their turn. The orator had wheeled round. There was a moment of rigid motionless suspense. Then the small fellow slowly bent down without taking his eyes off the advancing C.R.S. He picked up a stone.

In the silence could be heard a very short *tac-tac-tac*. The young Arab seemed surprised, hesitant. He dropped the stone, bent down lower, fell on his knees. His head drooped nearer and nearer the ground, touched it, as if he were going to pray. And he remained motionless, while a stain of blood spread on the pavement.

All heads—the North Afs', the strikers', the cops'—had turned toward him with an expression of blank surprise. And then they veered round in unison toward a pale, petrified C.R.S. man whose tommy-gun was smoking. The cops, as if on a word of command, moved up to their colleague, surrounded him. Their eyes were darting in all directions at once.

Fernand thus found himself free and alone. Upright before the prostrate wounded man, he seemed to be receiving his offering, his prayer or his submission, and he stood as still as a statue. But behind him the men had resumed their interrupted march, they marched on as if in a dream, wordlessly, without a glance at the police, although the latter had lowered their tommy-guns against them. The trucks had emptied, the North Afs had jumped down in silent clusters, and were advancing in their turn. The cops backed away so as not to be caught in the circle which, slow and implacable, was closing on them like a pincer.

A bleak silence reigned, in which there only echoed the muted crunch of soles on the pavement as if on snow-covered ground. In a moment, the motionless wounded man was screened from the policemen's sight by a circular wall of rigid, expressionless, inert backs that seemed riven to the ground. And then the wall quivered, opened. It drew aside and Fernand appeared, walking with slow steps as he slightly tottered under the weight of the wounded man whom, unconscious, dead perhaps, he carried in his arms like a sleeping child.

Behind him the wall closed again, got under way, and the silent

234

throng seemed to follow in his track—the blood trickling drop by drop to the pavement, dotting it with crimson splashes, like the trail of some tragic hop-o'-my-thumb. Fernand walked up the avenue, turning his back on the factory, and with him came the North Afs and the strikers in brotherly unity and, behind them but at a distance, followed the C.R.S., furious to be thus intimidated, enraged by their own impotence, for they realized that but one ill-advised move and, notwithstanding their arms, they'd be savaged, lynched.

The long column thrust into the town, compact and silent, but above the noise of steps there was another unwonted sound, a vast sigh, a vague, hoarse rumble which filled the avenue like a groan. The passers-by stopped. The women pulled their children into shops or doorways. From the windows one might have seen that this column, too, was split in its middle—but nobody would have dared to call this space a *cordon sanitaire:* it was stippled with blood.

The heavy rumbling noise brought Mirambeau to his door. The procession was passing under the plane trees, along the quiet canal. He recognized Fernand and, in a split second, grasped what was happening. He went out as he was: hatless, in his alpaca jacket, in his slippers. He joined Fernand and wordlessly fell in beside him. There was the whole Boulevard Le Nôtre still to march through, the Town Hall Square to cross, before reaching the hospital in the rue des Quintes-Feuilles. This was the busy center of Chaulieu, resounding with the noisy hum of a modern city. But it was as if the marchers were preceded by a tattoo of silence. A hush descended far ahead of their approach. Motorcars drew up at curbs, cut their engines, people stopped still along the walls. They stared at the strange pair coming toward them, the bareheaded old scientist, square and upright on his stumpy legs, and the man in blue dungarees carrying a sleeping young Arab in his arms. Many recognized Mirambeau and greeted him in confused surprise. Only after the pair had passed, followed by its impressive suite, did they begin to wonder whether they had not been saluting a dead man too.

Fernand and Mirambeau walked together into the hospital. The procession, still mute, remained outside in the roadway, waiting for news. Its tail end, too long for the short street, sprawled over into the Town Hall Square. After a few minutes, there was a slow ebb toward it. Without any need of words, a group of some ten strikers and as many North Afs were the only ones to remain waiting outside the hospital, while their companions turned back, invaded the square. The C.R.S. had regrouped below the steps outside the Town Hall, to defend its entrance no doubt. The crowd faced them without a word. It filled the entire center of the square. Its size swelled every minute, as if the news was flowing through the streets and rallying all those in the town whose hearts could stir with indignation. The silent throng, their eyes glued to the façade of the prefecture, in one massive stare, seemed to exude a rather terrifying calm. One felt they were only waiting for the one fatal word to unleash their anger and, shouting, storm to attack.

The young Kabyle tribesman did not die. But his compatriots refused to work, lined up with the Chaulieu strikers. Nor did the Italian and Polish reinforcements dare to disregard the common front. In reprisal there were ruthless measures of expulsion under all sorts of flimsy pretexts, giving rise to distressing family dramas —many of the men were married to Frenchwomen. These iniquitous expulsions stiffened the workers' resistance, sealed their solidarity, which less cruelty might possibly have disrupted. The enraged reflex of impotent power almost invariably gets the better of its cunning. It was obvious the strike had now settled down to a long run.

Mirambeau, in the meantime, scoured the town to collect funds to support it. In this he was more successful than with his watch committee, having to appeal less to prominent persons and more to ordinary people. One day he climbed up to Olga's flat, in order to tap at least her should Egmont persevere in his eccentric refusal. He found no one in. He learned that Olga was in Paris "with her patient." He was glad of this, presuming the young woman had at last decided to have Egmont examined. But this was not so.

For some time past their mode of life had changed while Egmont's experiments assumed a new, ever more startling form. The semicataleptic state which used to accompany his "plunges" was now no more than a transient phase, a fleeting moment; most of the time—as on that evening when he had gone on dining and moving about—one might have believed, seeing him, that he was merely deeply preoccupied, but awake and present.

"You've never had sleep-walking fits in your childhood?" Olga asked him.

It was the word which seemed to fit best his automaton-like behavior.

"No," said Egmont, "not to my knowledge, anyway."

As, at the same time, his returns to full awareness became progressively less frequent, Olga most often found herself facing a somnambulist, and this created a disturbing and harassing problem: what to do with him? She did not dare to take him for a stroll, as she never knew what sudden fancy might come over him —the only time she had tried to make him take a whiff of fresh air, they had heard, through an open window, a mother calling her child to rest: "To bed! To bed!" Egmont had walked on for a few more steps, and then proceeded calmly to unbutton his jacket, his waistcoat, started to pull off his tie, and if Olga had not been quick-witted enough to break his reflex by making him step off the curb and on again two or three times, he would probably have undressed in the street—as it happened to her at times when, her mind on other things, she wanted to slip on a different blouse at teatime, and would catch herself a minute later in briefs and brassière, about to roll off her stockings, or winding her watch for the night.

So there was nothing to do but decide to keep Egmont at home. Fortunately, he always showed himself most conveniently docile and submissive. He would sit for hours motionless in the easy chair, his legs crossed, with blank eyes which suddenly, however, would fasten on her as soon as she murmured his name or changed her place. His leg would move a little while he followed her with those filmy-blue eyes. What was he waiting for? If she said nothing, he eventually turned his eyes away and fell back into the stillness of this quiet repose. He often yawned with boredom but seemed to find no relief from it other than falling asleep. A light sleep from which he woke at the slightest noise, lifted his head, listened, sometimes went to the door to hear better, but when the noise stopped, he would lazily return to sit down with a pitiful yawn.

It also seemed to Olga that he was no longer complete master of his returns, that they became ever more irregular and unpredictable. Mealtimes had definitely lost their power to call him back. Egmont appeared to "surface" not so much when he wanted to as when he could. He did not at first seem particularly frightened by this; on the contrary, his rare emergence into full consciousness became for Olga and him a sort of special treat. For every day they marveled more at what Egmont called his victories. His flesh grew firmer, as if his body was undergoing intensive training. He gained weight without putting on fat: rather, his incipient paunch had disappeared at the start. Then, week after week, the whole body had recovered the bloom, suppleness, and manly vigor of an accomplished athlete. Olga's tests confirmed the perfect health of his organism. On certain evenings, taking advantage of his unconsciousness, she would hold him naked before her, making him turn round and round under the light, for the mere joy of contemplating this revival which Egmont himself, as he said when awake, experienced as "electrifying." One day he started bounding and jumping over the chairs, filling the room with bursts of laughter; another day he seized his sweetheart, carried her off like a feather, and imposed his love on her till she had to ask for mercy.

But these flashes of consciousness did not last, and he never spoke of his mysterious life to Olga, it made him somber. Less and less could he remember what happened from the moment he left her. This impotence filled him with a sort of rage that was mingled with anguish. This was a novel feeling, and it troubled her. When she questioned him, he shook his head impatiently, murmured indistinct words, growled some vague phrases. One day when she complained that he had really stayed away for too long, he had flung at her with irritation: "Do you think I always do as I please?" The words, hardly uttered, had surprised him as much as her. He had turned his eyes away but for many minutes he could not control the nervous twitching of one eyebrow.

Chapter Twenty

For three days now the mistral had been blowing, the mulberry trees moaning, the boughs of the planes writhing in harsh entreaty; there was the blue ridge of the Lubéron which barred the horizon; the brown earth, golden and blood-red under the newly verdant old vine stocks; there was that vast, stern, sun-drenched plain; those long calm lines carved by the black cypresses; there was this ecstasy mingled with sadness, this too, too solid beauty. . . . Pascale, curled up on the divan, in her little room with its bare whitewashed walls, was reading her father's letter over and over and over again.

. . . I believe he would be happy if you returned. Why didn't you tell me, my little girl? I looked what I am—a very absent-minded and rather foolish father. He finds it hard to speak: they broke his jaw as well. Abominable habits, the Gestapo's ghastly heritage. Naturally, both police and prefecture swear it was an accident, that he fell down the stairs from fatigue while being led back after questioning. Robert has no witness bar himself to establish the truth. There are, fortunately (what a word!), the crushed fingers, not to be explained by the fall, which prove they have been trampled on with nailed boots. Mirambeau and myself are moving heaven and earth to prevent the case being

hushed up. Robert had to be moved to a hospital and they certainly won't dare refuse his release from custody. Mirambeau has become a lion-eater. With a man called Fernand he's tearing through the town to get backing for the strike, the factory could not reopen, and there's talk of the Coubez lot being willing to compromise.

We have another worry: Egmont and his friend Olga. I can't explain to you. Their resuming their old bond would be rather a good thing for both of them. But they have done so in alarming circumstances. Egmont's burned feet have long been healed. Nevertheless, he does not leave his room, where he spends his time in a state of voluntary prostration which borders on catalepsy. According to Mirambeau, he claims to be engaged in an absolutely staggering organic investigation. Even less comprehensible is Olga's conduct. She has got young Crozatier to take her place and stays with Egmont day and night. Total confinement. We thought at first that she was trying to tear him away from his demented enterprise; it now appears that the contrary is true, that she is perfectly compliant, perhaps even about to sink into the same lunacy. Crozatier tried to see her and hand back the patients she had entrusted to him for a month, but she sent him packing. We are really worried. . . .

Her chin in her cupped hands and her elbows on the mantelpiece, Pascale was staring at herself in the looking glass. Are you a monster? she thought, opening wide her eyes: Robert was in the hospital, his ribs smashed, his jaw and hands broken, and she thought only of Egmont. Egmont? Not even: of Olga. She thought of Olga with hatred and rage. Was this unfathomable Slav going to wreck Egmont's life forever?

"Robert is in the hospital," she repeated aloud, walking up and down between the whitewashed walls. But she thought of Egmont, of Olga. The mistral whistled in the old Roman tiles. A shutter slammed monotonously in the sunlight. "He is in the hospital," she said, but she pictured Egmont motionless on his bed and that Olga constantly at his side. "He is in the hospital." She started packing her suitcase.

She packed it without being able to collect her wits. A sort of giddiness was drilling into her. She dropped the slip she was about to fold, let it fall to the ground. The divan lured her. She lay down on it.

What doesn't Daddy understand? she thought, with closed eyes, lulled by the monotony of the relentless mistral. Egmont . . . poor Daddy, she herself knew so well what was happening. This flight, this attraction . . . *Under wilted roses my heart lies in slumber* . . . And that ghoulish Olga sucking his last breath, his last drop of blood . . .

Why did I leave? she wondered remorsefully and accused herself of cowardice. I have deserted him. Sheer weakness. She ought to have stayed near him, whether Egmont wished it or not. Robert? He would have got over her, she would have got over him: was it even love? Infants' calf love, that was all. He loves my freshness, which will fade, I love his solidity, which reassures my inexperience. The rest? A flutter of the senses, no more, two young, starving bodies. So brittle, all this, so ephemeral. We mustn't marry, not that, above all. So many dreadful couples in Chaulieu who made a mistake at the start. Mustn't add one more. I should have given myself to him, to quell his hunger, and then become good pals again, quite simply, as we should have been. Didn't do it on account of Daddy, mostly. Poor Daddy, he'd never have noticed, since anyway he hadn't noticed. Still, that's not a reason, it's true.

Is there still time? Robert in the hospital, Egmont in limbo, on Olga's wings. Too late . . . Oh no! Refuse to resign yourself. Too easy, my girl. Nothing is ever too late, nothing, nothing, as long as one's alive. Pack your case. Go on, get up! But you're afraid, that's the truth. Admit it. Abjectly terrified to suffer and cause suffering. Oh, you're a great one for suffering in writing, for singing hymns to pain, in writing, but when it comes to facing up to suffering, in the flesh and blood, Robert and you, Egmont and you, there's no one . . . A dying duck in a thunderstorm, that's what you are. You've run away and you don't dare to leave these four protective walls any more. You are going to write more letters, I can see it coming.

No. That's not possible. Even your fear is no longer strong enough. There, that's better, you're getting up. Pretend you're calm, perfectly calm, that's it. Pick up your slip, all crumpled on the tiles tinted like clotted blood, fold it carefully, like this, good, good . . . And sing, recite, never mind what, Racine, or Baudelaire . . .

> *Four horses stuck in a bog,*
> *Three monkeys tied to a clog,*
> *Two pudding ends would choke a dog . . .*

Never mind. Go on. Don't think, above all. Your case is almost packed. Your toilet bag . . . your stockings . . . your handkerchiefs . . .

> *And a gaping, wide-mouthed, waddling frog.*

You'll say Daddy has suddenly called you back. You're being offered a job. You are so glad. You'll kiss them, you'll laugh. You'll have plenty of time in the train to tremble your fill.

Egmont whispered:

"Not the shadow of a doubt: I'm being observed, spied on. I'm hunted down like a smuggler, you see. Hunted down."

He clenched his fist:

"I'm being watched like a convict!" he shouted in a half-tone. "Ah!" he cried with exasperation, "that's silly, of course, it doesn't mean a thing, but how else can I express myself? I have no other words, up *here.*"

He forced himself to be calm, mocked:

"I'm being watched . . . Who could possibly watch me? Yet that's precisely it. I've been able to see too much. No, that's silly too. I don't see anything, of course, it happens quite differently— and yet, all the same, I *am* being watched!" he shouted in the same tone in which he would have said: *Eppure si muove!*

He strained to explain his meaning:

"You remember, we talked of it: reckless explorers in the virgin forests of the Amazon . . . It's that very sensation: you don't see, don't hear a soul, and yet you feel, you know that thousands of eyes are watching you, following you. The most your ear may catch at times is the cracking of a branch, of crushed leaves, the most your eye may perceive are moving lianas. . . ."

He broke off to say with a wide, vague gesture of his hand up and down over his chest, his stomach:

"I've always felt it, always. Since the start. But then it was only . . . a sort of surprise, a slight curiosity. . . . Whereas now . . ."

He resumed in a low tone:

"It's a relentless surveillance. . . . You understand, as long as the traveler has not seen anything, not chanced across anything essential, he's left in peace. . . . But if he's suspected of having observed some secret practices, inviolable rites, then all is changed. . . . Obstacles suddenly hem in his return. . . . First a fallen trunk, a destroyed footbridge . . . A diverted path, a camouflaged crossing lead him astray, throw him back ceaselessly into the chaos of a monstrous, inextricable vegetation. . . . He'll get out of it once, perhaps twice, but if he persists it becomes obvious that there can be no two ends to this kind of game, that one morning he will find himself tied to a tree, fettered in some lair. He must drop his pursuit or take this risk with open eyes."

"I warned you," said Olga tonelessly.

"It's true. I didn't believe it. Do I believe it even now? It seems too silly, said here, in this room. The braggart Tartarin and his 'They' . . . 'They watch me . . .' It forms part of something so much more . . . enormous. Enormous and collective. I'm think-ing of Sunday church, during mass, you aren't being watched, nobody's looking at you, nobody's paying any attention, but if you happen to get up at the wrong moment, there are at once five hun-dred pairs of eyes. . . . So just try and run off with the alms box, eh? Or go and lure the choirboys away for a stroll . . . It's this kind of surveillance that I feel, getting ever more pressing, more weighty, more anonymous. . . . One of these days they'll take me by the scruff of the neck."

"What do you dread?" asked Olga, frightened. "Dying?"

"That's the last thing to fear, you know that. On the contrary, I'm helping to keep death away. I'm helping more every day. Aren't you checking me regularly?" he asked anxiously.

"I am," said Olga. "It's still amazing. Especially the cardio-grams. Your arteries are softening. You're consuming your fat as if you went in for callisthenics every morning. You've got the skin of a youth."

"And my beard, did you notice?"

"No, what of it?"

"I haven't shaved for three days. It's growing less fast already. I manage to curb it. When I think that I used to have no more power over my own hair than over the grass in the Parc des Recollets! What impotence!"

"Then what makes you afraid?"

"At dinner the other night," said Egmont. "That wasn't on purpose."

"You didn't mean to 'go away'?"

"No. You could see for yourself. It happened in spite of me. I felt quite well that I wasn't managing to surface completely. Something was clinging to my feet. . . . I must have seemed a perfect dotard."

"Not at all!" protested Olga. "You ate very properly, without dirtying yourself, even without using your fingers."

"Did I really?" said Egmont with a pleased smile.

"You ate like a gorilla I once saw at the music hall when I was a little girl. My mother said: 'You don't eat as nicely.' Afterward, he rinsed his fingers, smoked a cigar, and even washed the dishes."

"I washed the dishes?"

"No," said Olga with her husky laugh. "What would Virgil have thought? But you obeyed me implicitly. Maybe you'd have washed the dishes had I asked you."

"Ah," murmured Egmont, "that *is* reassuring."

"What is?"

"That I obey you so well. Whatever I may say, the idea of . . . that I . . . it scares me stiff," he admitted in a whisper.

"Oh, you see!" said Olga, shaken.

"Listen," said Egmont in a stronger voice, "if ever . . . if ever I should not 'surface' any more . . . promise me one thing."

"Yes . . ." she breathed. "Say it."

"Have me put away in an asylum."

"What an idea!" cried Olga revolted. "An asylum!"

246

"You'll call it a nursing home. Never mind the name, as long as you recover your freedom. What is there to fear for me? You'd only be putting away a carcass. Olga, you must promise me to do what I ask. Promise me now, at once. Swear it."

It was a long struggle, but in the end she promised, not without making strong mental reservations. Then he suggested:

"Let's dress. Pull the curtains a little. . . . I thought as much: it's a lovely day. Let's go out, take a walk. Oh Olga, let's catch a train to Paris? I'd like to see the embankments, the Place Furstemberg, the Church of St. Julien-le-Pauvre. We'll munch waffles in the Luxembourg, sit on two iron chairs, and look at the Medici fountain. We'll re-embody our ghosts of former days, when you shed tears on my shoulder for the first time. I shall recapture the scent of your hair. What do you say?"

"I say yes," said Olga.

Later she thought: What should I have done? Could I have stopped him by force? Should I have? In all sincerity, I must own that even today I still acquiesce. Has it been just a succession of weaknesses? The politicians have shown us how peoples can be brought to surrender bit by bit, without even flinching, what they would have defended with their blood had it been wrested from them at one stroke. That's how they can be led insensibly into servitude, to butchery. Is that the way things have happened with me? In the early days I'd have fought like a tigress had I known what lengths he'd go to. Now he's there, and I am resigned, unless I actually relish it in my secret heart. Unless I even envy him . . .

The Parisian escapade had lasted for three days. A three days' ordeal for Olga. Yet Egmont had promised himself to give her those days without any "plunges." But, as he had said, he was no longer really master of his plunges and re-emergences. It seemed

as if fatigue, a relaxation of attention, was enough at times to produce a change of state, so that Egmont suddenly was absent without having consciously willed it. And as his absences were no
longer accompanied by catalepsy, it often happened that Olga did
not realize at once that Egmont had left her: a whole stock in
trade of old reflexes, well-worn habits, continued to respond to
signs and stimuli from outside. When they were walking, he became hardly more heavy on her arm, carefully turned his head
before crossing a road and let the traffic pass. It even happened
that Olga would ask a question thinking he was "there," and after
an overlong silence the answer nevertheless would eventually
come in a slurred, somnambulant voice, the way she had heard
certain subjects of Burgeaud's, undergoing a narcotic test, continue valiantly counting to a hundred although they had fallen
asleep at thirty-five. Once, as they were walking up the rue des
Ecoles, Egmont had suddenly turned up a small street on the left
to the door of an orthopedist's. His hand was already on the doorknob when Olga restrained his arm: the place, formerly an Indo-
chinese restaurant, had been one of their haunts. Another time he
stopped before a shopwindow, his blind man's stare glued to
shelves which, in the old days, had displayed books on art, but
were now sporting buns, rolls, and brioches. And his mouth had
slowly opened, and saliva oozed at the corners of his lips.

On their way back, in the train that was taking them to Chaulieu, Egmont remained in motionless silence beside Olga for half
an hour, apparently looking out of the window, when he suddenly
said tonelessly but so loud that their fellow travelers started: "It's
impossible!" and subsided into his silent stupor. He came out of it
two hours later, and during those hours Olga racked her mind
with conjectures.

"What is impossible?" she asked when at last they were in their
flat. "Can you remember?"

"You are sure I said that?"

"Yes, with a sort of despair, or discouragement."

But, as usual, Egmont at first did not recollect anything. However, a glimmer seemed gradually to pierce this leaden skullcap: "Ah," he murmured, "I see . . ." He seemed to be staring at the old vine stocks on their shelves with dilated eyes. "I was outrun," he said. He kept silent for a long time before murmuring: "Suddenly reduced to panting in vain pursuit, like a white mouse in a wheel." He said again, as if dispirited: "Too swift, too complex, too vast. Couldn't keep up." And as if this ghost of a memory was enough to exhaust him, he closed his eyes and fell silent.

Several hours passed before he declared: "No. I must try. Must persevere. I'll get there. Your first day on skis, how could you dare to hope that you might later race down the slopes with a squirrel's ease? I'll catch the rhythm. Matter of time. I'll get them all in hand, however swift they may be," he said defiantly.

"Who?" asked Olga.

He shrugged:

"They, nobody, what do you expect me to answer? I'm talking of events in the neighborhood of my pituitary gland. Question of trying to irrigate a small stretch of the liver. But it also depends on messages received from the spleen and a whole series of ganglia. They're making a mess, but when I start meddling, the mess gets worse. What didn't I catch!" he said with a sort of laugh. "If I meddle again, I'll get myself . . ."

Suddenly, at these words, he stopped with a strange, unusual abruptness. And Olga saw his look draining away, as if pulled from the back of the eye, while his head inclined to one side and his hand remained suspended in an unfinished gesture. It lasted only a few seconds but for the first time Olga measured the extent to which Egmont was henceforward poised on the borderline of two worlds. The look re-emerged, and a smile.

"I've just been down to see," he said, "to make sure. . . . It's just as I said. Everything more or less in running order, but if only I could intervene, I'd prevent those bottlenecks. Yet the fact is I am like a policeman on the Place de la Concorde attempting to order the traffic by attending to each car in turn, taking the wheel himself. . . ."

"You've been down to see, you say," cried Olga. "So this time you *have* seen something? You do remember?"

But Egmont became glum again, shook his head:

"Yes, you can imagine what! If I am obliged to talk of cops and cars . . ."

"But you only stayed a minute!"

"If it were only a second, it would still be the same. You know how it is: you have a brilliant idea in your half-sleep, and the moment you open your eyes to jot it down you find nothing but ashes. . . ."

That same night, however, Olga heard herself being called. Egmont was awake at her side, was shaking her a little with impatience. He said—he stammered:

"Olga, I've got hold of something. Listen, listen quickly . . ."

He jerked the tips of his bent fingers against the inside of his thumb as if trying to hold on to a slippery fish—just long enough to show it.

"Life isn't what we think," he said in a very low tone, as if afraid to be overheard. "Our flesh—" he whispered—"our flesh does not live."

Olga naturally awaited his explanations. And the fear of not having time enough, of finding this fleeting truth slip through his fingers, twisted Egmont's face.

"You," he said, "you live. A man, a dog, a snail, they live. But a piece of flesh doesn't. A living cell, what we call that, is only . . . is . . ."

He searched, panting. "It's . . ." he repeated, and at last he threw out like a find:

"It's choreography—a waltz, a fandango! Do you understand?"

Olga shook her head. "Not very well. What do you mean?"

"It doesn't exist, a cell. A fandango, a ballet, do they *exist?* Do you think of a ballet existing or dying? That's what I mean. . . . The dancers exist, they exist in flesh and blood, but the ballet? Yet conversely, the choreography remains, even when each dancer has been replaced by another. The ballet doesn't exist but it remains immutable, whereas the dancers exist but they pass and change. Do you understand this time, do you?"

"I think so," said Olga. "That's known, isn't it? The architecture of amino acids, of the molecules constituting the albumin . . ."

"No!" Egmont interrupted her with impatience. "It's not a question of that, you are talking of the dancers, the public, the stagehands, I'm talking of a fandango, a gavotte."

"Exactly, that's what I said: the architecture."

Egmont shook his head irritably.

"Not that at all. Maybe if you talked of 'structure' . . . But not even that. It's still too solid. At most, if you like, a blueprint, without bricks or mortar, an *idea;* sheet music without musicians, a ballet without dancers, choreography once more. Oh try to understand . . . You are the ballet master, your dancers are there, they execute their *entrechats,* their *jetés-battus,* and you, you compare what they're doing with what you have in mind. What you have in mind," he repeated, "you understand? That is life, and so you correct them here and there, you modify a movement, a figure, and that's why," he whispered, "that's how I can myself change a few bars, you see, a *pas de deux* into a *chassé-croisé,* modify the state of a tissue—because flesh and thought," he said with sudden animation, "are one and the same: utterly, completely the same, *no difference at all,*" he said almost shouting, "except that for thought, you are the ballet master, whereas for the flesh, you aren't any more; and not only aren't you, but you're strictly forbidden to meddle. . . ."

"Why forbidden? Do you know?"

"Why, because . . ." he said, his face even more twisted by anguish and impatience, "don't you understand, if you meddled . . ."

But he remained open-mouthed, like a stammerer before the intangible obstacle of a recalcitrant word.

"Well? Well?" said Olga, now carried away by impatience herself, and she shook him by the shoulder to make the words drop like plums.

"If you mixed up the figures . . . you can't mix up thought and flesh," he shouted, "you'd . . . you'd create . . . monsters, a magma, goodness know what, you'd bust up everything, oh, can't you understand?"

"But you're doing it!" cried Olga. "Isn't that what you're doing?"

"Yes . . ." said Egmont, and in a suddenly muffled voice: "and that's why God knows how it'll all end. . . ."

"Don't go on if you're afraid!" begged Olga.

"No, no, I must go on. . . . And I'll bring you back all I can, you'll try to keep it and put it in order. . . ."

"But you didn't want to! You said: I no longer wish to know, I want the very opposite, to become like a lettuce again, live the life of a turnip. . . ."

"Yes, that was wisdom, but it's impossible."

"But why?"

"Ah . . . because I'm a Man. I cannot change that. And they know it. Oh, they know it very well."

"Who?"

"Nobody, all the others, how can I tell?"

"You make it sound like the werewolf."

"But it *is* the werewolf; you've found the word! You can't see the werewolf, since it doesn't exist. And yet his presence is everywhere, his tracks cover the ground, and those who walk abroad at night to chase him disappear and die. But there it is: if you aren't a cringing dog in a corner, you can't stay in when you hear him prowling."

"I no longer understand what you're talking about."

"Oh, that may be better, perhaps," said Egmont.

A few moments later he said again:

"If only we could introduce, insert the figures of thought into the organic ballet figures . . . then we could do *everything*. Olga, do you understand? Everything! Become what we want, and create what we want, change heredity, the brain, what you will. And not only within us but, step by step, we'd change the rocks, the water, the sky. . . . And it's such a near thing!" he exclaimed, with dilated eyes.

"This time," said Olga, shivering, "I'm beginning to grasp a little better why you're so afraid. . . . The fear of Prometheus on the verge of snatching the forbidden fire . . ."

"They won't let me snatch it, I'll be put in chains before," said Egmont in a murmur.

"Then don't try," she implored.

"How can I not try—unless I am a dog?" he repeated.

"But if you know you'll be chained?"

"Prometheus must have known it too."

"In that case, it's madness."

"You are right," he said with a sigh, "It's madness to be a Man."

These were almost his last words. Olga was later to compare Egmont, after that night, to a bather caught in weeds, who still manages to lift his head at times long enough to breathe and utter a shout—before being submerged again. And she compared herself to an onlooker on the riverbank, whom horror roots to the spot, depriving him of the presence of mind to run for help. When Olga at last decided to send for Burgeaud, it was almost a week since Egmont had recovered full consciousness for the last time.

Chapter Twenty-One

First there had been that unexpected visit: Dutouvet's daughter. That child who, two years ago, with plaits down her back, was still in Closter Cloots's class! Olga had not recognized her immediately. But the way she said: "I want to see Daniel! . . ."

"He's resting, my little Pascale," said Olga.

"No!"

The girl flung the word with such force that Olga remained speechless.

"Let me in! I want to see him!"

Olga had recovered herself: "Must I repeat . . ." but Pascale came closer and said through clenched teeth:

"I warn you that from here I shall go straight to the police and we'll all come back with a doctor. Do you prefer that?"

Olga smiled unruffled.

"What do you imagine? You are crazy. Go and call anyone you like."

She made as if to close the door. Pascale begged:

"Let me come in. At least listen to me!"

Olga shrugged, without ceasing to smile, stepped aside. "This way," she said pointing to a door. They soon found themselves seated facing each other in a small room full of books. "But she's about to pass out!" The young girl was ashen, her teeth were chattering. Olga hurriedly opened a small cupboard, produced a flask and a tumbler.

"Drink this. Come on, quick!"

The girl drank. She seemed to recover. But she looked at Olga with swimming eyes which she opened wide like two anemones.

"My word," said Olga softly, "I thought I was going to have two patients on my hands."

"Don't lie!" said Pascale with violence. "You haven't treated him as a patient for ages," she added dully.

"All right," said Olga smilingly, "Unload the lot. What's the matter, little girl? You love him?"

"I won't allow you to—"

"I thought you were more or less engaged to Robert Pélion?"

The young girl paled again so suddenly and so completely that Olga once more took fright. She gripped her hand, tapped the palm hard.

"Well, well, what a drooping daisy! Do you often get like this?"

She had made her lie down on the little divan, she was holding one hand which she stroked absently with her finger, and she watched with pitying tenderness the woeful young face staring at the ceiling in blank misery.

"I wanted so much to hate you! Why can't I?" said Pascale almost plaintively.

"Because you need me to help you," said Olga gently.

"You think so?" stammered Pascale. "How could you help me?"

"I don't know that, you do," said Olga in the same gentle tone.

"You think so?" repeated Pascale even more softly.

She asked after a long pause:

"Has Egmont talked to you about me?"

Olga slowly shook her head.

"Never?" said Pascale, and her voice broke.

Once again Olga motioned no.

"Why did he never tell me that he loved you either?" murmured the girl.

"He no longer did," said Olga. "Not for ages."

"And now?"

"Neither."

Pascale seemed to meditate.

"And you?" she said at last.

"I don't know," said Olga. "I may be infatuated with him all over again. But it isn't certain. It's too difficult to know."

"But why?" said Pascale sitting up to look at her.

Olga smiled:

"You'll understand this sort of thing in time. It's the sentimental form of an old law of physics: the conservation of energy."

Pascale blinked. Olga smiled even more:

"You love your garden," she said, "in proportion to the care you give it. You never love it as much as under hail or frost, when you see all your work in danger of—"

"Egmont's in danger!" cried Pascale with renewed fierceness. "And what are *you* doing?"

"Who's talking of danger for Egmont?"

"Daddy is. Mr. Mirambeau told him . . ."

"I know what he can have told him. He told me that too."

"And you do nothing!" repeated Pascale harshly.

"No," admitted Olga. "Maybe that proves I love him," she murmured.

257

"If you really loved him, you would not have permitted this . . . this mental suicide."

"You talk of things you know nothing of."

Pascale suddenly took her face in her hands.

"It's my fault, all my fault," she moaned.

Olga bent over her with distressed concern. Her finger caressed the soft forearm, the crook of the elbow.

"Don't go believing such nonsense," she said into her ear, which shone transparent like a pearly shell. Olga brushed it affectionately with her lips. "Egmont found his motives in himself alone. In his curiosity, in his revolt. It's none of our doing, neither yours nor mine, poor little girl."

"It is, it is, I know it," insisted Pascale, her eyes crushed in her palms. She felt the lips brushing her temple, the unexpected caress shook her with a poignant emotion which threw her into Olga's arms.

"I am a monster," she gasped, "an absolute monster!"

Olga was now lulling her and repeating in a nanny's voice: "There . . . there . . . there . . ." Pascale was sobbing on her shoulder. At last she managed to say:

"Oh, help me, you've promised."

"You must unload the lot, little one, I've already told you so," whispered Olga affectionately.

Now she's talking to me like a child. Everybody always does eventually. Egmont did. Pascale slipped out of the too maternal arms.

"Can one love two men at once?" she asked with a tragic face.

"An old question," said Olga, trying hard not to smile.

"I know, but it's terrible," said Pascale.

"What isn't, here on earth?" said Olga gravely. "Everything is terrible. Human life is impossible, fortunately one doesn't know it."

258

"You learn it the moment you suffer," said Pascale.

"You suffer the moment you learn it," said Olga. "Human life is impossible, but it must be lived."

"In resignation?"

"In unsubmissiveness. That's what's so hard. Hard to distinguish, I mean."

"Unsubmissiveness?"

"From resignation. The two may look so much alike. . . . What should we call Egmont's attempt? You call it an escape, mental suicide. And perhaps it's true, probably it was, at the start. But now? He seeks after truth, and truth is out of bounds. To seek God in one's self in the silence of Carmel, stubbornly to seek there this evasive God, is that obedience or disobedience? It's hard to say."

"Seeking God . . ." murmured Pascale.

"We all do after our fashion—that nice young Pélion, old Mirambeau, Egmont, a Carmelite nun. But what we seek, this one calls God, the others don't, it's simply the Hidden Truth. Yet each one will accuse the others of resignation, they'll accuse Pélion of bearing with the silence of Heaven, the Carmelite nun of bearing with social want. . . . Egmont is now in the Carmelite's camp, though she'd accuse him of pride. . . . Someone must be having a good laugh at this muddle."

"What Egmont is doing . . . is a way of seeking God, you think?" said Pascale.

"It is if you like. It certainly isn't the most orthodox one. But it's surely the most risky."

"Ah! you see! He *is* running a risk!"

"Perhaps, but what risk? Of being lost to the world? So is a Carmelite. And suppose he finds what he seeks? Come," she said suddenly, and she got up.

"You are taking me to him?" said Pascale breathlessly.

"Isn't that what you wanted?"

"I no longer know . . . I'm afraid . . ." she confessed.

"And, true enough, there you are white as a sheet again! You're afraid of being impressed?"

"I don't know. . . ."

"There's cause to be, I admit. Now there, a little pluck! Come on."

They went into Egmont's room. He was sitting deep in an easy chair, in his dressing gown. He slowly turned toward the two women an owlish gaze, round and unmoving. Pascale had gripped Olga's hand as if she were on the brink of a precipice. She remained nailed to the threshold. Egmont let his gaze shift after a moment, his mouth opened in a long yawn, closed again with a dull moan punctuated by a click of his teeth. Then he again fixed the two women with his church-owl stare. Olga took a few steps, dragging Pascale after her, and one of Egmont's legs, crossed at the knee, started swinging more swiftly and more widely as they advanced. When they stopped, the leg kept still.

"Look," said Olga. "You'll see."

She went to take a tin box out of a drawer. Does he recognize me? wondered Pascale in terror. A little? Not at all? Olga went close to Egmont, opened the box in which wrapped candies sparkled. Egmont did not help himself at once, his eyes still on Pascale. Olga rattled the box. Egmont's hand rose in an inattentive yet uncannily precise movement. It grasped a candy, which Egmont then unwrapped abstractedly. He made a pellet with the silver paper, which he flicked away with his thumb, and started chewing the candy with oxlike rumination.

"That's all that remains," murmured Olga. "Old gestures, all sorts of automatic actions—if I hand him a newspaper he'll even start reading it, as we sometimes read a whole page of a novel without understanding, our minds on other things. In short, he lives normally, or almost so. All the appearances of a man—except just what makes a man: unsubmissiveness. But look," she said again.

She switched on all the lights. Egmont raised his head toward the ceiling. The firmness of his flesh, the glowing complexion were revealed in such splendor that Pascale started with a shock.

"Is it possible . . ." she whispered, and she looked at Egmont's face with a kind of petrified ecstasy.

And suddenly she felt a heavy lump inside her melt and loosen, dilate and vanish like a puff of steam, and leave her lighthearted for the first time in many days. She thought confusedly: "But did I ever love him?"

Olga lifted the sleeve over his arm, bared the hollow of his elbow.

"Look," she said once more, with a strange pride in which Pascale was not sure she did not also spot a slight provocation. "And look at this neck. This whole body . . ."

She drew aside the opening of the dressing gown, baring the manly muscles that were swelling the top of his chest. Her hand slid to his shoulders under his gown.

What followed happened very fast. Pascale did not have time to take in a comprehensible reality. She still saw two blind eyes fixed on her, a round, vacant gaze. But Egmont had half risen. Olga jerked away from him with a twist of her waist as if he were holding her back. She flung at Pascale in a changed voice:

"Go now. Go away! Quick!"

It was so unforeseen that Pascale did not move. She stayed there in a sort of passive stupor. Olga took her by the shoulder, wheeled her round, pushed her to the door almost brutally. In the instant before turning her head, the girl saw two hands slip under Olga's arms, seize her at the hips, but behind Olga a stony face kept its dazed, birdlike stare riveted on Pascale. The last thing she saw was Olga being dragged backward but managing, with a kick of her foot, to slam the door fast.

Through the partition, Pascale still heard a dull stamping, a muffled thud on the bed, a panting murmur.

She stopped her ears with terror. She would have liked to scream but couldn't. She fled in a rush.

Chapter Twenty-Two

Mirambeau talked to me about it," said Burgeaud,
"but I'd never have believed . . ."

He removed his spectacles and eyed Olga thoughtfully.

"You *are* a funny girl," he said.

"You're blaming me a lot?" said Olga without raising her eyes.

Burgeaud shrugged his shoulders. He took Egmont's wrist
again, but it was more to keep himself in countenance, for he'd
already done so several times.

"It's crazy," he murmured. For the third time he unrolled an
electrocardiogram with his other hand. "That the last one?" and
as Olga nodded: "Taken when?"

Egmont was stretched out on the divan, bare to the waist. His
eyes were closed. Was he asleep? Olga hoped so. The incident that
had occurred during Pascale's visit had left her with a mortifying
memory. She had rung up her colleague that same evening. Burgeaud was probing Egmont's thighs, stomach, chest.

"How old exactly?"

"Fifty-four. Or just over."

"It certainly is staggering."

Burgeaud replaced the blanket over the stretched-out body, took a chair, sat down. He crossed his legs, seized one ankle which he stroked slowly.

"And he's been sleeping like that for a week . . ." he said.

"He's not sleeping," said Olga. "Maybe he is at this moment. And at night. But in general it's something quite different."

"You couldn't wake him? I mean, eh . . ." Burgeaud groped for the right word with his fingers. "Bring him round?" he said.

"No," she said. "I've tried a dozen times, you can imagine. It's impossible. Wasn't it you who told me of that brainless dog, Cannon's I believe?"

"It wasn't I, but I know. Do you mean to say that Egmont is like that dog?"

"Exactly. When I shout, he contracts his eyelids and ducks his head between his shoulders, when I try to shake or pinch him, he defends himself, parries with his arm or his fist—but that's all. His conciousness has no part in it."

"Ah!" said Burgeaud, "Yes, I see. Well, so we'll have to resort to more forceful methods," he said looking very straight at her.

"Yes," she stammered. "Do that." She added a little shame-facedly: "I'd rather not be present, though."

"My dear friend," said Burgeaud, "you've incurred shertain responshibilities for him which it might be proper to shoulder with me at present."

"That's true," she said, flushing. "I'm behaving like a dishrag."

Burgeaud smiled and rose; he went and gave Olga's bent nape a friendly pinch.

"It's for you too," he said, "believe me."

"I know. You're right. I am ready," she said, lifting her head. "Whenever you like. No," she whispered. "Turn round."

Egmont had sat up. He was peering at the neurologist with his sightless eyes. They seemed to observe one another silently for over a minute.

"Contraction of the pupils," murmured Burgeaud. "Periblepsy, palpebral paresis. The whole works."

There was a pause.

"You're really worried?" said Olga, disquieted.

"There's shertainly a breakdown at the level of the striate bodies. Is it organic or not? That's the question. Let's take him to my place."

"What do you want to do?"

"An electroencephalogram. After all, we must know where we stand. My car's downstairs. Can he be got into it?"

"Ordinarily he's very docile. . . . Come," she said.

Egmont cocked his head, one might have said he cocked his ears.

"Come on," she repeated, and he rose. "Get dressed," she said. She handed him his trousers. But he folded them and placed them on a chair. "No," said Olga and put them back into his hands. He passed one leg through, then the other, and without waiting for her to tell him so, he dropped his slippers, his eyes searching under the chest of drawers. Finding nothing there, he seemed vaguely uncertain and remained motionless and apathetic. Olga made him sit down, went to fetch a pair of shoes, handed him one. He put it on, then the other. He tried to tie the laces, but bungled the knot. He seemed to lose interest and Olga had to finish it. After making him get up again, she stood behind him with a sports jacket into which he slipped his arms obediently. He felt the pockets several times. He looked at his wrist as if seeking his watch. Olga pushed him with one finger toward the door and when he started walking, she accompanied him, steering him from time to time with the pressure of her hand, as one some-times does a friend who, walking as he keeps up a lively conversa-tion, might bump into a piece of furniture. Burgeaud followed, his mouth pursed in perplexity.

"Eckshtremely shingular," he admitted later in his drawling voice, as he scanned the electroencephalograms. "The encephalon is in a waking state, no doubt about it. No trace of shleep, or in-hibition. And it responds to sound, to light, to pain. Never seen that. And no discernible break with the thalamic area, as I sup-posed. It's flabbergasting. I'd give a lot to know just how that shop's ticking at this moment."

"You see," said Olga gently.

"What do I see?"

"That such an exploration is not sheer madness. Nor my weak-ness in letting him go on. Your curiosity proves it."

"No. What good is this eckshploration if its results escape us?"

"They may not always. If presently—"

"Not a chance in a million."

"You give him up as lost?" cried Olga, going pale.

"I didn't mean that. The encephalograms show nothing that denotes an organic lesion. I mean if he comes round again, if we manage to pull him through, we won't get three sensible phrases out of him."

"That's not so sure," said Olga without conviction.

"What usable stuff did he bring back before he checked out for good?"

"Not much," she admitted after searching her mind.

"Obviously," said Burgeaud. "Inherent contradiction. The nerve connections, the synapses which compose the mind can't be

266

grasped by the mind, since they conshtitute it. A Chinese lantern can't project its own silhouette."

Olga persisted however:

"Still, Egmont did see things. . . . He does at this moment, I know, I'm certain. . . . I did myself. . . ."

"I don't deny it. Fabrice also 'saw things' when fighting at Waterloo. But he didn't see Waterloo."

"Enough to inspire Stendhal, though."

"That's it. Egmont might turn it into a novel. Nothing serious. To observe usefully, I repeat, there must be dichotomy, a divorce. We can observe Nature only to the extent to which we keep it at a distance."

"Observe, yes, but know it?" said Olga. "Aren't there things that we can only know by taking part in them? All the learning of a virgin science graduate won't teach him physical rapture. Egmont knows things of which we'll never have an inkling."

"Nor he," said Burgeaud.

"What do you mean, nor he?"

"The one who discovers them is no longer Egmont. When he becomes Egmont again, he'll lose them. If the dead Lazarus knew God, the restored Lazarus remembered nothing of it. Egmont will always awake with empty hands. Or full of illusions, which is worshe. This lunatic venture cannot serve anyone, not even him."

"But this power he has over his organism? This new youthfulness you can see?"

"I see above all the price he's paying. I see a prize ox. I prefer to age and call myself Burgeaud."

"Why should he remain a prize ox? He may recover his name and keep his youthfulness."

"That would shurprise me a lot. It's just a momentary palace revolution. As long as he is master of his hormones, of his humors, he also remains master of his power. But the moment the usurper vacates the premises, his reforms will be short-lived. Hormones and various secretions will function, as before, in the way that suits his age."

"He'll still have cured his gangrene," said Olga. "That's something positive, anyway."

"I'm not saying there is nothing positive. I'm saying that the road he shows is the wrong one. I have always detested yogis, hermits, anchorites. Like any form of individual salvation. When the tribe is starving, I don't like those who hunt on their own account."

"Even if they advance the science of hunting?"

"Any science, even hunting, means repeating, verifying, and, above all, communicating to the rest of the tribe. Egmont's hasn't helped anything to advance; that's another illusion, since his experience is untranshmittable. Moreover, it's a dangerous illusion: what keeps the wild beasts at bay is the hunters' cohesion, it's mankind's advance behind this armored line on which they break their claws: human reason. To hunt alone with bared chest is not heroism, not even foolhardiness, it's sheer folly, a damned nuisance to the beaters. It would be a disastrous example, were others to follow it."

"You're pretty damning."

"Never enough for this treacherous snare, this arishtocratic make-believe of lonely heights whence you defy the skies. Ludicrous bravado. If he's not roped to others, the braggart will end as Egmont has done, in a clownish slither, while the sky'll be none the worse."

"You're harsh," said Olga again.

"The only heights that threaten the sky," said Burgeaud, removing his jacket, "are the Tower of Babel which the human mind is building obstinately despite tempests and earthquakes."

He went to a cupboard and extracted a white coat from it.

"All these little smart alecs," he continued in his slow drawl, slipping his arms into the sleeves, "who out of pride leave the yard to go and build their private little towers in a corner, are not only traitors but idiots. I can't approve Egmont."

"Still, there's something you forget," said Olga after a moment.

"I'd be only too glad," said Burgeaud. "What do I forget? Pass me the gauze and scissors," he ordered.

He cut off a strip of gauze and twisted it into a roll.

"Those Babel stonemasons of yours," said Olga, helping him to insert the roll of gauze between Egmont's teeth, "didn't they long ago forget why exactly they're building their tower? If they can so easily be set against each other, isn't it because they have gradually come to take this building for an end in itself? The sky must have a good horselaugh at times, despite its awful silence, to see the builders brain each other with their piers and pediments because some prefer granite and others marble."

"Yes, well?" He passed her a swab of cotton wool seeped in surgical spirits.

Olga softly dabbed Egmont's brow and temples, then straightened herself, still staring down at him.

"Isn't there need from time to time," she said, "for one of these men to fling against the silent sky the cry of his revolt, to remind the others of what they're doing there? Even if that cry serves no other end? Even if it bursts his veins like Roland's at Roncevaux?"

"That's true," said Burgeaud, looking at Egmont, motionless in his tragic stupor. "Provided, that is, he can make himself heard."

Chapter Twenty-Three

H er head as empty as a bell and, like it, beating and droning, Pascale remained in dumb confusion before Mrs. Pélion, very small and red-eyed, who was saying to her:

"You cannot go in. He's too weak. He mustn't see anyone. You are so kind to have come. He'll be glad."

"May I sit down?" murmured Pascale.

"Why, surely. I'm keeping you standing. You see how I am: always thinking of something else. I'm just an old and anxious mother. I didn't even notice how pale you are. Have you been poorly?"

"What do the doctors say?" inquired Pascale with an effort. "Are they worried?"

"I don't know, they won't tell me anything," confided Mrs. Pélion, clasping and unclasping her small, wrinkled hands. She had sat down, too, in an armchair, all tubular and plastic. "No skull fracture, I was so afraid, apparently there's none, but severe concussion due to violent blows, that's all I've been able to get out of them. I worry so much, dearie," she stammered, and her poor red eyes became blurred. "Your father has been very good, he sees to everything," she said, laying her hand on Pascale's. "He had him put into this nursing home. He's so much better here than in a hospital."

"Does he . . . does Robert talk to you?" asked the young girl apprehensively.

"They make him sleep all the time. I'm afraid his mind'll get all muddled. But it seems that his head'll get better quick that way. Still he does talk to me now and then. Not for long. He tires so quickly. So quickly," she sighed.

"Did the . . . the others get arrested?"

"Those who beat him up? What an idea! They're all over the streets and cafés. They say they'll get him put back in prison. Would you believe it, they're even suing Mr. Mirambeau for slander, because he's been up to Paris to talk to a minister! They pretend my Bob confessed, only he didn't have time to sign his confession because he had that accident, as they call it. But he'd already denounced his accomplice, they said, a certain Fernand, that's what Mr. Mirambeau told me. They would like to arrest him too."

"Arrest Mr. Mirambeau!"

"Goodness no, not him! That Fernand. On account of the strike that's been on for weeks now. I didn't understand very well. My poor Bob, I've always been telling him, you do too much, you'll get into trouble. Still I wouldn't have thought the world was so wicked. His workshop, his head, and now they want to lock him up as well. Isn't there any justice?"

"Mrs. Pélion," cried Pascale suddenly, "tell Robert I'm here. Let him know, please!" she begged.

"But my dear—"

"I beg of you. Please."

She wrung her fingers, her hands, with nervous impatience.

"The doctor would be angry with me," said Mrs. Pélion with inflexible gentleness.

"I'm not asking you to let me see him," gabbled Pascale. "Only to tell Bob I am there. Tell him I've come."

"But I'll tell him so presently . . . when you've gone. . . . Otherwise he'd want to talk to you, sure as sure: you've turned the head of that big son of mine, you know," she said with a sweet smile. "Now there she goes crying. Look, dearie, you must be sensible. There, there, you must understand. . . ."

"Only say I'm here," repeated Pascale obstinately, dabbing her eyes, her nose, with an imploring glance.

"All right, all right," sighed Mrs. Pélion, and she got up. "However, I'll say you've gone."

"No!" cried Pascale, flinging her hand forward. "Oh no, Mrs. Pélion, don't! I swear I'll stay here, that I won't go in, not even if he wants me to. I swear it. But tell him I'm here."

"But he'll get all fidgety! I really oughtn't to—oh dear, there she goes crying her heart out again. . . . You won't go in? You promise?"

Pascale shook her curls, blowing her nose. "Promise," she mumbled in a damp, shaky voice. Mrs. Pélion left the waiting room.

All one could see of the injured man was a swollen slate-colored eyelid, the corner of a split lip. The rest of the face was tightly bound in a stiff, thick, crisp dressing. Mrs. Pélion went close to her son whose eye half opened. The split lip twitched over a gurgling voice:

"A 'isit?"

The old lady nodded yes. She hesitated:

"I don't know if I should tell you . . ."

The eyelid closed brusquely.

272

"Then 'ont."

"But I promised," said Mrs. Pélion. "And she's crying her eyes out. Your mind's still made up?" she asked reproachfully. "You really don't want to see her?"

"She's crying? . . ." wondered the voice through the dressing.

"Fit to burst. She so much wanted me to tell you that she'd come. That she's here."

" 'oor kid. She'll think herself in love 'ith me again."

"How do you know she isn't after all?" suggested Mrs. Pélion gently.

"She's a child," he said. "She takes e'erything 'or love. She'll drive ten men to drink 'efore she'll finally love one."

"Why not you?" said his mother.

The dressing gave a negative twist.

"What she loves is . . . Her heart bleeds with the discovery that men suffer, grow old and die. Her whole childhood rebels against it. She feels so much pity she could burst. It's terrible. How can you make her see she's not in love with me? That she's in love with the pain she's caused me without wanting to?"

"Don't you think that love is a great sight simpler than that? When I met your father—"

"Call her all the same," said Pélion softly through his bandages.

There was so little room left on his face that the old woman took his hand to kiss, the one that was sound, that hadn't had its fingers crushed under nailed boots.

"You are a good boy," she said.

Her son held her back and asked:

"You haven't said anything of Closter Cloots?"

"No . . . why should—"

"She used to be in his class. She was very fond of him."

"Oh!" she said, "I see."

"Go and fetch her," said Pélion.

She went out. Pascale's eyes were dry, a little hollow. When she saw the old woman come back, she started twisting her thumb, bending it, turning it.

"I thought as much," said Mrs. Pélion in a plaintive voice. "Now he's all of a fidget. He insists on seeing you. I ought to have told him you'd gone."

Pascale remained silent, she pulled her thumb almost out of its socket.

"You'd better go in to him now," said Mrs. Pélion. "It'll upset him less than. . . . Go on," she said with a sigh, "go on, go, he's waiting."

But Pascale did not move, as if she hadn't understood. The old woman's eyebrows went up over a surprised little smile. "Well?" she murmured.

The young girl left her armchair, caught one sleeve on it, tripped, took a few steps. She turned:

"You aren't coming?" she said anxiously.

"Presently, dearie. I've got to see the nurses. Besides, you'll be more at ease. Go on . . ." she repeated, with a little flick of her hand as if to chase a wasp.

Pascale gripped the door handle, turned it slowly.

She went in, closed the door and remained leaning against it, motionless and wordless, and with wide-open eyes.

"I frighten you?" shushed a cracked voice out of a corner of the mouth, the only feature, with the slate-ringed eye, visible amidst a ball of linen. "There'd be cause to . . ."

"Not frightened," breathed Pascale.

"Well, then, come closer, talk to me," she gathered amid the gurgles.

The young girl moved away from the door with an effort, walked toward the bed, her eyes still wide.

"Never seen a casualty in your life?" said the squashed voice.

"Oh yes. It's not that. Not at all," said Pascale in a less strangled tone.

"Ah . . ." said Pélion. "Then what is it?"

"Did they hurt you very much?" she said without answering.

"Don't know if they did. Can't remember anything after the first blow. The head, that hurts all the time. Luckily I sleep a lot. Don't you want to sit down?"

She sat down near the bed, on the edge of a chair.

"You rather look as if you'd like to run away," said the voice, whether mocking or melancholy one couldn't tell.

Pascale shook her curls energetically.

"No! Only to . . . to hide myself," she said very low.

"Hide yourself!" wondered the boggy voice. "Who from—me?"

"No, me," said Pascale.

"When will you stop feeling guilty," said the voice. "Why do you make yourself so unhappy?"

"I am a monster," said Pascale.

"Monsters never think they are," said the voice, amused. "You thought you loved me, it wasn't serious, that's no reason to . . ."

"But I do love you!" said Pascale vehemently.

"No. You know very well whom you love."

"That isn't true, I love nobody!" she protested in despair.

Pélion looked at her with his single eye and said:

"Yes . . . that's probably the first true thing you've thought."

Pascale breathed hard before asking in a hushed voice:

"Have you seen him?"

"Whom?"

"Egmont. Have you?"

"No. Not since . . . why, what is it?"

"It's absolutely awful."

The single eye looked at her. She went on with an effort:

"He's not asleep, you know. He comes, goes, takes things, looks at you. . . . You'd say a man like any other."

"Then what's so awful?"

"I don't know. He looks wonderful, you'd think he was your age, almost. And Olga claims that . . . she's sure he's happy, that he lives in an unimaginable universe."

"Well, then?" he repeated.

"It's that idea, perhaps, which is so awful: that he leaves us this gorgeous animal and goes away to be happy outside this . . . this world of ours. . . . Makes you think, I don't know, of someone quitting, of a rat in a cheese smiling at the cat to butter him up. . . ."

"Funny you should have that feeling, I'd have thought . . ."

He broke off.

"What would you have thought?"

"No," he said as to himself. "It's really quite natural. Your heart opened to a victim, it shuts up when the victim compounds with the killer. . . . If tomorrow I went and signed up with the police so as to be left in peace, you'd loathe me in turn, despite my smashed head. Wouldn't you?"

"I don't know . . . perhaps . . ." she murmured.

"Is it long since you last saw Closter Cloots?"

"Very long. Not since I left school, I suppose. Why do you ask?"

"Because he's about to peg out. Attack of uremia. They're afraid he won't pull through."

Pascale had dropped her little jaw, one could see a soft, pink tongue between small teeth.

276

"Mis-ter Cloots! . . ." she said very softly with stricken slowness.

"Poor chap. He knew he'd had his, and thought the others didn't. But we knew he was even sicker than he believed. I was in his class, too, before you."

"Mis-ter Cloots! . . ." Pascale repeated, stunned.

"Mirambeau saw him yesterday. It seems he's changed beyond recognition in a few days."

Suddenly Pascale took her two cheeks between her clenched fists and, looking at Pélion with distracted eyes, she cried—it was almost a scream:

"I won't have it!"

She got up and Pélion saw her come and go, fluttering against the furniture with the awkwardness of a moth, as he had seen her do once already, on that strange day when Egmont . . .

"Can't one do anything?" she cried, pounding her cheeks with her closed fists. "Are they all going to die? Why are we put into the world if it's to see them die one after the other, one after the other. And Mr. Mirambeau will die too . . . And so will Daddy!" she cried.

Pélion saw her stamp the ground like a furious baby.

"I don't want to love anyone ever again," she cried. "Not any one! No one at all!"

Chapter Twenty-Four

A̶ll this would be stark lunacy if it weren't so commonplace," said Burgeaud, adjusting the electrodes. "An illusion is no lesh an illusion for having pershisted for thousands of years. It all boils down to this sensation of self. If we hadn't that we'd have no problems. The question, therefore, is to burst the bounds of that sensation. To pass beyond the illusion. To understand that the human mind, though individually localized, yet remains a joint heritage. When you've grasped that, things become clearer."

Olga assisted him in silence. She had recovered both her senses and her coolness, as always on the verge of grave decisions.

"Now what is it we are going to do?" went on Burgeaud. "To express it conveniently, we'll say: trying to re-establish the mental cohesion of the poet Egmont. In actual fact, we are going to try to reconnect reflex conductors which, in their vast majority, were created from outside, don't belong to him personally, belong to the slow cerebral construction of a millennial mankind. The connections produced by Egmont himself are only a shlight froth. As priceless a froth as you like. But in the way a rainbow is: without the huge sun, not the leasht little rainbow."

Everything was ready for the electric shock. Egmont lay prone with open eyes in the somnambulant coma which neither insulin

278

nor cardiozol injections had managed to dispel in the previous days, hardly a slight spasm had shaken him for a moment.

"Mankind, nevertheless, remains a collection of lonely men," said Olga.

"That's precisely why," said Burgeaud, "we're going to bring Egmont back to mankind."

He placed the electrodes on Egmont's head. Olga thought: What an odd fellow. Can't help being a bit of a prof, with that perverse passion for holding forth. Luckily, his penchant for paradoxes prevents his being a bore. She was thinking of Burgeaud in order not to think of Egmont.

"We'll begin," said Burgeaud, "with a discharge of a few seconds in the bulbar region. We're groping like blind men: more or less like thumping a radio set when it starts whistling, until the right contact eventually clicks. It'll do so by chance, yet our thump is still a tribute to human science: since this contact existed in the conshtruction of the set, even if we've no idea where it's faulty. Ready?"

"Ready," echoed Olga in a voice she tried to render firm.

Egmont's body was shaken by a brutal fit of epilepsy. His back bent like an arch. The eyeballs shot out. The mouth twisted, foamed. Olga could not help hiding her eyes behind her palms, while the seconds dragged on like hours. At last Burgeaud switched off the current.

"Not much we can do now except wait," he said. "What do you say to a glass of Calvados?"

Dutouvet felt an arm clasp his knee, the weight of a head on that arm. Pascale often came to crouch like this at his feet. It did not disturb him in his reading, he stroked the thick curls with a tender, absent hand. But tonight, after remaining silent for a long, very long time, she murmured:

279

"Daddy . . ."

He lowered his book. Pascale managed to say in a quite small, shaking, oppressed voice:

". . . I'd like to become a Carmelite."

He promptly laid his book on the table and raised the girl's chin with one finger.

"What are you talking of? Carmelite! But you've no religion, no faith!"

"That's true. . . . But I would like to, all the same."

"Now then, now then," said Dutouvet between laughter and concern. "What's going on?"

"Human life is impossible," said Pascale.

"Where did you read that?" asked Dutouvet. "In Simone Weil?"

"No . . . Olga said it. . . . Life is impossible but it must be lived. Why must it? Egmont has refused to. . . . Oh, Daddy, Daddy, I want to have no part in all this! Do let me enter Carmel!"

Dutouvet felt out of his depth.

"No part in what?"

"In all this sorrow! People suffer, they die, and there's nothing to be done . . . nothing but watch them grow old and then take their place. I don't want to take anyone's place!" she cried. "I don't want to see them die. I don't want to!" she cried and pressed her father's legs with all her might.

"But you'll also see them die in Carmel," said Dutouvet with worried tenderness.

"That wouldn't be the same . . ." said Pascale, without raising her head, and she again hugged her father's knees.

"Why ever not?"

"I don't know . . . we'd all be dead anyway. . . ."

"And you think you'd be received in Carmel with ideas of that sort?"

"As long as I'd be seeking God. . . ."

"But you'd be seeking him to hate him, it sticks out a mile, my sweet. Nobody would be fooled. Leave this raving, and tell me rather what exactly's on your mind. Are you hiding some other griefs?"

"Is it very long since Grandfather died?" asked Pascale without moving.

"Twenty-two years ago. Four years before you were born."

"I'd like to be in India when you die. I'd like to run even farther away."

"That's kind, so you'd let me die all alone?"

There was a long silence, and then Pascale stammered:

"One day I wished you'd die. When you didn't let me go hitch-hiking to Nice with the older girls. I said to myself: good thing he's old. Afterward I'll do as I please."

"If my father had died as often as I wished him to, you'd have seen a jolly hecatomb," joked Dutouvet, tenderly pinching her neck.

"And yet you loved him?"

"Deeply."

"Isn't that horrible?" she said, lifting her forehead.

"It's very commonplace, above all. All children—"

"But isn't it horrible it should be so commonplace?"

Dutouvet fell silent, he scratched the middle of his beard with a smile of amusement at finding himself flummoxed.

"You so soon stop thinking of it . . ." he started.

"So when Grandfather died you didn't reproach yourself? You had no remorse at all?"

"No, only grief."

"No revolt? You accepted it? And you didn't feel like a murderer? How dare people live once they understand they're only living because the dead they loved have yielded them their place?"

"At the age I was then, you come to understand other, less bitter things as well," said Dutouvet.

"That means one must have hardened!" said Pascale violently.

"I didn't say less cruel things," said Dutouvet gently.

Pascale half opened her lips, passed the tip of her tongue over them.

"Ah . . ." she breathed a surprised, attentive sigh.

"You are right in all except one point," said Dutouvet. "It's good to love your dear ones to the point of rejecting their death so vehemently. But there are better things to do than scream—or run away to the ends of the Earth. And . . . less easy ones."

Pascale gazed at her father with eyes full of pathetic expectancy.

"For instance," he went on, "to give a meaning to their life."

He placed his hand on the youthful wrist.

"The death of a loved one is unbearable—but even more unbearable is the thought that he may have suffered for nothing. That his life was absurd and vain—impossible, as you say."

"It isn't impossible?" said Pascale feebly.

"If I'd thought it were, I'd have drowned you at birth," said Dutouvet. "You are my little proof," he said with a smile, "that I hold life to be both possible and good."

"In spite of so many miserable people? In spite of suffering? In spite of death?"

"I said possible," he qualified with care.

"You said good," insisted the girl.

"Yes, it is," confirmed Dutouvet. "Providing you admit it has some meaning."

"But what?" she exploded. "What can it mean?"

"It needn't be decipherable."

"So it's an act of faith. That I can't," said Pascale.

"You don't want to," he corrected her.

"It comes to the same."

"Let's say, if you prefer, you don't know how. Human life has indeed an intelligible meaning, even though death appears to deny it, even though it is too early to guess its aspect. It's not a question of a credo. When you were reeling off your A B C, you did not demand that literature should be proved to you first, it wasn't an act of faith. From century to century, mankind painfully learns to read. We shall discover gradually what book there is at the end."

While he spoke, he saw on the still pale lips the first furtive ghost of a smile. Pascale blinked her eyes and murmured, as if completing the sentence:

". . . and what literature . . . ?"

"And what literature, you've grasped my meaning very well," agreed Dutouvet, pressing the soft, fresh arm on his knee. "And what creation. The true, ultimate human creation, of whose alphabet our arts and sciences are still painfully spelling out the first letters."

"But if it's so remote . . ." she started, but she broke off.

"Well?" asked her father, encouragingly. He rolled a silky curl around his forefinger.

"Where does one get the courage?" she said. "Or the compulsion? When I was very little, you were there to explain to me, to compel me too. I'd never have learned to read if you hadn't forced me."

"You yourself have made the distinction: man's honor is this rewardless courage, it's living without knowing as yet the reason for living."

"But if there isn't any, at the end?" cried the girl. "No reason whatsoever?"

"There is *our* reason, which reasons precisely to discover it."

"Vainly, up till now," said Pascale bitterly.

"At the age of six, you vainly struggled to decipher your primer: could you divine Rimbaud, Tolstoy? They nevertheless existed. What the future has in store for the human mind is as much beyond its present narrow bounds as *War and Peace* was beyond a child's primer."

"Aren't there perhaps other roads than those of reason?" said Pascale after a pause. "More direct roads?"

"No. Above all don't go and listen to all those potshooters who keep gleefully announcing the bankruptcy of reason—under the pretext that, on this hundred-billion-years-old Earth, the mind, aged a mere twenty thousand, and modern reasoning, with less than three hundred, have not yet managed to penetrate to the mystery of the World! Believe me, little one, those who hasten to despair of reason prove only their impatience: they lack heart and guts, that's all."

"Like Egmont?" breathed Pascale almost inaudibly.

Dutouvet leaned back a little, then said softly:

"Let's not be in a hurry to judge him. It may be more complicated than that. Certain impatiences may have their greatness."

Pascale rubbed her cheek against her father's knee, pondered, and said:

"You're entitled to be impatient when you get old."

"That's not what I had in mind," corrected Dutouvet. "The right to be impatient—yes, of course. But I meant that there are types of impatience which are not uncertainty, despair. Which, on the contrary, spring from a too ardent mind, which sees too far and wants to press on. . . . That sort of impatience is not eager

284

to abdicate, to return cravenly to 'our mother Nature' despite her ferocity. But the very opposite: it's the impatience of a manly protestation, of anger."

"And Egmont's you think is anger?"

"I don't know," said Dutouvet, foraging in his beard with one finger. "This reckless adventure in which he's caught is perhaps revolt in its purest state, since there he is at grips with the enemy in the very heart of this sack of meat. But by the same stroke he is lost in his organic universe, his mind and spirit sacrificed to the barren and somewhat obscene triumph of blind, exulting flesh. . . . Does it mean, in the last analysis, revolt or total submission? I cannot tell."

"I hope it's revolt," said Pascale in a low tone.

"You hope it with your youthful ardor—and perhaps you are right. Although at Egmont's age, I wonder. . . ."

"But when death is at your door," Pascale burst out, "and you realize what remains to be learned and that you haven't got beyond A B C as you say, and you know it, why, it's a hundred times more unbearable. A hundred times more so than when you're young!" she cried, pressing her father's knee convulsively. "I think I'd be shaking with desire, and panic, and rage, and greed!"

"That's no longer the way you think when you grow older," he said softly.

"Why?" she protested. "You become resigned? That's even more frightful!"

"Not at all, the very contrary, my bucking colt," said Dutouvet laughingly, tugging at her curls as if at a bridle. "At that age one's come to substitute determination for anger. You'd rather have seen the victory yourself, true enough, but the main thing is not so much seeing it as helping to bring it about."

285

"But how?" said Pascale, turning her big eyes on him, and her father raised his eyebrows questioningly. "How can you pass from your primer to *War and Peace*?" she inquired. "If even a genius like Einstein really got only as far as A B C? What sort of brains would we need?"

"Our friend Burgeaud would tell you: Einstein didn't exist, it's just the name of a crossroads. The business of the crossroads depends on the traffic on the streets that converge there—but that traffic is still a thin trickle, it's hardly increased since Plato's days. Wait only till the traffic grows, and we'll be hearing more about the Einstein Crossroads!"

"But when?" asked Pascale. "It's ages since Plato. If you have to wait such an awfully long time . . ."

"Look who's in a hurry! But I don't mind, that's right at your age. Now look," he said, pulling out his fountain pen. He took a sheet of paper from the table, drew a horizontal line on it. "That's time," he said. "At the left end is prehistory; a little closer, Plato; there, in the middle, are we, our contemporary era. Among the mass of men, the brains that really work are still very few, not surprising that knowledge limps miserably," he said, tracing a line which hardly lifted itself above the former. "It'll take thousands of years at this rate, won't it, to make it reach the top of the sheet?"

"Yes," sighed Pascale. "It's hopeless."

"Only here's where things change!" said Dutouvet in a comic chant, and his pen sketched an ascending curve. "Because for the last hundred and fifty years, the number of active brains, the sum of exchanges, have begun to increase in a geometrical progression and, with them, knowledge. It's beginning to climb almost vertically, knowledge is. To tend toward the infinite. You see that?" he said, letting his pen glide to the top of the sheet.

Pascale watched entranced the hyperbolic graph creeping for so long, so very long, and suddenly soaring to giddy heights.

"But . . . since when?" she asked.

"You want to know where we are? Is that it? Well, roughly here, I'd say"—and he made a cross toward the middle of the rounding of the curve. "The change isn't very noticeable yet. But you'll see," he said, "you'll see, in a century's time, perhaps in much less, it may suddenly go very fast. The mind becomes explosive."

Pascale was still looking, one finger stroking her cheek which slowly rose to a smile.

"You think that's possible?" she murmured as if dazzled.

"Possible? Say it's evident. Look," he said again, turning the sheet over. "We'll divide this paper into centimeters, thirty lines across, twenty down. Each square is worth a year. That doesn't make a lot, does it? What would you put at the bottom of the sheet? Napoleon III? Lafayette? No, it's already Joan of Arc. Two more sheets, there's Nero. Ten, and there's prehistory. A schoolboy's thin copybook, Neanderthal man. A fat notebook, the apes. But to see the Earth being born you'd need three hundred thousand copybooks, one hundred and fifty million sheets! Can you imagine? Fifty sheets to pass from the Lascaux cave paintings to Giotto, that's half a minute, only a quarter of a sheet to pass from Papin's digester to uranium fission, that's a quarter of a second. What do you say? Can you imagine where man may have got to in one more sheet or two?"

"Isn't that rather terrible?" she said between a thrill and a shudder. "Mr. Cloots was telling us—oh! do you know he's . . . he will . . . that he is so ill?"

"Yes, poor fellow. What did he tell you?"

"He said that that's just what's so awful! That science is moving so much faster than moral progress."

"Yes, that was true not long ago. It still is, alas. Only it will be decreasingly so. When all science was—and it's only just ceasing to be—an isolated product, the product of a few dispersed minds, while all the other brains, or nearly all, were still at the stage of the brute, hardly rough-hewn by dim mystic glimmerings, what could they be expected to do with those discoveries? But that's already no longer true. Already the most rudimentary brains are beginning to gain height in their turn. It is still a very slow, almost imperceptible movement, an incipient movement. But it'll go accelerating like the fall of a body—an upside-down fall, toward Heaven."

"But if that's true, Daddy . . . if it's true, then our time could . . . it should soon become one of the most exciting ones since the world existed?"

"That's what I'm trying to tell you."

"But then, but then . . ." said Pascale thoughtfully, and she stopped.

"Well?"

"You mean it would need millions of brains, hundreds of millions who'd all start thinking together—really thinking?"

"That's the whole question," said her father. "Up to the middle of the century, the last one, how many brains were there in a thousand who'd been given the means to think? One, two, perhaps less. And suddenly today we no longer find one, but ten, a hundred, perhaps one day even a thousand out of a thousand brains will start thinking, nurturing each other. That opens perspectives, doesn't it? Can you imagine the sort of swarming at the crossroads then? What an Einstein of those days will be like?"

"So the main thing, the most important one of all, is schools?"

"It's the abolition of want in general. And of stultifying work. Hand in hand with a policy of educating the masses which still remains to be worked out. It all dovetails. And there are poor mutts," he suddenly warmed up, "who dream of Malthusianism— who are frightened of overpopulation, of hordes and invasions! Who don't see that as humanity grows in numbers, it grows in knowledge and in wisdom, at a rate that will soon become stupendous. The Earth too small? Why, soon, in two or three hundred years, plowing the earth, even with tractors, will seem as primitive as hunting seals with reindeer-bone harpoons. Because Man will long ago have discovered how plants transform solar energy and thus be able to do without them. And there are people still frightened by the advent of the masses, people sincerely ready to defend, at the cost of their lives if necessary, their petty privilege of filling the columns of their diehard daily with their mumbled A B C's, or their little esoteric poem or their little abstract painting once a week. They take themselves for aristocrats and don't see that they resemble helots—who, because they know how to carve a heart on a tree trunk would think they were the custodians of the highest possible form of culture, would flatter themselves that they were the fine flower of Man's mind. They believe they're defending the mind and stifle its blossoming; they are so proud of their tiny seed that they're afraid of the tree!"

Pascale had risen. While he was speaking, she had sat on her father's knees, had put her hands on his shoulders, and watched him, listened to him with a little laugh, a coo of delight, her eyes wide open with gay surprise. When he had finished, she threw her arms around his neck, cheek against cheek.

"Oh Daddy, Daddy, you really believe what you're saying?"

"Do I!"

"Then there'd really be only one thing to do? One thing alone?

To fight and fight to wrest this stranglehold from those millions of poor brains, those wretched brains that cannot think?"

"That is indeed the very top priority."

Pascale remained silent for a long while.

She was still stroking her cheek on her father's, on his beard, with a coaxing movement. At last she said with a gentleness that gleamed with hope:

"You think I'd be right to marry Robert?"

Chapter Twenty-Five

The prefect himself pushed the armchair forward—
it was an enormous, heavily gilt, atrociously *Empire* armchair.
Mirambeau sat down on it. He contemplated the allegory of Harvest suckling Industry, in which rouged nipples and buttocks broke the austere lines of standing corn and steel girders, with their oafish obscenity. Must official art under all systems of government invariably lead to such rot? he thought.

"I am happy," said the prefect, "to have at last an opportunity of meeting you. I have not been here long, that must be said in my excuse. When I was appointed to this post, the Minister said to me: 'It's the home of Mirambeau.' You are the glory of Chaulieu, you see," he said with a smile.

Mirambeau did not smile. He looked at the prefect with a rather inexpressive mien, and seemed to be waiting. The prefect continued to smile. He had a dissymetrical face, quite refined on one side, rather crude on the other. A long, slightly flabby nose divided it askew. Even the eyes did not stand on the same plane. Bulging flush under the fat eyelids, they rather inclined to twinkle, although the left eye had a sharp, cold glint. The hair was fair with a hint of ginger. The man was not yet really bald but soon would be.

He held out a box of cigars: "You smoke?" Mirambeau declined with a gesture. The prefect shut the box and put it on a massive desk behind him, picked a cigarette out of a leather box.

"I'm unfortunately pretty much of an ignoramus in matters of science," he said with a pleasantly shamefaced smile, "still I am well aware of the importance of your work." He struck a match. "I knew it by repute before coming here," he said, and he had resumed his seriousness. "Would you do me the honor of showing me round your laboratories one day?"

"Whenever you wish," said Mirambeau noncommittally. "I'm hardly ever away. Just let me know."

"Would you have any objection," said the prefect, bending forward, elbows on knees, "to my investing the visit with a certain ceremony? What I mean is," he added more quickly on seeing the old man's eyebrows rise, "would you mind it being a somewhat official visit rather than an informal one?"

"I don't quite see the reason . . ." started Mirambeau.

"You know that you have been mentioned for the Prize of Nations?" said the prefect in a semiconfidential tone.

Mirambeau raised several fingers, dropped them again in a gesture of ignorance. The prefect slightly flicked his cigarette while glancing at him over his elegant hands.

"I've perhaps let the cat out of the bag," he said with a little laugh. "But I'm acting practically on orders. The French government attaches great importance to this candidature. I know, I know!" he said to forestall a movement by the old scientist which obviously meant: Candidate? No, not I. "I know," he repeated, "that isn't quite the way of it. Let's say the government would warmly welcome, for understandable reasons of prestige, the prize going to France this year after being so long denied to us."

"It would be better," said Mirambeau, "to persuade the republic that she can't do without scientists. The prestige of a prize will never make up for the shocking want of scientific research."

"As if I didn't know," sighed the prefect. "It's a maggot of mine. The education budget is disgraceful. Unfortunately, the opinion of a provincial civil servant does not carry much weight. . . . But today," he went on in a firm voice, "I'm not speaking for myself alone. The government wishes to make no secret of its very high opinion of you."

"Very nice of them," said Mirambeau with a straight face.

"They wish," said the prefect, appearing not to have heard, "to make it publicly known abroad. They also wish," he added with a chuckle of connivance, "to show those gentlemen of the Institute. You do not lack opponents there, you'll not be surprised to hear. Your laurels won't let some of your colleagues sleep. They can't forgive you your scandalous fame that's spreading to the five continents on the strength of a memoir of a hundred pages, when twenty volumes haven't enabled others to reach beyond the confines of the Seine-et-Oise. But above all they find you personally a bit alarming. It's laughable and of course you don't care. However . . ."

With the back of his hand the prefect stroked his clean-shaven chin, which was determined if a trifle plump.

"However, the repercussion such a prize would have, I repeat, for our town and for the whole of France is something you cannot disregard. Allow me to say—you haven't the right to disregard."

He must have read in Mirambeau's eyes a gleam of amusement, for he went on hastily:

"I know, you must be thinking 'What can I do about it?' And, indeed, at first glance, your outstanding merits should set you above such pettiness. But it's not only a question of you yourself, I repeat. And you know as well as I do that in these world-wide competitions, calumnious reports can weigh against otherwise brilliant titles. It would be a calamity for French science." He grimaced: "There's also much talk of a German geologist, who may well have been a Nazi . . . It would be a calamity," he repeated.

He lowered his plump chin for a moment, with the result that a second one bobbed up above his stiff collar. He seemed to ponder, then raised his head with a puff of smoke.

"Mr. Mirambeau," he said, "you must certainly be wondering what I'm driving at. I shall not beat about the bush: it would be unworthy of you and me. You guess no doubt what I have in mind?"

"Well, I have an inkling, but I'm afraid . . ."

"Mr. Mirambeau, you must . . . that action for slander that's been brought against you, you must help me to get it dropped. It would really be too absurd. After all, isn't that your view too?"

"That should be easy for you," said Mirambeau in his even voice.

"No, because you're making it difficult. Let's admit it quite frankly."

"I gathered," said Mirambeau, "that the action was in fact filed by your departments?"

"Exactly. I am naturally obliged to defend them when they are attacked, that's the least of my duties. Now you have gratuitously maligned them before witnesses, in various ministries. What would you have done in my place? Suppose you were called upon, as I am, to maintain order and, consequently, to support those who help to maintain it?"

"How should I know? I've never found myself in that situation," said Mirambeau genially.

"I confess I find it hard at times to understand you. You are

294

a laboratory man after all," said the prefect in a tone of veiled reproach.

"And you'd like me to stay one," said Mirambeau, unable to suppress a smile.

"I would, when I find you act without circumspection. It surprises me in someone like you. I imagined you'd never accept as proven anything you'd lacked the material to verify scrupulously for yourself. Anyway, that was the integrity of judgment I expected of a mind of your caliber."

"When the police torture an innocent man there is no need of judgment, indignation will do."

"Were you present?" said the prefect.

"No more than you were, Mr. Prefect—I hope."

"But what would you say if I disparaged your work without even seeing it, ignorant as I am of biology?"

"Mr. Prefect," said Mirambeau, "if when visiting my labs you cared to criticize the arrangements of certain apparatus, the setup of certain experiments, I would not send you about your business. I should listen to you with respect and try to profit by your advice."

"But if you considered it erroneous, specious, uninformed?"

"I'll tell you something, Mr. Prefect. I have never forgotten Charlie's lesson."

"Whose?"

"Charlie Chaplin's. Most valuable lesson. 'The Pawnshop.' You've never seen it?"

"I'm somewhat short of time to go to movies."

"Ah? Pity. Mind you, at the time you couldn't have been more than twelve or fifteen. No French citizen should be presumed to have missed it. It ought to be shown compulsorily and free of charge in every village, every school. The country would have been spared many a misfortune."

"Forgive this gap in my knowledge," pleaded the prefect with a light laugh that sounded somewhat strained. "What was its point?"

"A fable. But this isn't the place to tell you. Suffice it to say that it restores the citizen's self-confidence and stimulates him to watch a little more closely the competence of the higher-ups. We might perhaps have avoided the loss of Indochina, the imminent loss of North Africa. It is by virtue of this fable that I occasionally poke my nose into unexpected places."

The prefect said in a tone that was meant to be bantering but grated a little:

"Then don't be surprised if it gets caught in a door one day!"

"I shan't be surprised at all," laughed Mirambeau. "I expect it."

"You do not make my task any easier," said the prefect bitterly.

"What task?"

"Of protecting you against yourself, Mr. Mirambeau. I explained to you the importance we attach to this year's prize and the worries that are caused us by—"

"I'd be sorry if you lost any sleep over them."

"Why do you adopt this tone, Mr. Mirambeau? Isn't it rather offensive?"

"There are, up and down the world, a vast number of offensive things," said Mirambeau, rising. "Did you ever go for a stroll down the rue Bérengère?"

"Rue Bérengère?"

"In the slums. You maintain order, you say? No: you maintain *an* order. There's room for much injustice and bloodshed in this small addition of an article."

296

"Mr. Mirambeau," said the prefect, "do me the pleasure of sitting down for another minute. If you please," he said with smiling entreaty. "Thank you. You studied in Paris, didn't you?"

"Your services are efficient."

"At the lycée Janson, if I'm not mistaken. We weren't contemporaries there, I'm your junior, but all the same . . . our minds were formed to have the same approach to things. Even if our opinions on those things may differ. Whether you like it or not, we belong to the same clan."

"I've never much cared for clannishness."

"Nor I, believe it or not. Still, there's no getting away from it: I may not be happy with this *rissole* of a nose my father bequeathed me, but that's the nose I have, and no other. Neither you nor I can do anything about it. And whatever you may do, you will have more in common with the most stiff-necked Coubez son than with the most decent of their workers, those people you want to make common cause with and who themselves so mistake their true interests."

"That depends what you mean by 'in common.' . . . But even admitting it, what are you driving at?"

"I would like you," said the prefect, "after all, to trust the specialist a little more. He does know more than you do, when all's said and done. And I would like you to be less certain of your judgment in matters outside the scope of biology. You are surely not a man who's satisfied to see the world in terms of chromos?"

"Why not?"

"That's the Jesuit priest's famous reply," said the prefect, laughing. 'Why do you always answer our question with another question?' someone complained. And he, too, answered: 'Why not?' "

"Chromos simplify, they do not lie," said Mirambeau. "There is no chromo squalor, no chromo injustice. There is squalor and injustice."

"That isn't what I meant. I mean that nothing is quite black or white. Do me the honor of believing that I am no less alive than you to social problems, to want, to injustice. But you know quite well that you'd easily find among the employers sincerely good and decent men, deeply devoted to the well-being of their workers. And that you'd also find among the workers sly opportunists, selfish cowards, would-be despots. You don't deny it?"

"Isn't that another sort of chromo?"

The prefect threw back his head and body with an air of surprise and incomprehension. Mirambeau explained:

"This, in two words, amounts to saying: Don't judge. Consequently, don't act. Let the specialists do their job and keep your inner purity nice and shiny. I am sorry, but I have lost the urge for that sort of purity."

"I'd like you to meet Antoine Coubez," said the prefect, changing his tone.

"I can't say I'm very keen. He's the brains behind the business?"

"Yes. The younger son. Janson man, too. And the Polytechnique. Hardheaded but with an eye to the future. One of the first to have understood that you can't fight revolt by prolonging poverty but by substituting prosperity. You play into the hands of unworthy political elements, Mr. Mirambeau, by yielding as you do to the dictates of your heart. Believe me, they are the very ones who nowadays speculate on poverty, and you are helping them to perpetuate it."

"Are you counting on the gifts of Antoine Coubez to sell me that gospel?"

"You have never talked in earnest with men like him, I'm sure.

You plug your ears so as to hear only one side of the record. Let me at least make you listen to the other. That's fair, isn't it? I wager that Antoine Coubez will surprise you. You certainly have no idea of the broad-mindedness of a man like him. . . . We might lunch together all three—tomorrow, if you like?"

Mirambeau scratched his cheek thoughfully, a slowly dawning smile splitting his moon face. He murmured: "Fancy . . . fancy." He thought: Things going so badly for them? Can they be out of breath? He said:

"Lunch, no. That would not do at all. But you can bring him to my laboratory, if it interests him. I'll show him round."

He rose, held out his hand.

"The other side of the record?" he said. "How many different ones have you got Antoine Coubez to listen to? This would be a fine opportunity. And fair, as you say. Pity our friend Pélion won't be available. Anyhow, I'll do my best. Is your Coubez a good listener?"

"I am sorry," said the prefect with a reproachful smile, "that you turn my words into a joke. I was very much in earnest."

They walked toward the door.

"But Mr. Prefect," said Mirambeau, "I am extremely in earnest myself. Certainly quite as much so as Mr. Coubez and his friends. Bring them along. We'll have a chat. I expect they're eagerly awaiting the opinion of a Nations Prize-winner-to-be, and burning to adopt it."

"You certainly like to have your little joke," said the prefect with a sigh. "Tomorrow then?"

"If you like," said Mirambeau.

He paid a silent tribute to Agriculture's breasts and Industry's buttocks, and went out.

While walking through the Parc des Recollets, he never stopped grinning. Unless I'm much mistaken, he thought, they count on me to save their face. They'll give in, that's on the cards. I'll have to let Fernand know. And announce the news to Pélion; that'll help to put him on his feet. Never say die! he thought, and the August sun seemed to wink at him through the branches with brotherly complicity.

Egmont had given no sign of a change after a second electric shock in the bulbar region. Burgeaud declared that he would now try the hypothalamic area.

Olga at first said nothing. But Burgeaud, looking over his shoulder, saw her pace to and fro. Her high heels rang out on the flags with thoughtful slowness. She said at last, without addressing him:

"By what right? . . ."

Burgeaud turned a deaf ear. Olga crossed the room, came back, resumed:

"And if it's a refusal? If he refuses to return? If he wants to stay where he is? If what we take for a failure is the result of his stubbornness? By what right would we insist?"

Burgeaud remarked, without turning round:

"The same right with which I jump into the river to retrieve a would-be suicide. Even if he resists."

"But it's not the same thing!" protested Olga. "Your suicide is about to die. Egmont isn't. What do you want to rescue? A poet? And if he no longer wants to write? Would you drag him by force from a hermitage, and make him write poems *by force?*"

"You've a thick skull," said Burgeaud. "The precious froth of his future poems, that, at a pinch, he may be entitled to blow off. But the champagne underneath doesn't belong to him. It's ours as much as his. He's disposing of it unwarrantably. I demand its return in the owners' name."

"You're muddling me," said Olga plaintively. "Besides . . . even if I were to follow you on those lines, Egmont is surely the sole trustee of his mind for life. He can devote it to any purpose he likes, can't he?"

"Short of depriving us of a capital asset that remains indivisible. That's what you refuse to understand."

"But has he deprived us? Hasn't he rather invested it in a lucrative undertaking: this carnal wealth, this fund of youth and vigor which you'll admit is stunning?"

"In that case, your proclaimed ideal must be for him to become an elephant, a whale. He'll never be big enough. Of what use is the youthfulness of this mass of beef to us, I ashk you? What contribution may we eckshpect of it?"

"But by what right do you expect a contribution?"

"Oh bother," said Burgeaud. "I've told you twenty times, I'm not going to shtart again."

Olga resumed her pacing and said shyly, bitterly:

"He *was* happy, I am sure of it. We are going to bring him back to all he loathes."

"That is not for us to take into account. Beshides, you can't possibly tell."

Thereupon, he began placing the electrodes in position. Olga helped him with a sigh. She shook her head from time to time. When they had finished, she murmured: "I can't tell you how ardently I hope we'll fail."

Burgeaud shrugged his shoulders and switched on the current. Olga closed her eyes as on the first occasion, stopped her ears. She opened them when she thought it was over. Egmont was resting, a little twisted to the right, a little foam on his lips, his eyelids closed. He was breathing spasmodically, with slight convulsions. She saw Burgeaud bending over him with a worried look. She quickly asked:

"What is it?"

He did not speak. He probed the muscles of the right arm, the right leg. He listened to the right lung, pulled a face. At last he murmured:

"Incipient hemiplegia. Let's hope it passes."

It was true that Egmont's mouth sagged a little to the left, as did the whole face. Burgeaud motioned to Olga to help him with a new encephalogram. They both worked in silence. Once again, in face of danger, Olga recovered her calm with her energy.

The needles quivered. Burgeaud watched the mysterious waves inscribe themselves on the roll. Over his shoulder, Olga followed the slow arabesques.

Burgeaud scratched his skull:

"It's not organic—and yet . . ."

The slender, sinuous serpent interminably scratched the recording strip.

"No break, it's staggering," muttered Burgeaud, "it's as if . . . I don't know why I'm thinking of a one-way street . . . as if the traffic could no longer proceed in the right direction. . . . I wonder if I shan't once more . . ."

He felt Olga's hand grip his forearm.

"I beg you," she whispered, with real distress in her voice, "let's wait . . . oh, do let's give him a little peace. . . ."

She passed a hand over her forehead. She was staring at Burgeaud almost with dread.

"If we could imagine what is happening to him, inside there. . . . I can almost see him," she stammered, with glaring eyes, "a man in the dark, jumping from rock to rock, chased by the fire of heaven . . . falling and picking himself up . . . and in pain and so lost. . . ."

Suddenly she went close to the body and shouted into his ear with all her might:

"Egmont!"

But not the slightest quiver passed over the inanimate, faintly twisted face.

Olga slowly straightened up, seemed completely shaken, utterly baffled.

"In any case," said Burgeaud kindly, taking her arm with affection, "we'll have to give him a couple of hours. Don't panic. . . . Let's go and down a tankard," he said, pulling her along.

He turned toward the old nurse who was listening to them in silence.

"If by any chance you see him give a sign of waking," he said, "send Toto for us. We'll be across the road, at the King Stag."

But they weren't sent for. That evening Egmont was still unconscious, in a deep, comatose sleep, moving neither hand nor foot, his mouth slightly askew, and his breathing almost imperceptible. This catalepsy lasted for several days. Olga hardly left his bedside any more, ceaselessly taking his pulse, his temperature, examining his heart, his blood pressure, despite the invariably normal results. Burgeaud had chided her at first: "I don't recognize you, upon my word! Are you going to turn into one of those nervy little women?" She remained impervious to his friendly mockery which tried to sting her pride; instead, she gave him a black scowl, and Burgeaud felt ill at ease, a little guilty. But damn it all, he thought, he's in no worse a state than before;

303

he's still more or less asleep; let him wake up first and then we'll see where he's got to. However, he did not venture to suggest a fourth shock.

The sixth day, toward evening—Burgeaud had forced Olga to go and have a drink with him at the King Stag—they hardly had the time to take a sip before young Toto came panting to fetch them. They hurried back. Egmont was asleep. However, he had moved. One cheek was resting on the pillow. An arm was raised above his head.

"He opened his eyes," said the nurse. "Oh, two seconds, that's all. And he tried to speak."

"You understood something?" asked Olga in a hoarse voice.

"No . . . he seemed to complain . . ."

Olga sat down by the bed. And she stayed there, motionless, watching, watching, watching him.

But a quarter of an hour passed before he opened an eye again. Only one. The other eyelid lifted without quite managing to open. But Olga saw a real look fastened on her. A light shone in it. The twisted mouth opened. With an effort, some incomprehensible sounds passed the cracked lips to which clung some saliva.

"Yes, my poor darling," said Olga, taking his moist hand into hers. "Presently. Don't tire yourself."

Was it an illusion, or did she see a glint of mockery pass through the single eye, a corner of the mouth lift in a hint of a smile?

". . . But hi . . ." she heard, "hi ham . . . so hlad . . ."

"You are glad?" cried Olga, rising, and she gripped him by the shoulders.

"Ho hawfully . . ." gurgled a twisted tongue between the stiff lips.

304

The single eye left Olga, traveled around the bleak, enameled room where, through the glass pane, one slender ray of the setting sun cast a pink and golden gleam. From the window came the murmur of the town.

". . . to be . . ." gurgled the voice in a shower of bubbles, and Olga had to bend low to hear him.

". . . here . . ." said Egmont, dragging the word out with relish, as if he were savoring a liqueur, the flesh of a peach.

Later, Egmont was to evoke for Olga the essence of those days, dramatic "but not tragic," he said. He had a tonic memory of them. He still articulated painfully, tripped over the labials, yet managed to express himself without too much difficulty.

Olga kept questioning him. Had he been aware of the electric shocks?

"No, not exactly," he said. "I was like a wounded soldier who recovers consciousness after dark. He doesn't remember the shock. Maybe I recollect . . . yes . . . a sort of distant storm, with gusts of wind to throw you against a house wall. But it remains very indistinct. What really happened, I don't know. I believe . . . Burgeaud, you say, spoke of 'one-way traffic'? That may be it, roughly. By dint, you see, of my disconnecting contacts behind me, always in the same direction, the contacts could eventually no longer work in the other, I suppose. The electric discharge must have restored them violently, but something must have jammed in a corner, I expect, and smashed other contacts. Happily they're being restored gradually. . . ."

Olga asked if he could more clearly recall those long days of unconsciousness, before the shock treatment. Or had he lost all remembrance of them, as Burgeaud had foreseen?

"All remembrance . . . no," he answered. "Actually, that's the term that fits best: I have some remembrance of having gone through a fabulous period—but without any real memories. A distant feeling of a medley of wonder, rage, dread, bliss, nostalgia. . . ."

"All that together?"

"Yes, as if I had at last got through the tunnel I'd been plodding along for months, to emerge in the dazzling brightness of an earthly paradise—and lost everything in reaching it: hearing, sight, and scent. A sort of 'dissolution,' you understand? Like smoke, like a puff of steam. With the same sensation of incredible expansion. Despite that feeling of stupendous existence, of fantastic multiplicity."

"But nothing more precise, as usual?" said Olga regretfully, and as Egmont shook his head with a rather glum air: "Burgeaud was sure of it. You prove him right," she said with a sigh. She asked again: "You have no regrets? For that paradise, I mean?"

"Good heavens, yes!" he cried. "But it's not a question of regrets or no. No choice. I don't know if you can understand. How could I not be haunted by what I have known? This intimacy, this freedom, this immense power? But they are futile, you see, a power turning helplessly around itself; and this too vast freedom worse than a prison; and the tunnel blocked up behind me—upon that blind, dissolved, evanescent me; and reveling in unheard-of riches, but they too wasted and nameless . . . That's what's so infamous!" he cried angrily. "That you must lose yourself in all this wealth to relish it, or stop enjoying it to comprehend it. Ah," he said laughingly, "I am babbling, forgive me. What gibberish! But it's really inadmissible!"

"You do regret, all the same," murmured Olga, without hiding her concern.

"No, that's not how it is, I told you. Remember, during the Occupation, the friends who crossed into Switzerland. That, too, was paradise on Earth, after hell. But they stifled in it. Remember their joy on coming back. It's the same I felt when, suddenly, I found myself back here. On this side of the tunnel. And yet all I was able to do was open one eye and utter a grunt. And yet I had every reason to fear that I should never, perhaps, be able to do more. But the old nurse answered me. And I grunted again. And she smiled at me. And we looked at each other. And God knows the poor woman is no beauty, but she smiled, and she saw that I saw her. You understand? I emerged from the tunnel and a human being was waiting for me and saw that I saw her. Oh, that was wonderful!"

Mirambeau left the hospital in the best possible of moods. In Pélion's room he had found a joyous party. The young Kabyle, recovered from his injury, Fernand, Albert, and a radiant little Pascale. They had drunk champagne in honor of the Coubez capitulation. The bonus had been won for all of the workers without distinction. In Saint-Vaize, too, a budding organization among the North Afs and the support of a progressive town council who threatened the distilleries with requisition had resulted in the reopening of the factory there. Upon a mere intervention by his lawyer, Pélion had promptly and easily obtained his provisional discharge, which now stood a good chance of becoming absolute. He admitted that everything was not yet rotten in the republic: an inquiry had been ordered into the circumstances of his injury. It looked as if the prefect had had his knuckles rapped. Nobody, however, nursed wild illusions. The dropping of the charges against Pélion would no doubt be equalized by the charges against his torturers meeting the same fate and the inquiry into the outrage against his workshop petering out. You cannot expect too much.

Mirambeau had found Pélion somewhat changed—to his advantage, he thought. Was it love, physical suffering, solitary meditation? He had lost some of his arrogance, his boyish self-assurance. Some pertinent questions about the scientist's research and—oh horror!—about problems verging on metaphysics, had revealed the opening of a skylight, perhaps a real window, on wider vistas. It was a good sign.

As he was once again crossing the Parc des Recollets on his way back to his laboratory, it seemed to him, he knew not why, that the park had gained in beauty. On the still waters of the pool, the revivifying blooms of the water lilies spread their drowsy flesh. A swan glided past, blue in the shadow. Mirambeau watched him with that old yet always novel pleasure which beauty affords, even conventional beauty. Anyway, he had stopped questioning himself about aesthetic problems for many years now, and was content to take a naïve joy in birds and flowers. He watched a little wagtail trip up and down over the lawn, bobbing its head and feathery rudder, and suddenly darting twenty steps to peck a midge in his bill. The last campanulas reflected their episcopal bells in the slate-colored lake. The brilliant blue of the lobelias crouched under the scabiosas' paler blue. Farther away, behind the black poplars, a scarlet stain of full-blown cannas blazed in the sun. Mirambeau inhaled a burned fragrance of resin and dry hay. He felt profoundly happy. It seemed to him that the sunny grass, the freshness of the pool, the antiphon of the flowers, the heady pungent tang of the breeze through the pine needles, the swish of the sparrows, the lilt of the butterflies . . . that all this serene festival around him was beginning to gain gradually on the bleak horizon where the workers' district slumbered in the sultry heat. Mingled with this slowly intoxicating perfume, he breathed a mounting scent of victory.